Praise for *The Great American Awakening*

After the elections of 2010, I was asked if I had any advice for incoming Congressmen and Senators. My advice was, "Be principled and do what you say you are going to do. If you ever need guidance, just follow the lead of Senator Jim DeMint." The Tea Party trusts very few of our leaders and Senator DeMint is one of them. He is a shining light because he is principled, does not waiver from his values and is as conservative as they come.

—Amy Kremer, chairman of Tea Party Express

As I stood with Senator DeMint behind the stage at the 9-12-09 protest and gazed at the swell of patriots who had gathered from all corners of America I felt the re-awakening of American Exceptionalism. This movement is transformational, not temporary. It is rooted in our nation's Founding Principles, with the knowledge that a better understanding of our past will better guide us into the future.

—Tom Gaitens, cofounder of Tampa Tea Party

Jim DeMint is a hero of the Tea Party movement because he's shown the leadership that the movement, and the American people, are desperate to see. He has given Tea Partiers real political clout because he's been unafraid to challenge the status quo, both on the Senate floor and with his Senate Conservatives Fund. But perhaps even more than that, he's given people hope by showing that with courage and dignity, and a firmness of principle, change for what is right can and will happen.

—Ned Ryun, president of American Majority

I believe the Tea Party movement is the best thing to happen to our country since the original tea party of 1773. Patriotic Americans are finally awake and now we have insomnia. Thank you, Senator DeMint, for standing with us as we take back our country.

— Joyce Krawiec, North Carolina FreedomWorks grassroots coordinator

★ ★ ★ ★ ★ **THE GREAT** ★ ★ ★ ★ ★

AMERICAN
AWAKENING

★ ★ ★ ★ ★ ★ ★ ★ ★ ★ ★ ★ ★

★ ★ ★ ★ **THE GREAT** ★ ★ ★ ★

AMERICAN
AWAKENING

TWO YEARS THAT CHANGED **AMERICA**, **WASHINGTON**, AND **ME**

★ ★ ★ **U.S. SENATOR** ★ ★ ★

JIM DEMINT

★ ★ ★ ★ ★ ★ ★ ★ ★ ★

NASHVILLE, TENNESSEE

978-1-4336-7279-8

Published by B&H Publishing Group
Nashville, Tennessee

Published in association with Yates & Yates, www.yates2.com.

Dewey Decimal Classification: 323
Subject Heading: FEDERAL GOVERNMENT \
POLITICIANS—UNITED STATES \
UNITED STATES—POLITICS AND GOVERNMENT

Scripture quotations have been taken from the
Holman Christian Standard Bible®, Copyright © 1999, 2000,
2002, 2003, by Holman Bible Publishers. Used by permission.
Holman Christian Standard Bible®, Holman CSB® and HCSB®
are federally registered trademarks of Holman Bible Publishers.

At time of printing, all Web sites were checked for accuracy.

2 3 4 5 6 7 8 9 • 15 14 13 12 11

Contents

To the tea parties and all those
who plan to join them.

Acknowledgments

First and foremost, I am thankful to my wife, Debbie, who endured another year of my using our limited personal time to help conservative candidates and write another book. Without her patience, encouragement, and understanding none of this would be possible.

All of us who are involved in political battles should have profound respect and admiration for the men and women in our armed forces who defend our nation. Because of their sacrifices, Americans settle arguments with elections instead of weapons.

My heartfelt gratitude goes to everyone who participated and voted in the 2010 elections. Those who were involved in tea parties, town halls, rallies, and other grassroots activities helped to wake Americans from their sleep and give citizens a way to channel their concerns into constructive political participation.

I am deeply appreciative for my extraordinary staff—both in Washington and South Carolina—who help me fight for conservative principles and care for the constituents I serve.

My Chief of Staff Bret Bernhardt and State Director Ellen Weaver led my Senate office through a difficult first six years and continue expertly to guide my office.

Ed Corrigan, executive director of the Senate Steering Committee, has been a fearless behind-the-scenes leader of the conservative movement in the Congress. He has provided me with invaluable advice and guidance in fighting legislative battles in the U.S. Senate.

Matt Hoskins, who assisted me in founding and directing the SCF, played a pivotal role in all our election victories of 2010. He saw the opportunity for a new, innovative fund-raising operation to support conservative candidates and was instrumental in ushering new Republicans to the Senate.

My Communications Director Wesley Denton, who has been with me since I came to the Senate, has consistently pushed a strong, conservative message to the press. Amanda Carpenter, my communications advisor, has also been a key player in helping drive our team's pro-freedom ideas into the media.

Throughout everything Julie Blackorby, my scheduler, has kept me on task and on time, which has allowed our entire office to be more efficient and effective.

Many other staff in my office and other congressional offices have served as the ground troops for the conservative cause in Washington. I am grateful to all of you and to members of many other conservative organizations who informed, equipped, and engaged Americans in the 2010 elections.

Above all, I am thankful that, while many of us are doing our best to save our nation, our future is in God's steady hands.

Foreword

I was supposed to lose Florida's 2010 Republican primary for the U.S. Senate, and I was supposed to lose big.

When I announced my campaign in the spring of 2009, the only people who believed I could win were my wife and four children. The endorsements for my opponent, former Florida Governor Charlie Crist, started rolling in from the Washington establishment just moments after he announced his candidacy.

At the beginning of the race, I was more than thirty points behind in the polls. People thought I was crazy to take on a popular incumbent governor in my own state, in my own party. He had the name identification, the money, and the political connections. But I knew in my heart he would not provide a clear, conservative alternative to a future of never-ending debt for our children.

In my mind there are only two good reasons to run for office. Either you run because something is wrong in the world you want to fix, or something is right in the world you want to protect. I wanted to do both.

At that time it wasn't even a matter of winning or losing the race. It was a matter of advocating for the principles of freedom I believed in. I know America is the greatest country in the world. But it didn't get that way by accident and won't stay that way automatically.

We were at a crossroads. Washington had been taken over by big-spending politicians from both parties who were willing to say or do anything to get and stay elected. Their credibility to be good stewards of taxpayer dollars was gone. There was simply no way the people who saddled taxpayers with costly spending bills, bailouts, and takeovers would ever advocate the ideas to reclaim America and put it on a path toward prosperity. If they remained in control, America would no longer be the land of opportunity and freedom for all people in the world. Instead, America would become an anomaly of history.

Like many parents, mine worked long and hard to provide for their children. My father labored as a hotel bartender for most of his life. My mother was a maid and Kmart stock clerk. They left everything they had in Cuba because they believed America was the best place for their children to live in freedom, grow, and succeed.

Because of all the sacrifices my parents made so I could grow up as a U.S. citizen, I'm acutely aware of how special it is to be one. I want nothing more than to honor my parents by giving my children the same gift of freedom and opportunity they gave me. Yet I fear our generation will be the first to pass onto their children a diminished country.

Early in my campaign I had no idea how I would ever raise enough money to be competitive in a Senate race. At times I doubted myself and questioned if the goal was really worth spending long hours on the road traveling to political events away from my family.

Then one morning my children came to me with quarters and single-dollar bills they had saved from their allowances. They had overheard me worrying and wanted to help. At that moment I knew I wasn't giving stump speech after stump speech in vain. I was not running to indulge my ambition; I was running to preserve everything that makes America exceptional so they and their generation could prosper.

Although I knew why I was running, I had difficulty convincing others to support me. As luck would have it, the day I came to Washington to court support from the powerful and influential National Republican Senatorial Committee was the same day Governor Crist announced his candidacy and received the NRSC's formal endorsement. Graciously, they still took my meeting. I explained, as respectfully as I could, they made the wrong decision.

Then I went to my next meeting, an appointment with South Carolina Senator Jim DeMint. I knew he bucked the party establishment and endorsed the conservative Pat Toomey against then-Republican Senator Arlen Specter in the Pennsylvania GOP primary. I thought if he had the courage to do that, maybe he would consider endorsing me, too.

Before the meeting DeMint had only watched a few of my speeches on YouTube, but he agreed to talk. When he asked why I was running, I told him about how my parents came to America as immigrants to give my siblings and me a better life. I told him I felt a deep obligation to do the same for my children and how determined I was not to let them down.

DeMint decided to endorse me soon after that meeting. A few weeks later, on June 16, 2009, I was back in Washington for a press conference where DeMint formally announced his support. He stood by my side as I talked with reporters about my biggest fear. "The spending that happens here on a daily basis, quite frankly, is not just mortgaging our future; it's selling off our future," I said. "To the point where my children and my grandchildren, who I can't even imagine yet, will work their entire lives just to pay the interest on the spending and the taxes that are coming their way. "

DeMint continued to stand by my side for the rest of my race, even as his colleagues, the pundits, and editorial boards said he was destroying the party.

His endorsement represented a turning point in my campaign. Soon after, I was endorsed by other leaders and landed on the cover of *National Review*. Slowly my fundraising numbers picked up. We gained more and more national attention and started closing the gaps in the polls.

Ultimately Crist decided to leave the Republican Party, but that move didn't improve his chances of beating me. That's because the race wasn't about conservatives versus moderates or Republicans versus Democrats. It was a referendum between our limited government, free-market American identity or a costly and intrusive big-government agenda my opponents supported.

There is a reason I so proudly proclaimed, "I will always be the son of exiles," in my victory speech after I won the right to represent the people of Florida as their senator. I said it to remind everyone of how special this country is. In most countries your fate is determined by who your parents are and other circumstances of your birth. In other places the sons of bartenders usually grow up to be bartenders, regardless of what other dreams they may harbor. But in the United States of America, the son of a bartender can grow up to be a United States Senator.

There's never been a nation like the United States, ever. The rights of the American people are not determined by the government, a king, or who your parents are. It's written in our founding documents that our rights come from God, our Creator. And it's up to us to preserve, protect, and defend those rights if we wish to keep them.

When I think about our duty to safeguard those God-given rights, I'm reminded of a speech President John F. Kennedy was never able to give. He was shot on his way to Dallas, where he was supposed to give it. The last lines of his prepared remarks said: "We in this country, in this generation, are—by destiny rather than choice—the watchmen on the walls of world freedom. We ask, therefore, that we may be worthy of our power and responsibility, that we may exercise our strength with wisdom and restraint, and that we may achieve in our time and for all time the ancient vision of 'peace on earth, good will toward men.' That must always be our goal, and the righteousness of our cause must always underlie our strength. For as was written long ago, 'except the Lord keep the city, the watchman waketh but in vain.'"

These words are truer today than they have ever been. America is not a great country because of the laws we pass or the men and women we elect. America's greatness comes from the passion of our people for the right to self-government and because of our God-given rights.

Some people snicker when I talk about American exceptionalism and how dearly I love this country. Or they say I'm too simplistic when I say God is real and is an ever-present, overwhelming force of love we can't ignore. These are truths I'll never be ashamed of saying, and I desperately hope no one is ever offended to hear. Thankfully, more people are responding to this message than ever.

When Senator DeMint was campaigning for me and other candidates for the 2010 elections, he often talked about the American awakening he believed was taking place. He saw the same thing happening throughout the country that I saw in Florida. As the federal government threatened to transform the country and fundamentally change what it means to be a U.S. citizen, Americans rose up and demanded a return to the constitutional limited government envisioned by our founders.

I will be always be grateful to Senator DeMint. His endorsement was invaluable to my campaign. Moreover, what he did to find and support conservative candidates in the 2010 election cycle provided an invaluable service to the country. When other people in our party cared more about popularity and power above all else, he insisted that Republicans stay true to their principles. Thanks to his willingness to take a chance on a new crop of committed conservatives, he won't be the only one in Washington standing up for the principles of freedom.

—Senator Marco Rubio

Election Day 2010:
Returns and Reflections

Tuesday, November 2, 2010

E lection Day 2008 felt like Christmas for many voters when Barack Obama was elected president. Two years later Election Day 2010 feels more like the day after Christmas, when everyone rushes to the stores to return unwanted gifts. Today Americans are going to the polls to return all the false promises of a presidency and Democrat majority that came wrapped with beautiful paper and bows in the last two elections.

Like every Election Day since I first ran for Congress in 1998, local media called to find out when I would be voting. My name is on the ballot, along with those running for Congress, governor, state senate and representatives, and candidates for many local offices. The media wants the perfunctory five seconds of video and snapshots of my wife and me voting at the school near our home. So Debbie and I are busy looking for our best voting day outfits.

My fellow South Carolinians are predictably interested in our state and local elections, but most of the suspense here and across America is focused on the potential change of power in Congress. Polls have indicated for months this election could be a political earthquake restoring Republicans to control of the U.S. House and giving Senate Republicans enough votes to slow the rampage of spending, borrowing, and government takeovers by the Obama administration.

I'm planning to vote and return home to reflect over the past two years and pray about the outcome of the election. What began two years ago with the historic election of our first African-American president and broad bipartisan hope for real change in Washington quickly deteriorated into horror as many Americans realized President Obama intended to change America, not Washington. His big-government, European-style, socialist agenda soon led millions of Americans to demonstrate in the streets and protest at town hall meetings.

My own alarm about the potential loss of America's status as the world's bastion of freedom led to a complete change in how I served in the U.S. Senate. The last two elections were disastrous for Republicans. After losing the House, the Senate, and the White House in 2008, I could no longer serve quietly behind the Republican leadership in Washington. We blew it! We betrayed the trust of the American people, and few of our Republican leaders would even entertain the idea we might have done something wrong.

Some Republicans in the Senate parroted the media mantra saying our party had become too conservative. This accusation made me want to pull out my already thinning hair. During the Bush administration, when Republicans controlled Washington, spending and earmarks exploded. We expanded federal control of education and health care, increased the national debt exponentially, while making almost no effort to fix the tax code, save Social Security and Medicare, or reduce the size of the federal government— all Republican platform promises. You could accuse Republicans of a lot of things, but you could never convict us of being too conservative!

Taking On the Establishment

After Obama defeated John McCain, who was considered a moderate Republican in 2008, and the Democrats expanded their majority in the Senate to sixty (the magic number needed to pass any bill), I decided it was time to declare war on the entrenched Washington establishment in both parties. This was a painful decision because it meant confronting some of my best friends. I prefer to persuade people quietly to do the right thing, but that approach hadn't worked in Congress. I knew if I had any chance of being effective, I'd have to leave my comfort zone and get more aggressive.

Just *how* aggressive, I had no way of knowing yet.

But in describing what has become for me a personal battle for freedom, please know that my intent in this book is not to be critical of individual congressmen and senators. My goal is to expose the "Washington establishment" as a powerful system of inertia that protects the status quo. This system includes powerful lobbyists, staff, agency bureaucrats, the media, as well as members of Congress and the seniority system that protects their power. The Washington establishment is driving our nation toward bankruptcy. Each day and with every vote, members of Congress decide whether to be a part of the establishment or a part of changing it.

Attempting to change the system is a brutal and painful process, as I reveal in this book. I tried for years to be a part of the establishment while trying to change it. That didn't work. It wasn't until I declared war on the establishment that I began to make progress . . . and enemies.

I knew I faced a lonely battle. Few senators were willing to take an aggressive public stand against intransigent senior Republicans or to join me in a direct assault on the source of the Republican downfall: earmarks and the culture of spending. This meant taking on the appropriators. Few Americans understand there are really three parties in Congress: Republicans, Democrats, and appropriators—those who sit on the powerful Appropriations Committees, which directs all federal spending.

The appropriators are Republicans and Democrats who believe one of the top priorities of members of Congress is to direct federal earmarks to their home states, congressional districts, and pet projects. These are not evil people. They are, for the most part, well-intentioned members of Congress who have been caught up in a system that rewards more and more spending, who over time become more concerned about "bringing home the bacon" than their constitutional commitment to a limited federal government.

Senior members on the Appropriations Committees effectively control both chambers of Congress. These are the people who direct almost all discretionary federal spending and hand out earmarks. Appropriators not only control spending and earmarks, but they also dominate elected leadership in both parties and are chairmen or ranking members of many policy committees. They have enormous influence because they decide which members get to "bring home the bacon."

Again, I want to emphasize my criticism is not directed at individual appropriators. They are doing the job the system expects them to do. My criticism is of the system many call the Washington establishment—a system that distracts Congress from the business of the nation with self-serving, parochial interests. Parochial interests conflict with the reforms needed to cut spending, reduce debt, and save our nation. Fortunately, more Americans are beginning to understand that earmarks and the resulting culture of spending are the root causes of our dysfunctional Congress and our crushing national debt.

Members of Congress who request earmarks inevitably become part of the problem. It doesn't matter what they say or even how they vote; they will not fight big-spending bills. They may speak against bloated spending bills to the press and even vote against them, but behind closed doors where the parties meet to determine their floor strategy, earmark seekers will not stand up and condemn the outrageous spending, borrowing, and debt created by these bills. They stay silent because they know if they offend the appropriators, they will not get their earmarks.

I know because I'm a recovering earmarker. Like anyone else in Congress who serves at the will of the people, I have felt the tug to use my position to fund various projects around South Carolina. Many opportunities present themselves to funnel resources back home, and those who make these appeals for aid are not always trying to line their own pockets or milk the system. They see a need, they see an opportunity, and they've been told the easiest way to get funding quickly is to ask for "free money" from Washington in the form of an earmark. It can be hard—and potentially job-threatening—to rebuff such a petition for help.

But money from Washington is not "free." It must first be taxed from a hardworking American who is struggling to make ends meet, or borrowed from nations like China and paid back with interest by our children and grandchildren. Additionally, over years and years of unchecked earmarking, our states have become accustomed to expect federal funding for every type of project from museums to charities to bike paths. We have slowly turned what should be state and local matters into federal issues. When did it become the job of a committee chairman from Alaska to determine where sewer plants are placed in South Carolina? When did it become the responsibility of a taxpayer in Alabama to pay for a museum in New York?

Think about it: if 535 congressmen and senators believe it is their job to get money for their states, districts, and pet projects, what will happen to the federal budget? It's no surprise we are over $14 trillion in debt. Members from both sides of the aisle are in on the game.

In fact, if you want bipartisanship, you'll love the Appropriations Committee. There is always plenty of bipartisanship when it comes to spending. Earmarks turn the whole focus of Congress toward self-serving, parochial spending projects—a direct conflict of interest with our oath of office to support and defend the Constitution of the United States of America.

It's as simple as that.

And when Republicans lost eight seats in the Senate, twenty-one seats in the House, as well as the White House in the 2008 elections, I recognized where the source of the anger was, and I decided it was time to shake things up.

I proposed several changes to the rules governing the Senate Republican Conference to reduce the power and influence of the appropriators. This seemed like common sense to me, considering Americans were screaming at Congress to stop spending and wasting money. But asking my fellow colleagues to give up their power to direct taxpayer funds to their favorite causes was simply too much to ask. They considered my proposals to be a personal attack.

I'll discuss this in more detail later, but suffice to say that our leadership responded with an organized effort to defeat these reforms and to humiliate me for challenging their power. *It worked!* I didn't get more than five votes on any of my proposals, and the disdain for my efforts was so thick in the air you could have cut it with a knife. Members and staff at the meeting leaked the story to the press. *Roll Call* reported, "DeMint's ideas reignited long-standing tensions with the GOP Conference and his fellow Senators, who often have tried to quiet his flame-throwing ways." My chief of staff, who is one of the most senior and respected chiefs on the Hill, was told by several of his colleagues he should resign.

But there was a silver lining to my humiliation. My Republican colleagues saw I wasn't easily intimidated and wasn't going to back down. Not only that, the experience forced me finally to accept a truth that had been obvious for years: my colleagues were not going to change. The only way to change the Republican Conference and the Washington establishment was to change the people in the Congress. A quote from former Republican President Ronald Reagan kept swirling around in my head, "If you can't make them see the light, make them feel the heat."

It was time to raise the temperature.

Fortunately, part of the heating element was already in place. After the 2006 elections when Republicans lost majorities in the House and the Senate, I got the idea to create a political action committee called the Senate Conservatives Fund (SCF) to help elect conservative senators. This would prove to be extremely valuable in the efforts required to meet the challenges from 2008 onward. (More on that later, as well.)

I also began taking this message to stop the spending, borrowing, debt, and government takeovers directly to the media instead of trying to convince my colleagues to support me. Most members of Congress are risk averse and will not take a stand until the polls tell them which positions the public supports. But when Republicans wait to find out what the public believes before delivering our message, the Democrats have an uncontested platform to shape public opinion. Republicans must know what we believe and lead the public in the right direction.

Shaping public opinion is no longer a pipe dream for the minority party. With today's alternative media sources, it is very possible. For example, only five Republicans in the Senate stood up to stop the Bush-McCain-Kennedy amnesty immigration bill in 2007. But working through conservative blogs, radio talk shows, e-mail lists, and other outlets, we were quickly able to inform Americans that the proposed bill did little to secure our borders and reform our immigration system. It simply rewarded more than ten million illegal aliens with citizenship, voting rights, and social benefits. Americans were rightly outraged when they found out the administration and Congress were not telling them the truth. Thousands of phone calls and e-mails opposing the bill collapsed the phone systems and computer servers in the Capitol. In a Republican Conference meeting one week before the final vote on the immigration bill, Senator George Voinovich, an Ohio Republican who supported the bill, defiantly responded to the public outrage, "I will not be intimidated by the American people." But in the end he was! When the final vote was called, he was intimidated. Voinovich walked to the well of the Senate and voted no on the immigration bill.

Taking our message directly to the American people also allowed a few of us to draw attention to the wasteful "Bridge to Nowhere" earmark and to increase public pressure against the culture of earmarking. Additionally, conservative media helped us create public outrage against the bailouts, the failed "stimulus" bill, the moratorium on offshore energy exploration, and to delay the government takeover of our health-care system.

As it turned out, I didn't have to go it alone. And that is the reinvigorating message of this book. This is where you enter the narrative—both through what many of you have done already in the cause of freedom, and through what many more of you are prepared to do in these crucial years in our nation and world. This is what began to change not only America, not only Washington, but me. For while I was beginning my one-man kamikaze mission within the Senate, millions of Americans were coming to the same conclusion I had: our country was moving with increasing speed toward a financial cliff, and we had to act decisively to save it.

The Wall Street bailout during the last days of the Bush administration was a loud wake-up call for many Americans. President Bush said he was suspending free-market principles to save the free-market system. I didn't buy it. Americans didn't buy it. But the bailout was jammed down our throats by a bipartisan majority in both chambers of Congress. The money was not used as promised, and over the next year Obama used the bailout money and other borrowed money to take over General Motors, Chrysler, AIG (the nation's largest insurance company), Fannie Mae and Freddie Mac (the nation's largest home mortgage companies).

After the public outrage over the Wall Street bailout, Republicans in the House held together against Obama's trillion-dollar government spending bill he called "the stimulus." But it passed the House with almost unanimous Democrat support. Republicans in the Senate could have stopped it. Instead a few Republican moderates, including Arlen Specter from Pennsylvania, sold us out. The bill passed.

Americans Join the Fight

By April 15, 2009, tax day, Americans were ready to fight back. Hundreds of thousands took to the streets across the country in what were called tea party protests. I was invited to speak at tea parties across South Carolina. Thousands attended, and audiences roared with approval when I was introduced as a senator who fought the bailout bill, the stimulus bill, and wasteful pork-barrel earmarks.

The isolation I felt in Washington disappeared as I realized millions of Americans were willing to stand and fight with me. They demanded Washington stop spending, stop borrowing, stop increasing the debt, and stop the government takeovers. They even demanded term limits for congressmen and senators! These freedom-loving Americans were my real colleagues. They convinced me to keep fighting the Washington establishment, despite the pain and long odds of success.

My first public act of rebellion within the Senate Republican Conference was my endorsement of Pat Toomey in the Republican primary against Specter. Opposing a fellow senator in the same party was unprecedented. The Republican leadership endorsed Specter for reelection, but I felt Specter had betrayed the party on too many occasions. I could not in good conscience support him against a proven and principled conservative like Pat Toomey. A few days after telling Specter I planned to support Toomey in the Republican primary, he announced he was leaving the Republican Party to run for reelection as a Democrat. Some of my colleagues blamed me for his defection, but Specter candidly said it was all about the numbers: his polls confirmed he could not win a Republican primary against Toomey.

As it turned out, Specter couldn't win a Democrat primary either. Even with the help of President Obama and the Democratic Party, Specter lost to Congressman Joe Sestak in the Democratic primary on May 18, 2010.

The Republican leadership in the Senate was strongly critical of my decision to support Toomey, reminding me conservatives could not win in Pennsylvania and stating Republican *principles* were not as important as

Republican *numbers* in the Senate. My Republican colleagues got even hotter when I said publicly I'd rather have thirty Republicans who believe in the principles of freedom than sixty who believe in nothing at all.

The temperature was rising.

In June 2009, I endorsed former Florida House Speaker Marco Rubio in the Florida Republican primary for the U.S. Senate. Rubio and I first met in DC in May 2009 after the National Republican Senatorial Committee rebuffed him. His commitment to America and our freedom was compelling. Rubio was just the kind of candidate Republicans needed. He was a young, charismatic, principled Cuban American ready to fight for his country. And he had the courage to play the part of David in a high-profile confrontation with Goliath. Rubio asked for my help, and I was honored to give it, as did millions of Floridians and patriots all over the country.

But our leadership endorsed another candidate, Governor Charlie Crist, who was one of the most popular governors in the country. At the time, he was also a prolific fund-raiser, which meant the National Republican Senatorial Committee wouldn't have to invest heavily to keep the Florida seat. But Crist embraced the Obama stimulus bill and proved he was more a political opportunist than a principled conservative. For me the choice was clear. It certainly wasn't for the others. My colleagues literally laughed at me when I endorsed Rubio because he was thirty points behind Crist in the polls.

Over the next six months the SCF and I continued to endorse conservative candidates who were opposing candidates selected by Republican leadership in Washington. I was not making many friends by taking this unpopular, unprecedented approach, challenging those who had served alongside me in Congress, but the system that had been built there was obviously not working. Broken, in fact. The only way to change it was to bring new ideals into Washington, people who believed in what most Americans see clearly every day when they get up for work or take their kids to school or sweat out their tax returns.

While making these endorsements, I was also waging another fight: Obama's health-care bill. On July 17, 2009, I participated in a conference call with leaders from a dozen grassroots organizations. When some of the callers expressed pessimism about our ability to stop the President's big-government agenda items, I encouraged them to stay focused on one thing: stopping his health-care takeover. "If we can stop him on this, it will be his Waterloo; it will break him, and then we can go on to freedom solutions that have always worked for America."

Someone on the call recorded my statement and released it to the media. President Obama attacked me for the comment, and "Waterloo" was soon all over the national news. Many Republicans in the Senate were critical of my direct attack on the President. Outside Washington, however, my comment served notice that there were at least a few Republicans in Congress willing to fight the government takeover of health care. "Waterloo" became a battle cry for all those who wanted to save our health-care system. Soon almost all Republicans in the House and Senate were fighting to stop the socialization of health care in America.

By August, Congress was in recess, and congressmen and senators began to hold town hall meetings all over the country. In South Carolina thousands attended my town halls to encourage me to keep fighting and to stay true to conservative principles. In other states thousands gathered to speak out against congressmen and senators who supported the health-care takeover. Obama's approval ratings dropped dramatically, and support for his health-care bill fell below 50 percent.

This vocal shift in the national conversation came to a visible head on September 12, 2009, when a national Tea Party was held in Washington. Numerous conservative organizations and grassroots groups teamed up for an event on the National Mall that came to be known as 9/12. Hundreds of thousands of Americans came to protest not only the health-care bill but the overall expansion of the federal government. I was honored to be asked to speak at the event. Before speaking, I spent most of the day mingling among the crowd and talking to people from all over the country.

Many of the marchers encouraged me with comments like: "Thanks for fighting. We're praying for you. What can we do?" These people were not partisan ideologues; they were afraid for their country and seemed almost desperate to stop Washington from pushing it over a cliff.

The 9/12 rally convinced me something deeply spiritual was happening in the nation. Call it a revival of the American spirit or an awakening of the American conscience—whatever their motivation, it was far deeper than political ideology. One lady who rode on a bus all night from South Carolina simply said, "I've never done anything like this before, but I had to do something."

Many in the crowd were clearly motivated by their faith, but they were not in Washington to ask the government to promote religion or morality. Their concern for our country's future seemed to have awakened their faith and stirred a sense of patriotism, civic responsibility, and a call to action. They knew their rights and freedoms came from God, not government; and they believed an expansive, debt-ridden government would destroy freedom in America.

But despite this incredible show of support for conservative principles on our front porch, Republicans in the Senate continued business as usual. At our weekly Republican Policy lunch on the Tuesday after the historic 9/12 rally, what had happened days before within a few feet of where we were sitting was not even mentioned. I couldn't believe it! At the end of the meeting, I stood up and said, "Friends, we have talked of the need for a 'big tent' Republican Party. Well, that 'big tent' came to Washington last weekend and invited us to join them. They want all the things we say we believe in: less government, less spending, less debt, and less taxes. But they are not going to embrace *us* until we embrace *them*."

I looked around the room.

Silence. No comment.

I shouldn't have been surprised. This is not atypical. Trying to change the Senate is akin to paddling up Niagara Falls. But I must admit, the stark contrast created by what I'd just witnessed on the National Mall, reflected against the stoic, unmoved faces and expressions of my own Party members, made me more determined than ever to redouble my efforts. I was certain now that no amount of prodding and poking and explaining positions was going to move this governing body toward decisive change and action. I was tired of beating my head against the marble walls in Washington. Debbie and I had struggled for many months about the decision to run for reelection in 2010. I didn't want to spend another six years in Washington with the same people I'd been working with for the last six years. Let me be clear again: many wonderful people serve in the Congress. From both parties. But too few believe in constitutional, limited government. Even fewer have the courage to stand for the proven principles of freedom when they are faced with demands from those who want more from government.

All of which brings me back to Election Day 2010. *Today.* The day we find out if Americans have answered the call. I can honestly say I have fought with all my strength and put it all on the line. What has happened in America over the last two years has been truly stunning. From the conflicts and drama behind the scenes in Washington to the revolutionary awakening of the American people, the battle for America's soul is a story every citizen should know. And it is the story I tell in this book.

This is my personal story, and it is written from my vantage point as a U.S. Senator. It is not intended to suggest in any way I was a central figure in this great American awakening. Millions of Americans led this effort, and no one person or group can take credit for the historic changes that occurred in the two years leading up to Election Day 2010.

Throughout the battle I have sensed the power of prayer from thousands of Americans, and it has profoundly changed me. What seemed impossible with human strength became a reality because of the hope, work, and prayers of the American people. I will be forever grateful for the opportunity to have played a small role in the fight to save freedom.

Chapter 1

Becoming an Outcast

November 4, 2008—January 20, 2009

O n Election Day 2008, the polls showed John McCain would lose badly to Barack Obama and Republicans would lose many more seats in the U.S. House and Senate. I was at home in Greenville, South Carolina, hoping for a miracle but preparing myself for the worst. The Democrats had been in control of both chambers of Congress for two years, and now they would have even larger majorities with a Democrat president in the White House.

The hardest part about losing for me was the belief among many that Republicans didn't deserve to win. Even after suffering major losses in 2006, the Republican Party did little to convince Americans we heard their message. Voters didn't like our Democrat-lite agenda. They didn't like our expansion of the federal role in education (No Child Left Behind) or health care (prescription drugs for Medicare), and they didn't like the way President Bush and the Republicans were managing the war in Iraq. Americans were especially upset about the growth of spending and debt under Republican leadership, represented by wasteful earmarks such as the infamous multimillion-dollar "Bridge to Nowhere" in Alaska.

Many Republicans denounced the explosion of government interventions into the private sector, but our leaders in Congress supported more spending and the Wall Street bailouts and were not willing to admit they made any mistakes. The Republican failure to respond to a clear message of "no" from the American people would now put our country under the control of liberals who neither understood nor respected the principles of freedom.

Since this was an election year, Congress had adjourned in early October so members could go home to campaign. My reelection was still two years away, so the early adjournment gave me time to finish my book *Saving Freedom* and to travel the state. *Saving Freedom* was my attempt to remind Americans of the principles that made America the most free, the strongest, and the most prosperous nation in history with commonsense principles like limited constitutional government, individual responsibility, free markets, and Judeo-Christian values. The book exposed how bad federal policy had caused the financial meltdown and how the bailouts expanded the government economy rather than save jobs and help the economy recover.

On the Sunday before the 2008 election, I enjoyed a brief timeout from politics. Wade Hampton High School, my alma mater, inducted me into their inaugural class of the Legion of Honor. Other inductees included former U.S. Director of National Intelligence Mike McConnell, theologian and best-selling author John Piper, award-winning newscaster Jane Robelot, and world-renowned opera singer Myra Cordell. After my mediocre performance in high school, I had to smile at God's sense of humor. I was humbled to appear on the same stage as these great people. Not even in my wildest dreams did I ever imagine returning here as a United States Senator.

I grew up less than a mile from the school in a family with a divorced mother, two brothers, and a sister. Our home sometimes seemed like boot camp because to survive as a single parent my mother enlisted all four of us for daily duties beginning at 6:00 a.m. She ran a ballroom dancing school in our home, and we were always on call if someone needed a dance partner. At age fourteen, I had two paper routes. At sixteen, I talked my way into an early-release work permit from my high school so I could leave after lunch to bag groceries at a local store. On weekends I made a little extra money playing drums in a rock-and-roll band.

My high school career was less than stellar. Had my senior class given an award for "least likely to succeed," I may have won it. But now I was being honored as one of their most accomplished graduates. I guess that's why 1 Corinthians 1:27 is one of my favorite verses: "God has chosen the world's foolish things to shame the wise, and God has chosen the world's weak things to shame the strong."

Still savoring my recovery from high school, I watched the less-than-savory election results at home with my high school sweetheart and wife, Debbie. The local Republicans were holding a victory party in Greenville, but we didn't attend because we feared it would be more a wake than a celebration. Within an hour of the polls closing on the East Coast, the election was all but over. For McCain to have any chance to win the election, he had to win at least one of the battleground states of Florida, Virginia, Pennsylvania, or Ohio. When all of these states fell to Obama, he clearly would be our next president.

By the end of the night, we lost four incumbent Senate Republicans and three open seat races. And we were in danger of giving up the crucial sixtieth vote to the Democrats. Sixty out of one hundred senators are required to pass controversial legislation. True, only fifty-one votes are needed for passage, but sixty votes are needed to end debate before moving to a final vote. Sixty votes in one party makes them essentially filibuster-proof. If the Democrats controlled the White House, a large majority in the House, and sixty votes in the Senate, all checks and balances of two-party government would be gone. Nothing could stop them!

Senator Norm Coleman, Minnesota Republican, would be our forty-first vote to stop bad legislation if he was reelected, but on election night Coleman was only a few hundred votes ahead of comedian-turned-Democrat candidate Al Franken for the Minnesota Senate seat. The day *after* the election, Coleman still led by about seven hundred votes, but the Democrat-controlled election commission in Minnesota kept finding more Democrat votes. Within a few weeks they found enough votes to declare Franken the winner.

Coleman appealed, a process that took months. But in the end he lost his appeal and his Senate seat. When Franken was sworn in as a U.S. Senator, he gave the Democrats their prized sixtieth vote, making it impossible for

Republicans to stop legislation without any help from Democrats, which wasn't likely. Democrats had a 256-to-178 majority in the House and Obama in the White House. The political left had an iron grip on the levers of power.

It wasn't hard to interpret what was happening here. The election confirmed just how angry Americans were with George Bush and the Congress. Because Bush was president, voters believed Republicans were still in charge of Congress even though Democrats had been in control for two years. Bush and the Republicans were blamed for the wars in Iraq and Afghanistan, the bad economy, the wasteful spending, and more importantly, the bailouts. In the last year of the Bush presidency, the federal government and the Federal Reserve spent trillions intervening in dramatic fashion in America's free-market economy. With mind-numbing speed Bush and the Democrat-controlled Congress opened the floodgates of spending and debt.

A brief time line below captures how quickly trillions were spent:

- March 7, 2008, the Federal Reserve gives $200 billion in low-interest loans to twenty investment banks and a $30 billion credit line to J. P. Morgan to bail out and buy Bear Stearns.
- July 30, 2008, Bush signs $300 billion bailout for Fannie Mae and Freddie Mac (the nation's largest mortgage companies).
- September 7, 2008, the federal government takes over Fannie Mae and Freddie Mac.
- September 16, the Federal Reserve bails out AIG (the nation's largest insurance company) with an $85 billion loan.
- September 29, 2008, the Federal Reserve increases lending to foreign banks by $330 billion.
- October 3, 2008, Bush signs the $700 billion Wall Street bailout called TARP, and Congress raises America's debt limit to $11.3 trillion.
- October 8, 2008, the Federal Reserve lends AIG another $37.8 billion.
- November 14, 2008, Freddie Mac loses $25.3 billion and receives another $13.8 billion bailout.
- November 23, 2008, Citigroup receives $20 billion more in bailouts.
- November 25, 2008, AIG receives another $40 billion bailout.

While Bush "abandoned free-market principles to save the free market" and McCain embraced the bailouts, Obama campaigned on what seemed like a conservative platform. He talked of tax cuts for 95 percent of Americans, less spending, no earmarks, and a more efficient federal government.

It was hard to imagine reality equaling the rhetoric.

Fighting Mad

I woke up on Wednesday after the election ready to do battle—not with Democrats but with Republicans. If we hadn't gotten the message now, we were completely deaf. The national media wanted to talk to me because they were interested in the rules changes I planned to offer in the Republican Conference to limit the power of senior members whose big-spending habits had, in my opinion, destroyed the image of the Republican Party and, along with big-spending Democrats, created a crushing and unsustainable debt load for our nation.

Obama's election was hailed around the world as a seminal achievement. Civil rights leader and Georgia Democrat Congressman John Lewis called the election a "nonviolent revolution." Hopes and expectations were extraordinarily high for Obama's presidency, but he would take office at a difficult time.

The stock market had its largest postelection decline in history. Auto companies were forecasting huge drops in sales and profits, and two of America's big three auto companies were asking Washington for $50 billion in loans. Housing sales continued to decline, foreclosures were increasing, and October job losses were worse than expected.

Distrust of Congress grew as radio talk shows filled the airways with reports of Democrats' plans to restore the so-called Fairness Doctrine to muzzle conservative media. Behind the euphoria of Obama's election, public alarm and anger were simmering. More and more people were wondering why Obama was being so reckless with our money. Myself, I was wondering why this was just now coming as such a big surprise.

During the week after the election, I did numerous radio and TV interviews. I was trying to make the point that Republicans had to acknowledge our mistakes publicly and begin to earn back the trust of the

American people with a bold reform agenda. On November 14, I traveled to Myrtle Beach to speak to about sixty members of the Republican National Committee from around the country, along with several national political reporters who were there to find out what Republicans planned to do to save the party. The theme of the conference was to "Renew, Reform, and Restore" the Republican Party.

I didn't pull any punches. The CNN story of my speech began: "South Carolina Sen. Jim DeMint on Friday became one of the first high-profile Republicans to publicly criticize John McCain following his electoral defeat, blaming the Arizona Senator for betraying conservative principles in his quest for the White House." But McCain was not the main thrust of my criticism. The article also quoted me saying, "Americans do prefer a traditional conservative government. They just did not believe Republicans were going to give it to them."

I told the Republican leaders in Myrtle Beach I planned to force votes on Senate seniority rules that have allowed a few bad apples to "rule and ruin" our Party. My proposals would place term limits on appropriators and elected Republican leaders.

As you might expect, this story did not play well with my Republican colleagues in Washington.

After every election both parties hold private meetings to elect their leaders and to formalize caucus rules. The Senate Republicans were scheduled to meet on November 18. Normally these meetings are filled with new "Senator-elect" members who are allowed to vote in our Conference even before they are sworn in. This year only two new Republicans replaced retiring Republicans: Jim Risch of Idaho and Mike Johanns of Nebraska. There were seven new Democrat Senators, not counting Al Franken. These postelection Conference meetings—especially this one—should be an opportunity for introspection, a time for Republicans to evaluate our performance in the last Congress and the last election and a time to adopt changes to make us more effective in the future.

But whether much introspection was taking place *inside* Congress, it was certainly taking place *outside* Congress with grassroots activists and conservative leaders across America. Just a few days after the election, a large cross-section of conservative leaders gathered at the home of Media Research

Center President Brent Bozell to discuss the future of the conservative movement. Bozell described the meeting in an interview on FOX News: "Conservatives have to reassert their position, and we are going to take over this country the way we did it with Ronald Reagan. But there is a lot of work that needs to be done. . . . The exit polls show that this country is every bit as center-right as it has been for a generation . . . and Barack Obama won as a conservative. That means he does not have the mandate to enact the left-wing agenda he wants to enact. The American people are still on our side. It becomes our job now to reconnect with the public."

Some changes were already taking place on the House side of the Capitol with conservatives Eric Cantor of Virginia assuming the post of Republican Whip and Mike Pence of Indiana becoming GOP Conference Chair. But in the Senate, where no such changes were likely to take place, I was at least hoping our existing Republican leadership would make some positive philosophical decisions to change the culture of spending and parochial politics in the Senate.

On November 17, 2008, the day before our conference meeting, the newspapers I read on my flight from South Carolina to Washington were full of stories about the Wall Street bailouts. The media discovered none of the bailout money was used to buy "toxic assets" as promised. We had been told the world economy would collapse if hundreds of billions of dollars of "toxic assets" weren't purchased within a few days. I was frustrated Republicans had led the bailout effort. Frustrated about a lot of things.

As the plane touched down at Reagan National Airport, the Capitol was in clear view across the river. As I contemplated the Republican Conference meeting, where I would be asking my fellow senators to consider a set of rules changes that I thought would indicate a wise, "we hear you" response to the election debacle, a sense of dread poured over me like a dark fog. Several of my colleagues had already encouraged me to withdraw my request for a vote on the rules changes. They said the vote would only irritate my Senate colleagues.

But I was more concerned with Republicans who were continuing to irritate the American people. One letter I received reflected what I was reading and hearing from thousands of letters, e-mails, and phone calls from people across the country. This letter was from Doug in Spartanburg,

South Carolina. One section captured the essence of his complaint and spoke for millions of Americans:

> My feelings and attitude took a drastic plunge and have never recovered from the 2000 election when the Republican Party betrayed Americans who voted for them! Voters who believed their loud and avowed campaign promises to: BALANCE THE BUDGET—ELIMINATE PORK-BARREL SPENDING, AND REDUCE THE SIZE AND INTRUSION OF GOVERNMENT. Voters, who placed their faith in them, voted them into office to do the job they vowed to do . . . and gave them control of the White House—and the Congress! Those lying criminals back-stabbed us at every turn for . . . 8 years!

Showdown in the Capitol

At 9:30 a.m. on Tuesday, November 18, 2008, the Senate Republican Conference convened in the Capitol for our leadership elections and to vote on my proposals to change our Conference rules. The leadership elections were a formality. It was all orchestrated in advance, and there was no competition for any position.

Next up, my rules changes proposal. Brace yourself.

The particulars of my proposal may sound boring and blandly procedural on their face, but trust me, they were actually quite controversial. A vote to change the rules for all Republican senators would have dramatic effects on hierarchy and influence among the senators.

At the risk of telling you something you already know, the Senate Republican Conference is the term used to describe all the Republicans in the Senate. There is a corresponding Democrat Conference or "Caucus" as they are often called. Each conference establishes its own rules for electing leadership, appointing committee members and leaders, determining term limits for leadership, and establishing other rules to guide how they operate. In the Republican Conference, our rules limit the time our committee leaders can serve to six years, except for appropriators. This is to reduce the concentration of power and potential corruption that inevitably occurs when a few people control any group or organization over a long period of time.

The Appropriations Committee, which includes thirty senators, is the Senate's largest committee and includes twelve subcommittees, each with a Democrat and a Republican leader. The "appropriators," as we call them, decide how all discretionary federal money is spent. They decide which senators get earmarks—the politically directed, parochial money that gives senators the opportunity to "bring home the bacon" for roads, bridges, college buildings, museums, local sewer plants, all kinds of press release and ribbon-cutting opportunities for reelection campaigns. Appropriators are generally our most senior members, so because of the seniority system, they also control most of our policy-making committees. And they compose the majority of elected leaders in the Republican Conference.

The appropriators decide which members get earmarks. So any Republican who opposes big-spending bills packed with everyone's earmarks will likely find himself on the backbench wishing he had not rocked the boat. Republican senators who betray our Conference on major policy votes will quickly be welcomed back into the fold, but those of us who vocally oppose earmarks have few supporters within the Republican Conference.

I proposed to limit the term of appropriators to six years. This meant I was making a frontal attack on those who controlled the culture of spending in the Senate. And because the votes on my proposals were the only other business on the docket other than leadership elections—for what would be the last Republican Conference meeting of the year—this was our last chance to show Americans we got their message from the election.

My proposals, in addition to limiting the terms of senators on the Appropriation Committee, included limiting the terms of our Conference leadership, having secret ballot elections for the leaders of our committees, and several other proposals designed to limit the power of appropriators and the seniority system. Knowing these proposals were not going to pass, I asked our leaders to put all of the questions on a single ballot. This would make it quick and easy for everyone to check yes or no on each question. Then we could all hand in our ballots, and it would be over. Right?

Not so fast! The leaders decided to make me present each question separately, to allow for debate and then to have a secret-ballot vote on each one. They were more than happy to see me squirm.

My first proposal was to limit the term of members of leadership to six years. It exempted our current leader, Senator Mitch McConnell of Kentucky, to prove my efforts were not directed at him. But five speakers were already lined up to talk about how this would be seen as a personal attack on McConnell and reported in the media as a vote of "no confidence" in our leadership.

I explained how a healthy rotation of leadership would be a signal Republicans were committed to serious reform. But all the speakers said any limits on the terms of leadership would be viewed as a rejection of McConnell. One senator suggested I withdraw that proposal, and I agreed. But when I tried to withdraw it, another senator objected, indicating that my proposal would have to be voted on.

Ed Corrigan, the executive director of the Steering Committee, the conservative group of senators I chair, tried to get my attention to remind me I did have the right to withdraw my proposal. A member of leadership shouted Corrigan down, "Staff cannot speak at Conference meetings!" In my ten years in Congress, I had never heard a staff member spoken to in such a derogatory way. As my designated staff at this meeting, Corrigan did have the right to speak to me. But the leadership ignored my request and held the vote anyway. I stood in front of the room for about five minutes while they counted the secret ballots: five ayes and thirty-six nays. The motion failed.

Another of my proposals was to limit the terms of members on the Appropriations Committee. Several senators were lined up to speak against this proposal, including appropriators Kit Bond of Missouri, Arlen Specter of Pennsylvania, Bob Bennett of Utah, and George Voinovich of Ohio. When they finished speaking, we had another secret-ballot vote. I stood alone again at the front of the room while the votes were counted. There were four votes for my proposal and thirty-five against. Motion failed.

I offered a few other technical proposals such as having secret-ballot elections for committee leaders to stop the election engineering and intimidation by senior members. That proposal was accepted by a voice vote, and I withdrew the others, just to put us all out of our misery.

The moment this meeting adjourned, I effectively entered a new phase of my Senate career. If I didn't realize it before, I certainly understood it then. I decided my work could no longer be with other senators. I would have to find ways to work with the American people to elect a new class of senators who would help me stop the spending, debt, and the expansion of the federal government.

I was now officially an outcast in Washington. A front-page *Politico* story that appeared after the meeting was headlined, "Republicans Chew on DeMint." In the article Utah Senator Bob Bennett was asked about my standing with Republicans. He responded, "I have no comment. That should be a comment in and of itself."

The next week I went to see McConnell hoping to clear the air and repair some of the damage. He graciously accepted my visit. I sat down and got right to the point, "Mitch, you kicked my butt. I want to work *with* you, not *against* you. I will continue to fight to stop the culture of earmarks, but I will always try to keep you informed about what I'm going to do. I will try not to surprise you." He smiled and reminded me, "Jim, you can't change the Senate."

Something happens to me when someone says, "You can't." I'm generally not very competitive unless someone tells me I can't do something that should be done. The meeting with McConnell seemed to have established a temporary détente with him, but I came away with a new challenge: changing the Senate. Yes, if the people in the Senate wouldn't change their minds, then I should try to change the people in the Senate.

Down, Not Out

The national media had little knowledge or interest in the drama I created within the Senate Republican Conference. They were only interested in the next federal bailout: the American auto industry. So there was no time to nurse my wounds from fellow Republicans. I took to the airwaves to make the case our auto companies should be forced to restructure under bankruptcy protection rather than be temporarily propped up with taxpayer money. Bankruptcy protection would allow the auto companies not only to restructure their debt and streamline their operations but also to throw out their gold-plated contracts with unions.

The Democrats insisted the bankruptcy process for the American auto industry would lead to the loss of millions of jobs. FOX News, radio talk shows, and Internet bloggers were helping me and other conservatives present the view that bankruptcy would, in the long term, allow our auto companies to reemerge as healthy, competitive, global companies. I left D.C. on Friday for the Christmas break believing any bailout of the auto companies would have to wait until Congress was back in session in January. President Bush could not authorize billions of dollars of spending without congressional approval.

Or so I thought.

On December 19, 2008, the Treasury Department announced it would use $17.4 billion in TARP funds, the Wall Street bailout money, to bail out General Motors and Chrysler. Americans were promised these funds would only be used to save financial institutions posing a systemic risk to America's economic system. In my mind this auto bailout was a clear violation of the law and an obvious sign that respect for the rule of law had fallen to an all-time low in Washington. President Bush didn't want the auto companies to fail on his watch, and he was willing to do whatever it took to make sure it didn't happen. To their credit, Ford Motor Company said no to the bailout, which made me even prouder of my ten-year-old Ford Crown Victoria.

The auto industry bailout was just another example of everything that was wrong about the way the people's elected officials were going about their business. It revealed more of the same basic misunderstandings—and more of the same unsustainable solutions—that were plaguing our nation's policies and exasperating guys like me who were fighting for just a little common sense to be applied to these problems. My world was starting to become a lonely place, and honestly, I didn't know how much more fight I had left in me, at least in this particular context and forum. I don't mind telling you, the 2008 election and the events surrounding the failure of my rules-change proposals took a personal toll on me. My actions damaged relationships with my colleagues. I began seriously to question whether the sacrifices required to serve in Congress were worth it. I walked away from a small business I built for fifteen years, and then spent years away from my family while my children were growing up to pursue elected office. My goal was to help restore the principles of freedom to America's governing philosophy, but now all my work seemed to have been in vain.

My despair didn't last long, however. God always has a way of picking me up, reminding me He is in charge, and getting me back on my feet. One morning the first week of December, I was at home going through a folder of constituent mail sent from my D.C. office. I came across a handwritten letter from Paul Weyrich, the conservative icon who ran the Coalitions for America and was a leader in the conservative movement for decades. Weyrich thanked me for a statement I wrote about him and had published in the Congressional Record. This was part of a tribute to Weyrich by conservative leaders from across the country. He said his wife framed my statement and put it on display in their home.

As part of this tribute to Weyrich, Morton Blackwell of the Leadership Institute wrote: "Next to Ronald Reagan, no single person has achieved more to advance the cause of American conservatism than Paul Weyrich. Paul Weyrich was the premier institution builder of the conservative movement. He held us all to his high standards. His achievements will benefit America and the world for generations."

When Weyrich was a Senate staffer in the 1970s, he was instrumental in creating the Steering Committee I now chaired. In his letter he wrote, "I can state without contradiction that you are the best Chairman we have ever had. When you combine your courage, insight, and willingness to act with Ed Corrigan's abilities, you are doing exactly what I designed the Steering Committee to do. I hope they keep you as chairman for a long time." That was a tremendous boost to my waning self-confidence because Jesse Helms, Phil Gramm, and other great conservative senators have chaired the Steering Committee. He ended his letter, "God bless you and thanks again—your Friend (for life)."

Weyrich died a few days after writing his letter to me. I was encouraged by the belief God used some of the last words of one of the great patriots of this generation to encourage me to stand up and get back in the fight. *OK*, I thought, *those sorry rascals may have beaten me in Washington, but I can beat them with the support of the American people.*

For the last two weeks of 2008, I was at home thinking, writing, and continuing to call into radio talk shows around the country. Communication was the key to activating the American people. The last chapter of my book *Saving Freedom* was e-mailed to my publisher a few days before their December 31 deadline. This chapter called on Americans to take action, even to "take to the streets" to demand the federal government stop the reckless spending, bailouts, debt, and government takeovers. I had no idea within a few months millions of Americans would actually take to the streets to protest our out-of-control federal government.

As Americans closed out 2008 and ushered in 2009, our economy was sliding deeper into recession, and unemployment continued to rise. The Democrat majority in Congress was pushing new legislation for a trillion-dollar government-spending stimulus plan. Illinois Governor Rod Blagojevich, disgraced by the accusation he tried to sell Barack Obama's vacated Senate seat, rejected appeals from Democrat leaders and appointed Roland Burris to the U.S. Senate. The Minnesota election board finally found enough votes to declare Democrat Al Franken the winner over Senator Norm Coleman.

It had truly been a wild year, and I welcomed the Christmas break. The week between Christmas and New Year's Day has always been the highlight of the year at the DeMint house. Debbie always makes the holidays special for our four children and me. Three of our children were now married to wonderful spouses, and we had our first grandson. Playing with my grandson was a good way to forget about Washington for a while but a powerful reminder of why I needed to go back to Washington with more determination than ever.

Holding together a marriage and family is hard work by any measure. Many times during our thirty-five years of marriage and over thirty years with children, we weren't sure we were going to make it. The physical, emotional, and financial pressures of making a large family work are sometimes too much to bear. But this Christmas, as Debbie and I watched our adult children with their spouses, we knew our sacrifice was more than worth it. They had all graduated college and were working hard to build their own lives and families. If we never accomplished anything else, we knew we would leave the world better than we found it because our children and grandchildren would make it better.

Back in the Battle

On Tuesday, January 6, 2009, I flew back to Washington to begin a new session. Debbie rarely comes to Washington, but she came with me not wanting to face an empty house and the post-Christmas blues alone. Our oldest daughter and her husband lived in D.C., so Debbie welcomed the opportunity to spend some additional time with them following their time with us in Greenville over the holidays.

After we landed, Debbie took the Metro to my daughter's apartment, and I headed to the Capitol to escort my recently reelected South Carolina colleague Senator Lindsey Graham for his swearing in ceremony. The Capitol and Senate office buildings were swarming with people from all over the country who came to the swearing-in ceremonies for many new Democrat senators. Receptions were everywhere. Republicans were walking the halls with their heads down while the Democrats were celebrating a new era of unbridled power.

On Wednesday, January 7, 2009, there was an all-day Senate Republican planning retreat in the Members Room at the Library of Congress. As I sat and listened to the presentations from our senior members, my mind drifted back to my first planning retreat as a U.S. senator in 2005. Then Republican Majority Leader Bill Frist of Tennessee liked my ideas about repositioning the Republican Party on the foundation of our original principles of limited government, free people, and free markets, so he asked me to present my plan at the retreat. This was unprecedented for a freshman to get a lead role in the planning process.

It was an exciting time for Republicans. George Bush was in the White House, and Republicans had a large majority in the House and fifty-five senators. The purpose of my presentation was to convince my colleagues to use this opportunity to pass the bold reforms most of us talked passionately about in our campaigns. This was the time to save Social Security by saving payroll taxes to create wealth for individuals rather than continuing to spend them on other government programs. This was the time to simplify our tax code and make our nation more competitive in the global economy. This was the time to make affordable health insurance available to every American by giving tax credits to those who didn't get their health insurance at work, expanding health savings accounts, eliminating frivolous lawsuits, and allowing interstate competition among insurance companies.

All of my colleagues nodded approvingly throughout my presentation, but it was quickly forgotten. There was never any effort to follow up on these or other reforms Americans expected Republicans to pass. Frist attempted to pass lawsuit reforms for health care, but not all Republicans supported him. Our senior members seemed satisfied to use our majority to get a larger share of earmarks for their states. When a few of us developed proposals to reform our tax code, Social Security, and health care, it was almost impossible to find senior Republicans to cosponsor the legislation.

In 2006, Americans told Republicans what they thought of our leadership; they voted many Republicans out of office. In 2008, Democrats expanded their majorities in both chambers of Congress and elected Barack Obama president. Now I was sitting at another Republican strategy retreat hearing the same message from the same senators.

I didn't feel welcome at the retreat so I only stayed for about an hour. I already knew the talking points: "Americans wanted Republicans to compromise and work together with Democrats. Barack Obama was too popular for us to criticize his proposals. We needed to keep our heads down and wait for the Democrats to overreach. We should not offer bold reform ideas that could be misrepresented by Obama because he controlled the bully pulpit." I didn't buy it. This was the time Republicans needed to stand together behind freedom solutions to provide a clear contrast with the big-government approach of the Democrats.

Before leaving D.C. on Thursday, I met with former Republican Representative Pat Toomey of Pennsylvania at a restaurant near my office. Toomey was a longtime friend from our time together in the House. He was considering running for governor of Pennsylvania but still had some interest in running for the Senate again. We were elected to the House the same year, in 1998, and served together for six years. Like me, he term-limited himself and ran for the Senate the same year I did, in 2004, but lost the Republican primary to Arlen Specter by one percentage point.

Toomey was an impressive candidate, a Harvard graduate who worked in international capital markets and started a family-owned restaurant business with his brothers. This gave him a practical perspective on fiscal issues. He originally ran for Congress because he wanted to do something to lower the huge tax burdens being imposed on Pennsylvania's small businesses. And when he came to Washington, he became a reliable advocate for limited government. He consistently fought to reduce the federal government's role in the private sector and decrease spending. Even under immense pressure from the Bush administration to vote for an expansion to the Medicare prescription drug benefit in 2003, he didn't buckle. Toomey and I were among only twenty-five Republicans who voted against it.

After Toomey lost his 2004 Senate primary bid to Specter, he went on to lead the Club for Growth, a group dedicated to electing fiscally conservative candidates and defeating RINOs, an acronym conservative activists assign to "Republicans in name only." Under Toomey's leadership, the Club for Growth became involved in many Republican primaries, opposing economically liberal Republican incumbents, such as former Rhode Island Senator Lincoln Chaffee. Chaffee refused to vote for President Bush in 2004, voted against tax cuts, and opposed Supreme Court Justice Sam Alito's nomination. Yet the Republican establishment supported Chaffee because he was "electable." Chaffee ultimately proved the Club for Growth right by abandoning the Republican Party after he lost his 2006 reelection to Democrat Sheldon Whitehouse. Chaffee changed his party affiliation to Independent and voted for Obama in the 2008 presidential election.

Regardless, the Club was not well liked inside the Beltway. Everyone from then-White House Senior Advisor Karl Rove to former House Speaker Newt Gingrich said their strategy was wrong. They wanted the Club for Growth to use their resources to beat Democrats instead of liberal Republicans.

But Toomey refused to back down. He answered his critics with an op-ed in *The Wall Street Journal* titled "In Defense of RINO hunting." Toomey argued that supporting Republicans who voted like Democrats was futile. "Winning for the sake of winning is an excellent short-term tactic, but a lousy long-term strategy," Toomey wrote. "Just look at the consequences of the 2006 congressional elections, when the GOP lost control of both houses of Congress. A Republican majority is only as useful as the policies that majority produces. When those policies look a lot like Democratic ones, the base rightly questions why it should keep Republicans in power."

There was no doubt that Toomey would fearlessly challenge Republican leadership when they were wrong. He'd been doing it all along.

"Pat," I said, "I could really use your help in the Senate; and if you decide to run, you will have my full support and all the resources of my SCF in the Republican primary against Arlen."

I knew this was no light promise I was making. But that doesn't mean I had fully grasped what honoring it would mean.

Inauguration Day

The next time I flew into Washington was the day before Obama officially became president. I had to come in on Monday because the Capitol Police warned members of Congress it would be impossible to get from the airport to the Capitol on Tuesday, Inauguration Day. They were expecting the largest crowd in history to attend the ceremony.

My boarding house is on the House side of the Capitol about a half mile from my office so my walk begins near the House office buildings, crosses in front of the Capitol, and then to the Senate office buildings. When I walked out my door on Inauguration Day, the streets were humming with crowds from one side of the Capitol to the other. The ceremony didn't begin until 11:00 a.m., but people were eager to get to their seats early.

When I arrived at my office, the hall outside my door was filled with constituents from South Carolina being served hot chocolate by my staff. A lot of folks back home were excited about Obama's election, and we had more than three thousand requests for inaugural tickets. Unfortunately, the Inaugural Committee gave each Senate office only a few hundred tickets to give to constituents. Those who received tickets were thankful.

On this day there didn't seem to be any differences between political parties, and the handshakes and hugs were all warm and genuine. I was honored so many of my fellow South Carolinians, Republicans and Democrats alike, felt comfortable celebrating in my office.

At 10:30 a.m., I joined all my colleagues in the Senate chamber to walk together to the inaugural platform. When I stepped off the Capitol steps onto the platform, I saw hundreds of thousands of people covering the National Mall for over a mile to the Lincoln Memorial. Michelle Obama and her two beautiful daughters were ushered to their seats, a picture-perfect first family. Rick Warren, a well-known evangelical pastor, gave the invocation.

The ceremony was patriotic and uplifting. President Obama gave an excellent speech about working together and unifying the nation. In one excerpt he focused on personal responsibility and values:

> Our challenges may be new, the instruments with which we meet them may be new, but those values upon which our success depends, honesty and hard work, courage and fair play, tolerance and curiosity, loyalty and patriotism—these things are old. These things are true. They have been the quiet force of progress throughout our history.
>
> What is demanded then is a return to these truths. What is required of us now is a new era of responsibility—a recognition, on the part of every American, that we have duties to ourselves, our nation and the world, duties that we do not grudgingly accept but rather seize gladly, firm in the knowledge that there is nothing so satisfying to the spirit, so defining of our character than giving our all to a difficult task. This is the price and the promise of citizenship. This is the source of our confidence: the knowledge that God calls on us to shape an uncertain destiny.[1]

The weather was cold but not uncomfortable. The sun was shining, and Americans were hopeful real change had finally come to Washington. I was hopeful, too.

Chapter 2

From Hope to Disillusionment

January 21, 2009—April 12, 2009

Two days after his inauguration, President Obama issued an executive order to close Gitmo, the $300 million prison built to house terrorists at America's military base at Guantanamo Bay, Cuba. He didn't announce where he would put more than one hundred of the world's most dangerous terrorists, but he clearly intended to move some of them to American soil.

Obama had promised during his campaign to close Gitmo so the decision itself was not a surprise. What *was* surprising—and disappointing—was his decision to do it with an executive order, with no congressional hearings, and with no plan. His move seemed more impulsive than thoughtful. The president's lack of management and executive experience was a concern before he was elected. Now, two days into his presidency, Obama began to confirm fears there was little substance behind his polished rhetoric.

Sources in South Carolina confirmed to me the Obama administration inquired with officials at the Charleston Air Force Base about the cost and logistics of moving some prisoners to the Navy brig in Charleston. The brig already housed Richard Reid, the infamous "shoe bomber." This lone prisoner required an entire section of the prison and millions of dollars in renovations to keep the area secure.

I immediately pledged to fight any attempt to move dangerous, international terrorists to Charleston. The city is a heavily populated area with military installations and a large commercial port. Holding terrorist prisoners in Charleston would be an open invitation for terrorist groups to attack innocent civilians or military targets to promote their deadly cause. Administration officials denied any intent to move Gitmo prisoners to Charleston, but we knew it was one of the sites they were considering.

On January 23, one day after announcing the closing of Gitmo, Obama issued another executive order reversing America's "Mexico City Policy," the long-standing policy banning American aid to organizations promoting or supporting abortion in other countries. The abortion debate in America elicits strong and deep divisions among reasonable people. Technological advances with ultrasound imaging and genetic research have shown that unborn children have beating hearts as early as five weeks after conception. This has caused more Americans to become pro-life when they understand unborn children are human beings. Even some pro-choicers have become more supportive of prohibitions on late-term abortions, partial-birth abortions, and abortions of convenience—particularly for the purpose of gender selection.

The majority of Americans agree government should not promote abortion with taxpayers' dollars. The president's order brazenly violated the strong consensus among pro-life and even many pro-choice advocates who agreed taxpayer funds should not be used to pay for or promote abortion overseas. Reversing this policy with an executive order seemed heavy-handed, even to many Obama supporters. President Obama's decision to use American tax dollars to promote abortion around the world was an affront, even to many who are ambivalent about the abortion debate. The willingness of the president to make such an important decision with so little explanation or emotion exposed the unseen, callous side of a man intent on transforming the cultural and economic framework of America.

With the nation's attention focused on Washington, and the media still fawning over every move made by the new president, few noticed a seemingly insignificant report from TWEAN News of Syracuse, New York, on January 24. Two dozen protesters in Binghamton, New York, wearing Indian headdresses similar to the band of eighteenth-century patriots who dumped tea in Boston Harbor to express outrage about British taxes, poured a few gallons of soda from a bridge into the Susquehanna River to protest New York Governor Paterson's new obesity taxes on soda.

The report quoted Trevor Leach, chairman of the Young Americans for Liberty in New York State, "We really want to see a sense of fiscal responsibility from the government and have them get their hands out of our pockets. The government has gotten out of hand and out of control in the last few decades and we're taking notice of that." This protest had nothing to do with President Obama. It was indicative of a latent but growing sense of outrage among Americans who believed government had become too intrusive in their lives.

Stimulating Outrage, Not Jobs

Days later President Obama signed the Lilly Ledbetter Law, a bill promoted by feminists to allow women to sue their employers for discrimination—*years* after the discrimination occurred—opening up a new playground for plaintiffs' lawyers.

Then on January 30, Obama gave a boost to the unions by issuing another executive order forcing federal contractors to expand unionization of their workforces. That order was followed by the announcement Obama would end the successful D.C. school voucher program giving many low-income, minority residents the opportunity to send their children to better schools. This was blatant and shameless pandering to the teachers unions.

I met with several African-American parents and their children whose lives were transformed when they left dangerous, underachieving government schools and began attending independent schools. These parents tasted the freedom of making their own choices about the best schools for their children, and they did not want to lose this new freedom. They were incredulous Obama bowed so quickly to the teachers unions by deciding to end a school choice program so beneficial to low-income, minority students.

Less than two weeks after his inauguration, Obama crammed through executive orders and laws to pay back his political allies: the antiwar left, proabortion advocates, plaintiffs' lawyers, and labor union bosses. The fresh sense of optimism from the inaugural ceremonies was quickly being replaced with foul, old Washington air.

Washington was worse than ever because the checks and balances of two-party government were gone. Obama and the Democrat Congress had complete control of the federal government and were making it abundantly clear their talk of bipartisanship was nothing more than empty campaign promises. Everyone seemed to be mesmerized by Obama and paid little attention to his political paybacks. Schools and streets were being renamed after him. The president was in office less than a week, and he was already being compared to FDR.

It was as if Obama thought he had a mandate to do whatever he liked. He went on to announce the census would, for the first time, be run out of the White House instead of the Commerce Department. This was part of an overall plan to consolidate their political power. In an effort to increase the number of congressmen representing urban, Democrat-leaning regions, the White House wanted to calculate population estimates based on sampling in those areas, rather than a traditional head count. The Census Bureau then caused another national commotion by wasting $2.5 million in taxpayer money on an ad promoting the census during the Super Bowl. These actions resulted in Republican Senator Judd Gregg of New Hampshire withdrawing as Obama's nominee for Secretary of Commerce.

On February 5, Democrat Senator Debbie Stabenow of Michigan announced Congress should hold hearings about adopting the Fairness Doctrine, a discredited federal regulation making it almost impossible for conservative talk radio to continue to espouse political opinions. Former Democrat President Bill Clinton quickly added his support of the Fairness Doctrine, saying too much money was supporting the right-wing talk show in America. This belied the preponderance of evidence confirming major television networks and most other media were liberal and biased to the core.

The discomfort level for many Americans was increasing daily as conservative media and Internet blogs reported one dubious action after another by the new administration. But with the mainstream media continuing to promulgate the impression Obama was America's knight in shining armor, President Obama's popularity remained high among the majority of Americans.

President Obama devoted the first weeks of his presidency to passing a near trillion-dollar stimulus package, by far the largest domestic spending bill in American history. I was stunned after my first look at the legislation. It was a giant slush fund for pet projects. The Democrats took all the ideas they had collected during their decade in the minority and stuffed them into this huge, bloated, and wasteful legislation. Millions of dollars were being spent on projects like turtle tunnels under highways in Florida and golf course renovations. We even found a $30 million item to save a wetland mouse in Speaker Pelosi's congressional district. The stimulus was great fodder for late-night comedy shows, but the implications of this legislation were deadly serious for millions of unemployed Americans: there were almost no incentives for real job creation in this trillion-dollar boondoggle.

To counter the Democrat big-government stimulus bill, I introduced "The American Option" jobs bill, and other Republicans introduced free-market alternatives to Obama's massive government spending plan. My jobs plan would have stopped the planned tax increases at the end of the year and lowered business tax rates to 25 percent. Instead of expanding government through higher taxes as the Democrats were planning, my plan left trillions of dollars in the hands of consumers and job creators.

Despite my efforts and those of other Republicans with similar proven solutions, Obama and his media allies mocked Republicans for not having any ideas to improve the economy. On February 6 in Williamsburg, Virginia, the president bashed critics of his stimulus plan by saying "the scale and scope" of his economic plan was right. He claimed his critics were hawking "phony arguments" and "false theories of the past" to chip away at the bill's programs. He said Americans had no more stomach for such "petty politics," and that they "did not vote for the status quo."

The only conclusion I could draw from his statements was that the president was defining limited government and free-market capitalism as "false theories of the past." Republicans were promoting proven economic solutions such as lower taxes and less government interference in the markets. The president's solutions were driving America toward a European-style of economic socialism. The fact is, most Republicans knew exactly what was needed to rebuild the American economy, but the national press ignored our ideas.

Government spending, borrowing, debt, bailouts, and takeovers were solidifying partisan differences in Washington, while dissolving partisan divides among the American people. Citizens across the political spectrum were increasingly concerned about the direction of the country. The February 2009 cover of *Newsweek* magazine declared, "We Are All Socialists Now." The sense of optimism and hope Obama engendered during his campaign was quickly turning to disillusionment.

The House passed its version of the economic stimulus plan before the end of January without one Republican vote. When the interest expense of all this borrowed money was added, the total cost of the bill was over $1 trillion. President Obama claimed it contained tax cuts for 95 percent of Americans, but the cuts were so minuscule as to make his claim laughable. The bill expanded federal spending and debt at an unprecedented rate and promoted mostly government and union jobs.

When the bill came to the Senate, there was some hope Republicans could stop or significantly change the bill passed by the House. Democrat Senator Ben Nelson of Nebraska publicly stated he was opposed to the bill. If he held his position, Republicans could—if we all stayed together—force the Democrats to create a more balanced and affordable bill.

But the defection of a few Republicans on major pieces of legislation was so routine and predictable as to produce snickers by the press when we promised to stand together on important issues. Early in February, Nelson along with three Republicans—Specter, as well as both Susan Collins and Olympia Snowe of Maine—announced they had reached a compromise with the Democrat leadership. In return for a nominal cut in total spending, they agreed to support the bill. The bill remained a massive government expansion plan packed with parochial earmarks and almost no stimulus to private sector jobs.

The sad fact is a few Republican big spenders (mostly appropriators) in the Senate were now defining our party for the American people. Whenever these Republicans defect to support big-spending, big-government legislation, the Democrats claim the bill is bipartisan. This implicates all Republicans for supporting wasteful spending, pork-barrel earmarks, and debt. I am convinced a few Senate Republicans were the primary reason the Republican Party lost our credibility with the American people and our majority.

All the same, President Obama came to the Senate Republican Policy lunch the first week in February to sell his "bipartisan" stimulus plan. The president told us if we did nothing, unemployment would increase to more than 9 percent. He already had the votes to pass his plan, but he wanted more Republicans to vote for it, presumably so we could share the blame if it didn't work. On February 10, the Senate passed Obama's economic stimulus plan with only three Republicans voting aye—Specter, Collins, and Snowe.

President Obama signed his economic stimulus plan—the American Recovery and Reinvestment Act—on February 17, 2009, promising it would keep unemployment below 8 percent. He also promised the money would not be earmarked for pet projects. The passage of Obama's stimulus plan blew a huge hole in the federal budget so Congress had to pass additional legislation to raise the national debt limit to $12.104 trillion to accommodate the massive increase in spending.

The next day, February 18, Obama announced the Home Affordability and Stability Plan and the creation of the Home Affordable Modification Program. This plan promised to spend $75 billion to help homeowners pay their mortgages. It also increased aid to the government-owned mortgage giants Freddie Mac and Fannie Mae from $100 billion to $200 billion—*double!*

This was getting absolutely ridiculous and out of hand. New government programs and spending were being announced so quickly, few could keep up with their costs or content. Americans were pinned against their seats in a speeding roller coaster going faster and faster at every turn—and always downhill! I guess the president's chief of staff, Rahm Emanuel, wasn't kidding when he had warned in 2008 that Democrats should "never let a good crisis go to waste," because we were all beginning to find out what he meant! In less than a month, President Obama and an unchecked Democrat Congress had increased federal spending, bailouts, and debt at a historic rate—all while blaming Bush for it.

The following day, February 19, 2009, on the floor of the Chicago Mercantile exchange, CNBC's Rick Santelli had seen enough. He exploded in a spontaneous rant calling for a tea party to revolt against the Obama administration's mortgage bailout plan. Fellow traders cheered when Santelli ridiculed the president for his tax cut of "a whopping $8 or $10 in their check." Then he challenged the president directly on his bailout of mortgage holders:

> Why don't you put up a Web site to have people vote on the Internet as a referendum to see if we really want to subsidize the losers' mortgages? Or would they at least like to buy cars, buy a house that is in foreclosure, . . . give it to people who might have a chance to actually prosper down the road, and reward people that can carry the water instead of drink the water? This is America! How many people want to pay for your neighbor's mortgage that has an extra bathroom and can't pay their bills? Raise their hand! President Obama, are you listening?[2]

He went on, "We're thinking of having a Chicago tea party in July! All you capitalists that want to show up at Lake Michigan, I'm gonna start organizing it."[3]

Santelli's rant became the "shot heard around the world" for America's new tea party movement. Cable news shows replayed the video for several days. The White House's overly defensive response added fuel to the fire when Obama's spokesman, Robert Gibbs, attacked Santelli in unusually personal terms. "I'm not entirely sure where Mr. Santelli lives or in what house he lives, but the American people are struggling every day to meet their mortgages, stay in their jobs, pay their bills, send their kids to school," Gibbs said. It was an obvious effort to intimidate the president's critics.

Cable news and radio talk shows had a field day discussing the relevance of "where Mr. Santelli lives or in what house he lives." Obama became the butt of jokes on late-night network television shows. FreedomWorks, a conservative grassroots organization, initiated an online "Angry Renter" petition to draw attention to all the struggling renters who were trying to live within their means by waiting to buy a house. Bumper stickers appeared across the country with the message, "Honk if you're paying my mortgage."

Behind the humor was a growing sense of alarm. John O'Hara, in his book *The New American Tea Party,* captured the concerns of millions of

Americans when he described the reaction of fellow traders to Santelli's outburst:

> "These traders weren't reacting to the reallocation of wealth so much as the prospect of the United States' decline," O'Hara wrote. "These were not ideologues or talking heads, nor were they activists or lobbyists. They were simply working people who wanted the freedom to continue working and to enjoy the fruits of their labor in a fair way. Santelli's complaint about the unfairness of rewarding irresponsible behavior of those who didn't play fair resonated."[4]

Americans were now beginning to feel the same frustration and alienation I felt with the people now running the federal government. And just as I had experienced, Americans who stood up against the Washington establishment were met with intimidation and humiliation. The president and the Congress believed they knew what was best for the great unwashed masses, and they had no patience with anyone who disagreed. They were going to cram misguided government programs down our throats whether we liked it or not. They were going to waste taxpayer money with self-serving parochial earmarks. And they were going to spend, borrow, and bury our country under a mountain of debt.

There was little doubt about what Obama and the Democrats intended to do. The only question was: were there enough freedom-loving Americans with the courage to stand up, speak out, and take our country back?

I didn't yet know the answer to that question. Our nation had been plagued with apathy for many years, and I was afraid the independent, self-reliant American spirit might be approaching extinction. For decades voters had overwhelmingly reelected the big spenders in Congress who brought home the bacon—the congressmen and senators who voted for wasteful, parochial, pork-barrel spending projects.

Were Americans ready to say enough is enough? Would the majority of voters actually say no to more government programs and spending?

I hoped the answer was yes. If Americans knew the truth about how the government was bankrupting our nation and if we could give them a way to stop it, I believed they would respond. So I appointed myself as a spokesman for freedom-loving Americans. In my media interviews I tried to speak *for* concerned Americans, not *to* them. Over the next few weeks I increased my efforts in the media to speak out on behalf of disillusioned and alarmed Americans. At this point I wasn't sure if I was speaking for a few hundred or a few million Americans.

In addition to dozens of talk radio and FOX News appearances, I debated Massachusetts Democrat Congressman Barney Frank, chairman of the House Budget Committee, on the Sunday morning program *This Week* hosted by George Stephanopoulos about the stimulus and mortgage bailouts. My debate with Frank was particularly revealing about the different philosophies at war in Washington. I said we needed to leave more money in the hands of consumers and businesses instead of raising taxes to grow government. Frank said, "No tax cut builds a road. No tax cut puts a cop on the street. No tax cut educates a child in the way that it ought to be done."

Frank is a fast talker, but he didn't have his facts straight. I responded, "Only 5 percent of this bill goes to roads and infrastructure, and you're trying to tell the American people this is an infrastructure bill." When he railed against big bonuses for Wall Street bankers, I argued the real problem was with the politicians who were giving Wall Street bankers taxpayer money to pay the bonuses.

It was hard to get a word in with Frank trying to dominate the time, but I was able to land a few jabs. I concluded, "Don't say it's a stimulus when it's a government-spending plan."

Americans to the Rescue

On February 24, 2009, President Obama addressed a joint session of Congress to present his first-year agenda. I didn't want to attend. Any hopefulness I'd felt from his inauguration a month earlier had faded. I resented Obama's "in your face" style, and I didn't want to go through the dozens of requisite standing ovations. In short, I now believed Obama had deceived the voters during his campaign. He was the most liberal member of the U.S. Senate and quickly became the most liberal president in a generation. But I had to show up at the president's first address to Congress. Anything less would be considered disrespectful. My beef was not with the office of the president but with the man sitting in it.

As expected, Obama gave a great speech. In addition to selling his massive economic stimulus bill, the president announced his plan to offer government health insurance to every American, punish the big banks for the financial meltdown by increasing federal control of the nation's financial system, pass an energy tax, and bail out millions of homeowners who couldn't afford their mortgage payments. Obama and the Democrats were in complete control, and they intended to expand government into almost every area of the private sector.

After detailing his plans to spend trillions of dollars creating new government programs, Obama pledged to cut spending by going through the budget "line by line." He added, "Yesterday I held a fiscal summit where I pledged to cut the deficit in half by the end of my first term in office. My administration has also begun to go line by line through the federal budget in order to eliminate wasteful and ineffective programs. As you can imagine, this is a process that will take some time. But we're starting with the biggest lines. We have already identified two trillion dollars in savings over the next decade." We all stood and applauded, knowing this was impossible in the context of all his new spending proposals.

Over the next few weeks Fannie Mae and Freddie Mac received billions more bailout dollars. The Treasury Department, without congressional approval, gave $5 billion to auto parts companies (union shops) and bought $15 billion in small business loans. Congress passed a huge annual spending bill with nearly ten thousand pork-barrel earmarks, despite Obama's promise to stop earmarks. The Democrats were continuing on a rampage of government spending and expansion.

But on February 27, the cavalry arrived in Washington, D.C.

The Conservative Political Action Conference known as CPAC, the nation's largest gathering of conservative leaders and activists, came to town for their annual meeting. I gave the opening keynote address for the conference. The opportunity to speak to thousands of like-minded conservatives was both exciting and therapeutic. Frankly, I needed their support more than they needed my speech. They came to CPAC discouraged after the disastrous 2008 elections, but they were still determined. I wanted to encourage them to stay in the fight and tell them I desperately needed their help to change the direction of the country. I reminded them there had never been a greater, more prosperous, or more compassionate nation than the United States of America. We had nothing to apologize for. We believe in personal responsibility, capitalism and free markets, Judeo-Christian values, and, importantly, limited constitutional government.

During the speech I said, "Obama is the world's best salesman of socialism." (The media later had a field day with that quote.) I challenged the roomful of cheering conservatives to "take to the streets to protest government spending, borrowing, bailouts, debt, and takeovers." They were ready for the challenge, and I left CPAC more convinced than ever Americans were ready to take back their country.

Were they ever. And ready to prove it.

A few hours later across town near the White House, roughly three hundred protesters gathered for one of the first modern-day tea parties. One organizer wrote:

> The participants consisted of men, women, teens, and families. Democrats, Republicans, and Libertarians waved Gadsden flags and signs decrying bailouts and pork or calling for the Fed to be audited. It was beautiful, it was real, and it was entirely unscripted. . . . Following the event, the mood was not one of anger but of hope, but it was a different flavor of hope than promised during the recent election. The event, while only a few hundred strong, showed those present and those watching at home that they were not alone. Little did we know this last-minute, first-time rally of ours would spark a nationwide "million-man" taxpayer protest.[5]

I remember seeing a short clip on one of the news channels about this small protest at the White House. The media, in typical fashion, treated the demonstration as an insignificant rally of a few discontented conservatives. Rallies and protests were commonplace in D.C., and no one in Washington gave much thought to another group of malcontents at the White House. But this tea party was the answer to my hopes and prayers. I thought I was a one-man band working alone to recruit Americans to save freedom in our nation and didn't realize thousands of citizens were already well ahead of me organizing over the Internet to fight for freedom. They were hoping and praying for a few members of Congress to stand with them!

And I was proud to be at the front of the line, with my hand up, my bags packed, and my commitment strong. I knew I wasn't going it alone. I was going out with full voice, with major backup, with the heart and soul of like-minded Americans from all over the country and from every walk of life, and with every intention of doing whatever it takes to put our nation back on its feet again. To bring us back to our senses. *To save freedom.*

The next evening at the closing of CPAC, Rush Limbaugh gave an eighty-five-minute speech. Rush had been the first conservative "voice in the wilderness" I heard before ever considering running for public office. He confirmed my belief our government had become disconnected from our founding principles. He mobilized conservative citizens like few, if any, before him, and was a catalyst for the Republican takeover of Congress in 1994. He then became an articulate critic of Republicans who failed to keep their promises. He essentially created modern-day conservative talk radio. Say what you will about Limbaugh, you can't deny he has changed the landscape of American politics.

Limbaugh, whose daily three-hour radio talk show has the largest audience of any radio show in history, expressed his desire for Obama to fail "if his mission is to restructure and reform this country so that capitalism and individual liberty are not its foundation."

Boy, did that statement strike a nerve in high places!

The White House launched a full-on offensive the next week attacking Limbaugh. A March 5, 2009 article from Reuters titled, "White House Enemy No. 1: Rush Limbaugh," framed the target with threatening precision and clearly exposed the plot being concocted:

> The White House has seen the enemy, and his name is Rush Limbaugh. President Barack Obama's team is helping lead an effort to cast Limbaugh, a polarizing, conservative talk show host, as the Republican Party's new face, using campaign-style attacks against a high profile target. . . . The goal is to convince Americans that the popularly known "Grand Old Party" of Abraham Lincoln is a shell of its former self and in the grip of its most narrow, right wing, in hopes of making independents and moderates think twice about switching allegiance.[6]

By doing this, President Obama again broke precedent with previous presidents by personally attacking his critics and mentioning Limbaugh's name. This type of banter was traditionally beneath the office of the president and made Obama appear immature.

But his attempts to radicalize Republicans didn't work, and Limbaugh came out the winner in this skirmish. Having a daily audience of millions of Americans made it hard for even a president to intimidate him. The president's attacks only increased the size of Limbaugh's audience. The next week he declared on his show, "They need a demon to distract and divert from what their agenda is; they need a demon about whom they can lie so as to persuade average Americans that they're the good guys." Conservatives like Limbaugh were making a difference.

In fact, all of us were. With everyone's help.

The first week of March 2009, I received a short letter signed by dozens of friends from our church. They were following my struggles through the national media and local radio talk shows, and most were on my e-mail list for regular updates from the front lines. Their message encouraged me to keep fighting and praying:

> Dear Jim, Your friends here at Mitchell Road Presbyterian have been praying for you and Debbie at a very serious time in the history of our country. We are very aware of the pressure on you by both the Democrats and Republicans for your conservative stand on issues. Right is right and wrong is wrong! And we appreciate your strong stand for the individual freedom we enjoy in our beloved country. Please keep up the fight for freedom and capitalism that made our country the greatest in the history of this world. And we pray for the gift of faith you have by God's grace. Stand tall in your faith. We are continually praying for your strength and God's wisdom at a very critical point in the future of our country.

The bottom of the letter was filled with signatures of old friends I served with as deacon, elder, Sunday school teacher, and board member of our church's Christian school. This was just one of many ways God continued to use friends and fellow Americans to remind me I was not in this battle alone.

By mid-March, tea parties were springing up all over the country. Thousands attended rallies in Orlando and Cincinnati. Yet major networks provided almost no coverage of the growing tea party movement. Still, the Internet buzz continued to grow. With the hated April 15 tax day approaching, thousands of Americans were busy planning hundreds of antitax and anti-debt rallies to demonstrate their frustration with Washington.

I had a feeling Washington could hear them coming.

Chapter 3

Americans Take to the Streets

April 13, 2009—May 31, 2009

On April 13, 2009, *New York Times* columnist Paul Krugman published an editorial titled, "Tea Parties Forever," in which he grossly misrepresented the origins and purposes of the tea party movement. Krugman declared, "Republicans have become embarrassing to watch. And it doesn't feel right to make fun of crazy people. Better, perhaps, to focus on the real policy debates, which are all among Democrats."

Krugman made no attempt to research or understand why Americans with a wide variety of political views were taking to the streets. His only goal appeared to be to demean concerned citizens. He wrote, "These parties—anti-taxation demonstrations that are supposed to evoke the memory of the Boston tea party and the American Revolution—have been the subject of considerable mockery, and rightly so."

The New York Times and virtually all of the liberal media assumed the tea parties were a creation of the Republican Party and right-wing conspirators because Democrats, union bosses, ACORN, MoveOn.Org, and other left-wing groups spend millions to organize practically all of the big-government demonstrations. Krugman continued: "It turns out that the tea parties don't represent a spontaneous outpouring of public sentiment. They're Astroturf (fake grassroots) events, manufactured by the usual suspects. In particular, a key role is being played by FreedomWorks, an organization run by Richard Armey, the former House majority leader, and supported by the usual group of right-wing billionaires. And the parties are, of course, being promoted heavily by FOX News."

I knew enough about the tea party movement to know it was not the creation of any political group. No Republican or conservative organization has the ability to get millions of people to show up at rallies. The tea parties are characterized by people who have disdain for the political establishment in Washington, including Republicans. Politicians are only allowed to speak at tea parties by invitation. Republicans and Democrats who voted for the bailouts are often booed at tea parties, town halls, and rallies.

As April 15 approached, literally hundreds of homemade Web sites in cities across the country were encouraging people to come to tax day rallies. Facebook was often the place where citizens could get event information. Amateur organizers were busy trying to figure out how to find locations, secure permits, and select speakers.

One of the organizers of the Chicago tax day tea party recalls being contacted by the scheduler for Republican National Committee Chairman Michael Steele. Steele was going to be in Chicago on April 15 and assumed the organizers would be thrilled to have the RNC chairman speak to the crowd. "Thanks, but no thanks" was the response. Steele was welcome to attend, but no elected officials would be speaking.

This was no insider movement. This was grass roots at its finest.

For my part, I began calling local radio talk shows in South Carolina to promote tea party rallies across the state on April 15. I was invited to speak at rallies in Columbia and Charleston and readily agreed. We hoped these larger rallies would have at least a few hundred people, but it was hard to find out how many people would participate. When we asked for details, the response was, "We just sent out a bunch of e-mails."

On Tuesday, April 14, I drove to Columbia to participate in the annual South Carolina Washington Night. The event usually attracts the entire South Carolina delegation: six congressmen and two senators. It is the only time during the year the South Carolina congressional delegation of both parties gets together, and it is always a contentious evening.

We all sit in a lineup next to one another on a stage in front of several hundred businesspeople from around the state. A moderator asks each of us questions posed by the audience. This year was even more awkward than usual as I blasted Obama and Democrat policies while sitting shoulder to shoulder with the Democrat House Majority Whip Jim Clyburn. Of all the representatives I was the only one who agreed that Republican Governor Mark Sanford was right to reject stimulus money. Sanford believed accepting money for government programs the state couldn't afford to fund after the stimulus money ran out was wrong.

"Everybody says that we can't live without money we didn't know existed three months ago," I told them. It didn't make sense. I said we needed to break our dependency on federal dollars, especially when they come with so many strings attached. The money would ultimately become a bigger burden on our state.

The Washington Night debate was over about 6:00 p.m., and I headed for my Columbia office to hold a tele-town hall meeting with people from across South Carolina. With technology now allowing elected representatives to communicate more directly with our constituents, I regularly call tens of thousands to update them on issues in Congress and to answer questions about whatever is on their minds. That night we talked to about eight thousand people around the state.

Most of the questions from fellow citizens were laser focused on the out-of-control spending, borrowing, debt, and government takeovers. Some of the participants were transformed from enthusiastic Obama supporters to alarmed and concerned citizens afraid for the future of their country. A few people heard about rallies scheduled for tax day, but none seemed to know many details about rallies in their area. This led me to conclude the rallies in South Carolina would be small and poorly attended.

I finished the tele-town hall and checked into a hotel in Columbia about 9:00 p.m., hoping to get some sleep before the long next day on April 15. As I set the alarm on my BlackBerry, a blinking red light flagged an article sent to me from my Washington staff. It was titled, "Federal Agency Warns of Radicals on Right."

I couldn't sleep after reading it. In plain English it admitted, "The Department of Homeland Security is warning law enforcement officials about a rise in 'rightwing extremist activity,' saying the economic recession, the election of America's first black president and the return of a few disgruntled war veterans could swell the ranks of white-power militias." A footnote attached to the report by the Homeland Security Office of Intelligence and Analysis defined "rightwing extremism in the United States" as including not just racist or hate groups but also groups that reject federal authority in favor of state or local authority. "It may include groups and individuals that are dedicated to a single-issue, such as opposition to abortion or immigration," the warning stated.

What? People who believed in smaller government and free-market sensibilities were now considered threats to the state? "Disgruntled war veterans" were deemed potential enemies of our nation? Preposterous! It was inconceivable to me that our Secretary of Homeland Security would characterize Americans who believe in federalism as extremists and put them in the same category as racists and hate groups. I couldn't believe my own government would classify people like me who were against abortion and illegal immigration as potentially dangerous.

The timing of this "warning" before the April 15 rallies was frightening. The Obama administration appeared to be setting up the tea party demonstrators as dangerous extremists. All of this made me even more worried about the next day's events. I prayed they would be peaceful and positive, but I couldn't help struggling to sleep.

Tax Day 2009

Wednesday, April 15, I appeared on a local Columbia morning television talk show to discuss tax day protests around the nation and to promote the rally in front of the State House. I spoke confidently about the growing movement of concerned citizens and the "great awakening" occurring in America, even though I was more hopeful than confident. The moderator attempted to minimize the significance of the rallies and focused his questions on the economy and reports the Obama stimulus was already working.

After the interview a member of my staff drove me to our Columbia office for several meetings before speaking to the rally at the State House at 1:00 p.m. When I arrived at the office, my state director told me several hundred people were already gathering in front of the State House steps. "This is going to be big!" he said. My disposition improved immediately. I was afraid to let myself get excited about the possibility of a real American awakening, but now it might actually be happening.

At 12:45 p.m., we left my office for the short drive to the State House. People with signs were everywhere! Some protesters had hats with tea bags taped to them, and there were a lot of homemade signs about bailouts, debt, and taxes.

As my staff guided me through the crowd, people began to hug me and shake my hand. I hugged them back like long-lost friends. It felt like a surprise birthday party, only better. This party, and parties like it around the country, were going to surprise a lot of politicians with some unwanted gifts in ballot boxes on Election Day.

Several in the crowd grabbed my arm with a genuine sense of urgency. They said three things I continue to hear around the country to this day: "Thanks for fighting," "We're praying for you," and, "What can I do?"

I still don't know how to adequately describe how this felt. When I was introduced to speak, the crowd stood and cheered for what seemed like five minutes. Almost instinctively, I folded my prepared remarks and put them in my pocket. This called for nothing other than a heart-to-heart talk with friends, not an impersonally scripted speech. I instantly realized this was not your average, run-of-the-mill moment. In fact, I don't know if I can ever recall being in a setting that felt so completely real, so thoroughly right, so honestly and unusually familiar, even in the presence of many I had never seen before. "I'm not here as a Republican, or a conservative, or a senator today," I said. "I'm here as a fellow American who is very concerned about the direction of our country. I know the last place to change is Washington D.C."

Someone from the crown yelled, "Amen!" as I spoke.

"The first thing to change is right here in the hearts and the minds of the American people," I continued, "We can take back our country!"

Standing on the Capitol steps behind me was Governor Sanford. It was my job to introduce him when I finished speaking. Sanford had been a friend since we served together in the U.S. House. He was a little quirky and I wasn't close to him, but he had a reputation at that time as a man of faith, integrity, and strong character. He was quickly becoming a national conservative leader, and I was honored to introduce him to the roaring cheers of our fellow South Carolinians.

After the rally in Columbia, I immediately went to Charleston. The Charleston tea party rally was held downtown in front of the century-old Custom House, a historic location. When I looked through my Charleston office window, more than a thousand people appeared to be lining the streets below. The street in front of our building was closed to traffic and filled with people. This was a real surprise for Charleston. We waited for Sanford to arrive. Our speaking rotation was the same as in Columbia. Sanford and I walked out of the large second-floor door beneath tall marble columns and stood several steps above one of the local organizers as he spoke. Down on the street I saw young couples with children in strollers. There were also businessmen in suits, tourists in Jimmy Buffet attire, and seniors bearing hats laden with tea bags. Across the street, on a third-floor rooftop bar, customers with drinks were watching from a ledge.

I was again amazed at the energy and enthusiasm of the people who stood in front of me. When Sanford and I finished speaking, I walked down the steps and waded into the crowd. Everyone was cheerful, friendly, and thankful for the opportunity to express their frustration with America's leaders. I heard many of the same pleas expressed in Columbia, "Thanks for fighting; don't give up," "I pray for you every day," and "I've never done anything like this before; how can I help?"

There were Democrats, Republicans, and Independents, but none with much affinity for any political party. All were ready to "throw the bums out and start over." I responded to one participant I'd be the first bum out the door if all the rest of them would leave with me, but she was insistent I stay in the Senate and keep fighting. The energy and enthusiasm of the crowd were contagious. The tax day tea parties recharged my batteries!

The Media Trashes Tax Day Tea Parties

In the aftermath of the April 15 tea parties, much of the liberal press continued to insist the movement was motivated by self-serving conservative or Republican groups.

The Atlantic reported, "Three national-level conservative groups, all with slightly different agendas, are guiding it." CNN reporter Susan Roesgan became infamous for berating a tea party activist who was holding his young son. Her on-air lecture to the young man on Obama's policies was so over-the-top she later lost her job.

Speaker Pelosi called the tea parties "Astroturf" and claimed they were organized and funded by "some of the wealthiest people in America." Pelosi seemed to live in a fantasy world. Her comments were delusional. She consistently made statements with no basis in fact. Her outlandish statements about concerned citizens were incredibly irresponsible for someone in her position as Speaker of the U.S. House of Representatives.

CNN, MSNBC, and other media outlets consistently used the derogatory term "teabagging" when describing the protests. Brent Bozell, president of the Media Research Center, said the media coverage of the tea parties was "insulting." Bozell exclaimed, "I've never seen anything like it, the oral sex jokes on (CNN) and particularly MSNBC on teabagging. . . . They had them by the dozens. That's how insulting they were toward people who believe they're being taxed too highly."

On April 16, MSNBC's Keith Olbermann and his guest Janeane Garofalo were in rare form, showing visible contempt and hostility toward tea party demonstrators. Garofalo called the protestors "a bunch of teabagging rednecks," then added, "This is about hating a black man in the White House. This is racism straight up." *Racism?* Really? The tea parties had nothing to do with racism, and Obama was only a part of the problem. Americans were waking up and they were angry with the whole political establishment in Washington.

Estimates of the total attendance at rallies nationally ranged from 250,000 to a million. (Typical spinning of true numbers.) The media reported two thousand people attended rallies in South Carolina, for example, but I know for certain—having seen it with my own two eyes—there were more than two thousand at just the two rallies alone where I spoke in Columbia and Charleston. Hundreds, if not thousands more attended rallies in small towns across the state. And two days later, on April 17, at another rally in Greenville, there were well over a thousand more.

But no matter who was counting, the real story was this: for every American who attended a tea party, there were many more who felt the same way. That was the best news of all! Over half of Americans had a favorable view of the tea parties, and a Rasmussen poll reported 32 percent of Americans had a "very favorable" opinion of the events. Very few elected officials in that poll were viewed "very favorably" by a third of their constituents.

Back in Washington the next week, I introduced legislation along with Republican Senators David Vitter of Louisiana and Jim Inhofe of Oklahoma titled, "Protecting Taxpayers from Bailout Fallout." We were trying to stop the weekly issuance of new bailouts from the White House, which were becoming commonplace enough by now to make us all wonder if the "free money" merry-go-round was ever going to stop. Yet our press conference announcing the legislation attracted little attention from the media, and we couldn't find one Democrat to help us protect Americans from more taxpayer giveaways. Obama was emptying the Treasury, taking control of our markets, and Republicans simply did not have the votes to stop him.

This was almost more than I could take during a week. I had been dreading already, the week I decided to tell Arlen Specter of my support for his opponent Pat Toomey in the Republican primary. Despite his consistent sellouts of the Republican Party, Specter and I had a good relationship. Once when I was speaking at a Republican event in Pennsylvania, he wrote on my program, "One day you will be president." It was an odd statement coming from someone who disagreed with almost everything I believed in. Nevertheless, Specter and I stayed on speaking terms, and I knew that would soon end.

On Thursday, April 23, I saw Specter on the Senate floor. Between votes he left the chamber and headed for a private "Senators-only" room, just off the Senate floor. I followed him out and found him writing at a small table in the corner of the room. I sat down next to him and said, "Arlen, I just wanted to tell you face-to-face that I will be supporting Pat Toomey in your Senate race." He barely made eye contact, but I continued, "I value your friendship." He cut me off and said, "I've heard enough," then stood up and walked away.

I sat there for a few minutes staring at the floor feeling sick and guilty. How did a guy like me, who loved people and was known my whole life for being friendly, get myself in a position where I was making so many enemies? I certainly didn't feel like I was fulfilling my goal to show everyone the love of Christ! This was ripping my heart out. Was it really worth it?

I didn't know it at the time, but Specter was already in the process of making his decision to drop out of the Republican primary and run as a Democrat. The polls showed Specter trailing Toomey among Republicans even before Toomey began his campaign. Specter apparently thought, in the heavily Democrat and union-controlled state of Pennsylvania, he would have a much better chance of defeating Toomey in the general election.

The next week I scheduled an interview with a reporter from *The Washington Examiner* to announce my support for Toomey in the Pennsylvania Republican primary. As we were sitting down to begin the interview, our BlackBerries began buzzing with news Specter was going to leave the Republican Party. The story, "Did DeMint's Endorsement of Toomey Set Off Specter?" was posted later that day. The piece said: "DeMint had not yet gone public with his support for Toomey by the time Specter switched. DeMint said Specter's switch 'shows that there were no principles attaching Arlen to the Republican Party, but the Republican Party was the means to get elected.' DeMint continued: 'I would rather have 30 Republicans in the Senate who really believe in principles of limited government, free markets, free people, than to have 60 that don't have a set of beliefs.'"

The article also noted that a recent poll showed Toomey would handily beat Specter in the primary by over twenty points.

Although I had not publicly opposed Specter, I was blamed for driving Specter from the party. Several Republican leaders were quoted in media accounts saying in various ways, "DeMint is so focused on principles he can't understand we need more Republicans to stop the Democrats. We need more numbers, not principles." But I was experiencing a Republican Party with neither numbers *or* principles. When I was elected to the Senate in 2004, we had fifty-five Republicans in the Senate, a large majority of Republicans in the House, and a Republican in the White House. We had the numbers and we didn't do squat!

I was assaulted by a horde of reporters with their quotes from Republicans criticizing me. Some of my colleagues took my quote about wanting principled Republicans as evidence I wanted a smaller party, but they lost sight of the fact the best way to rebuild a majority in the Senate was with a core group of Republicans committed to the conservative ideals that gave us the majority in 1994. I *still* believe that!

But people in Washington had little patience with my quaint thoughts about "freedom." In an interview with CNN's Rick Sanchez, he paraphrased my critics and accused me of "shrinking the electorate to an extreme—to a point where a regular Republican can't win. What do you make of that argument?"

I responded, "Quite the opposite. We're seeing across the country right now that the biggest tent of all is the tent of freedom, and what we need to do as Republicans is convince Americans freedom can work in all areas of their lives—for every American, whether it's education, health care, or creating jobs."

Sanchez lost it! "What the hell does that mean? I mean, the biggest tent is freedom? Freedom? I mean you got to do better than that!"

Like most politicians and members of the media, the concept of freedom was a complete abstraction to Sanchez. To him freedom has no relevance to policy discussions. If there is a problem in America, the government should fix it. If you don't want the government to fix it, you're against fixing it.

I knew I was wasting my time explaining freedom to Sanchez, but I did hope to convince some of his viewers. So again I explained, "What has worked in America are free people and free markets. And what we see now is a government expanding into all areas of our economy, increasing spending and debt. . . . Americans who are normally not even political are coming out to tea parties and protesting. These aren't Republicans or Democrats. These are concerned Americans."

Not one Republican in the Senate came to my defense. Disappointing, though not surprising. Most of the media accounts quoted Republicans saying I was hurting the party. Fortunately, *The Wall Street Journal* accepted my editorial attempting to set the record straight. It was titled, "How

Republicans Can Build a Big-Tent Party." In the article I spoke directly to Republicans:

> To win back the trust of the American people, we must be a "big tent" party. But big tents need strong poles, and the strongest pole of our party—the organizing principle and the crucial alternative to the Democrats—must be freedom. The federal government is too big, takes too much of our money, and makes too many of our decisions. If Republicans can't agree on that, elections are the least of our problems.
>
> If the American people want a European-style social democracy, the Democratic Party will give it to them. We can't win a bidding war with Democrats.[7]

Despite all the criticism and condemnation, I emerged from the Specter defection more confident in my position. If Specter was just as comfortable as a Democrat, then there were obviously no perceptible differences for him between Republicans and Democrats. And if Republican leaders preferred Arlen Specter to Pat Toomey, then we obviously needed new Republican leaders. I knew we needed to find more people like Toomey to challenge Republicans who didn't believe in principles.

On May 12, I met one. I've already mentioned my support for Marco Rubio, but this was my first time meeting him. He had just announced his candidacy for the U.S. Senate and was in Washington to meet with The National Republican Senatorial Committee (NRSC), hoping to get some support. But the Republican leadership, as I said, was recruiting Governor Charlie Crist to run for the Senate, and they had no interest in talking to Rubio.

Crist was one of the nation's most popular governors and a prolific fund-raiser. By raising his own campaign cash in a large state like Florida, Crist could save the NRSC millions of dollars that could be invested in other races. But Crist embraced Obama's stimulus and proved to be "fluid" on many other Republican positions. He was considered by many to be a political opportunist, not a principled conservative.

When I sat down with Rubio, I didn't know much about him. I knew he previously served as Speaker of the House in Florida's legislature and had a record as a consistent, principled conservative leader. I also knew Rubio wrote a book about one hundred conservative state policy ideas during his time as speaker, and he proved himself to be effective because over half of his ideas became law.

Having just left a meeting with many Republican senators who were congratulating themselves for getting Crist to announce his run for the Senate, I walked into my meeting with Rubio. He was young and eager to make his case. I told Rubio most folks in Washington were telling me he would soon drop out of the Senate race since Crist entered, and there were rumors he would run for Florida's attorney general instead. Rubio told me he had no intention of dropping out. He and his wife had already decided the nation's future was too important.

His parents had fled Cuba as refugees, coming to America with great hopes of a nation promising a better life for their children. When they arrived in the United States, Rubio's father worked as a bartender, and his mother worked as a department store clerk. The Rubio family knew what it was like to lose their country. Rubio was afraid Americans were on the verge of losing their country and desperately wanted to stop the Washington politicians who were guiding America into the abyss. He was tired of seeing Washington tax and spend America into generational debt that could cripple our economy and send us over a financial cliff. He wasn't going to sit idly by as his children's future slipped away. He was ready to fight for America, our Constitution, our freedoms, and our way of life—no matter who entered the race.

Rubio's passion and genuineness left me speechless. Nearly everyone in the room was tearing up. After so much time in Washington among cynics, Rubio's courage and clarity were astonishing.

Even after the beating I took for announcing my support of Toomey against Specter, I decided immediately Rubio was just the kind of candidate Republicans needed to win back the trust of the American people and draw Independents and disaffected Democrats into a bigger Republican tent. And Rubio could do it while explaining the power of conservative principles, not watering them down to win approval from the liberal press.

It was unbelievable to me the Republican leadership in Washington was not even willing to give Rubio a chance to compete in the Republican primary. Of course, Rubio was only polling in the single digits against Crist at the time. That alone can make potential backers think twice before hitching their wagon to a candidate, even one they philosophically side with and believe in. I knew it would be a tough fight, but electing conservatives like Rubio was essential to preserving freedom. If I could help give Rubio the opportunity to be heard, he would connect with voters and might win against the odds.

Chapter 4

Falling Farther into the Abyss

June 1, 2009—July 31, 2009

The summer began with depressing news. On June 1, 2009, General Motors, once America's shining star of economic achievement, declared bankruptcy. President Obama blamed it on the recession, but GM was losing billions of dollars before the recession, even at the height of the economic bubble in 2007 when they sold more cars than any time in their history. The blame for the demise of the world's largest automaker could be laid almost entirely at the feet of big union bosses and complicit politicians.

For years American automakers had become less and less competitive with foreign producers as benefit packages for union workers forced prices up and union work rules pushed quality down. State and federal laws guaranteed the political clout of union bosses, who funneled huge amounts of cash into the campaign coffers of Democrats.

Auto executives had little control over cost and quality. General Motors spent more on gold-plated union health benefits than they did on steel to make their cars. Early retirement programs for GM employees resulted in more retirees receiving benefits than active workers. GM became a job security and retirement benefit program for unions; making cars was their side business.

President Obama would not allow General Motors to go through the normal bankruptcy process provided by the law. Legal bankruptcy could have restructured union contracts to make GM more profitable. Instead Obama gave GM another $30.1 billion of taxpayer money (they had already been given $19.4 billion) in return for a 60 percent ownership. Obama nationalized GM!

Even worse, instead of treating bondholders fairly by giving them an ownership share, Obama in yet another election payback to unions, voided bondholder claims and forced GM to give union bosses nearly one-third ownership of the company. America's largest auto company was now owned almost entirely by the federal government and union bosses.

"As General Motors goes, so goes the nation" was the old adage that kept going through my mind. If this was true, then America was now a socialized economy controlled by politicians and union bosses. How could nongovernment automakers compete with "Government Motors" and their control of credit, regulators, compensation, benefits, and unlimited bailouts?

The bankruptcy and government takeover of GM was a devastating psychological blow to Americans, yet the media minimized its importance. The major television networks reported the "bankruptcy" as a normal course of business and offered little commentary on the unprecedented nationalization of a major American manufacturer. I joined several Republican senators for a press conference calling on the president immediately to submit a plan to return GM to the private sector, but we were largely ignored.

The takeover of General Motors by the federal government and unions was the final straw for many Americans. For months we had watched one bailout after another: the takeover of the mortgage industry, the takeover of the nation's largest insurance company (AIG), a trillion-dollar stimulus plan that seemed to be tranquilizing the economy, and now the collapse and takeover of America's largest automaker. Frustration was boiling over across America.

A growing number of these alarmed Americans were pastors. On my way back to South Carolina that week, I flew to Norfolk, Virginia, for a pastors' conference titled, "Rediscovering God in America." The organizers asked me to speak to hundreds of pastors about the connection between faith and public policy. This was another opportunity for me to engage America's spiritual leaders in the fight to save freedom—including freedom of religion—in America.

Pastors in America face an artificial dilemma: the court-fabricated mandate requiring the separation of church and state. There is no such mandate in the Constitution. The First Amendment prohibits the federal government from interfering with the practice of religion in America, but there is no prohibition on faith leaders being involved with public policy or political campaigns.

Pastors and church boards have been intimidated into keeping silent about government-imposed immorality, like gay marriage, incentives for unwed births, illegal immigration, bailouts, and the corruption of big government. There is even a federal law, which I've tried to change, giving the IRS the power to take away a church's tax-exempt status if pastors or church officials advocate for a political candidate. This threat has led many pastors to ignore the frightening and irresponsible growth of big government.

Big government *is* a religious issue. History shows in nations where there is a big government, there is a little God. When people are dependent on government, they are less dependent on God, and their spiritual fervor fades. Without the foundation of biblical principles, the culture becomes more dependent, violent, and lawless, requiring even more government control. Socialism and secularism go hand in hand, as do faith and freedom.

I told the pastors in Norfolk their country needs them to lead. Just as pastors led America's original fight for independence, the nation needs spiritual leaders more than ever. Big government is a moral and religious issue, and pastors must teach their congregations and communities how to participate responsibly in public affairs. Pastors must stand up against the laws and court rulings stripping them of their rights to participate in America's political process.

The Senate Conservatives Fund

While pastors and spiritual leaders were joining Americans with a growing sense of concern and activism, there was almost no sense of urgency, passion, or energy among Senate Republicans to fight the rampage of spending and debt by Obama and the Democrat Congress. Sure, some Republicans expressed opposition in speeches on the floor of the Senate or issued press statements opposing various policies. But when all the Senate Republicans met privately, there was never an impassioned cry for "all hands on deck" to stop America's march toward socialism.

At this point I had little standing to lose with my colleagues, so I developed a plan to do everything I could do to elect a few more senators who believed in constitutionally limited government and the principles of freedom. I knew my endorsement of candidates alone wouldn't be enough to help them get elected. Endorsements from one politician to another rarely have much impact with voters. But if I could raise some money and increase voter awareness for a few strong, underdog candidates, it might be possible to elect some new senators who would speak up for frustrated, freedom-loving Americans.

This was certain to pit me against the NRSC, the political arm of Senate Republicans to protect incumbents and elect Republican challengers. Senator John Cornyn from Texas was the chairman. Cornyn is a good friend and an effective conservative senator. He felt it was his job to protect incumbent Republican senators. Cornyn and our entire leadership team were convinced "moderate" Republicans were much more likely to win general elections, especially in the Northeast and swing states like Florida. The NRSC would not endorse Toomey, for example, against incumbent Specter. Soon after their endorsement of Specter, the NRSC made official their endorsement of moderate Republican Crist in Florida. They were nothing if not consistent. Consistently playing it safe. Governing by averages.

I freely admit there are states controlled by unions and dominated by Democrats where it is difficult for conservatives to get elected. But I firmly believed after America witnessed the unmasked agenda of Obama and the Democrat majority, conservatives who stood on principle and told the unvarnished truth could win in any state, anywhere.

After the NRSC's endorsement of Crist, I decided I could no longer work with them during the primaries, choosing instead to put all my efforts behind my own political action committee. I had once been one of the top fund-raisers for the NRSC, and I would be back on their team after the primaries, but now it was time to focus all my energy in helping underdog conservatives in Republican primaries.

Election laws allow members of Congress to form PACs to raise money for other candidates. PACs are heavily regulated and subject to strict reporting requirements. No group or individual can contribute more than $5,000 a year to a PAC, and the names of all contributors must be disclosed.

PACs run by members of Congress are known as "leadership PACs." They are primarily used to endear one member to another by making contributions to one another's campaigns. Those who give the most from their PACs to their colleagues often end up in leadership (thus the name, "leadership PAC"). Sitting senators also use their PACs to help elect new senators when seats are open. But when an incumbent senator is running for reelection, it's extremely rare for a sitting senator to support his colleague's opponent. It happened after Joe Lieberman lost the Democrat primary in Connecticut in 2006 and decided to run as an Independent (technically, he was no longer a Democrat). Many of Lieberman's Democrat Senate colleagues then used their PACs to support the Democrat nominee. Lieberman won anyway. But again, this is the real exception. Almost unheard of.

I didn't let that stop me, however, from using my SCF to elect new senators. This PAC only supported candidates who would fight for a balanced budget, term limits, an end to the culture of earmarks, and other tenets of limited government and individual liberty. My plan was to endorse, promote, and raise money for candidates who would help me change the Senate.

On June 8, 2009, SCF endorsed its first candidate for the 2010 elections: Toomey. To those in the media, SCF was just another leadership PAC, and Specter was now a Democrat, so there was little fanfare about the endorsement. But even without garnering a lot of notice, I knew in my heart this endorsement was the start of something big. My goal was to make an endorsement by SCF more coveted by candidates than an endorsement from the NRSC.

With little promotion other than my personal Twitter account and a small e-mail list, SCF raised more than $20,000 for Toomey within a few weeks. This confirmed my belief that thousands of Americans would support conservative candidates if they could find them. I hoped to make SCF the

"Good Housekeeping Seal of Approval" for conservative candidates for the Senate.

The next week SCF formally endorsed Rubio as well. Unlike in Toomey's case, this endorsement did create a media stir because the NRSC had just endorsed Crist. Traditionally the NRSC stayed neutral in Republican primaries. But the Republican leadership in the Senate decided to ignore Rubio completely and throw all their weight behind Crist. This would be one of many head-to-head battles with the Washington establishment.

The media handling of the Rubio endorsement signaled to me our strategy to make SCF bigger than me could actually work. Press stories referenced "Senator DeMint and the Senate Conservatives Fund," and a few focused almost entirely on SCF—which was just what I'd hoped for. The more SCF was positioned as an organization separate from me, the more credibility it would have with the media and voters.

And as the controversy between SCF and the NRSC created national news over the next several days, the spike in media coverage proved a huge help to Rubio, resulting in thousands of hits on our Web site. The money started pouring in for him.

Fallen Brothers

Things were moving fast in the Senate aside from all the endorsement controversies. Obama nominated Sonia Sotomayor to replace Supreme Court Justice David Souter. It is customary for Supreme Court nominees to have courtesy meetings with as many senators as possible before their confirmation vote.

I met Sotomayor on June 9, 2009. We talked for a few minutes, and I found her very likable. But she was a controversial nominee, and her statements suggesting her decisions would be based on "empathy" rather than law created a media stir. She was also quoted saying, "I would hope that a wise Latina woman with the richness of her experiences would, more often than not, reach a better conclusion."

I didn't spend a lot of time asking her about her previous decisions as a lower court judge because it was apparent she had been well coached not to answer my questions. She kept her answers vague, but when I asked her,

"Do unborn children have any rights at all?" she told me everything I needed to know. Mulling over my question, she briefly paused and finally said, "I never thought about that before."

Come on. That just could not be.

Abortion is one of the most controversial issues a judge can face, and I knew after many years on the bench—even if she'd never made a specific ruling on it—she had certainly *thought* about the question at least. The fact she was willing to look me in the eye and act like the rights of an unborn child had never crossed her mind told me she was not a person of integrity. President Obama may have won the right to make his own nominations to the court, but I also had the right to say no.

Despite my objections and the objections of thirty other Republicans, Sotomayor was confirmed as the next justice of the Supreme Court.

After my discouraging meeting with Sotomayor, I was looking forward to some positive, nonpolitical fellowship with friends at our regular weekly dinner that evening. Since there was usually a mixed group of Republicans and Democrats, we didn't talk politics except for some good-hearted teasing about our "radical" positions on issues. We talked instead about our marriages, our families, our faith, and our interests outside politics.

Usually it was a relaxing time to talk and laugh with friends, but this night was different. My fellow Republican Senator John Ensign of Nevada shocked and saddened all of us at the dinner table when he confessed to an affair with a married campaign staffer the previous year. He wanted us to know before the offended husband took the story to the media.

Ensign is a good friend whom I admire and respect. We played tennis together and worked together in the Senate on conservative issues. In my dark days after the "rules change" fiasco, Ensign was sometimes the only senator who would sit next to me when I presided as chairman of the Steering Committee at our weekly Wednesday lunch. We prayed together and shared many highs and lows for more than ten years. So my first reaction to his confession of adultery was a sense of betrayal. How could he have kept up the pretense of honesty and openness while being unfaithful to his wife?

But whenever I'm tempted to judge others, I remind myself of my own sin and how much I rely on God's grace to forgive me every day. It was easy to think, *John's sin is much worse than mine*, but God doesn't make a distinction between sins. The Bible is clear: "All have sinned and fall short of the glory of God" (Romans 3:23). So I quickly got over the idea I was somehow more righteous than him and vanquished the thought he had done *me* wrong.

Once I got beyond thinking about myself, I was overwhelmed with sadness and concern for Ensign, his wife, his family, and everyone involved. The next week Ensign held a press conference in Las Vegas and confessed his affair to the whole country. He took full responsibility for his actions and made no excuses. He admitted what he did was morally wrong, saying it was "the worst mistake of my life." He apologized to his wife and children, to his Senate colleagues, and to the country. In God's eyes John was completely forgiven, and he committed himself to rebuilding his marriage. But in Washington his trouble was just beginning.

Trouble was also brewing for another friend, South Carolina Governor Mark Sanford. I served with Sanford in the U.S. House for two years before he left to fulfill his term-limit pledge. In 2002, he was elected governor of South Carolina. Four years later in 2006, he was reelected overwhelmingly. Though unpopular with South Carolina legislators, Sanford was fast becoming a national conservative icon for his strong stand against government spending and high taxes.

While I considered Sanford a friend, we were never really close. Sanford occasionally sent me notes of encouragement from the governor's office when he saw a news story quoting Republicans criticizing me for trying to stop earmarks or some other wasteful spending. He knew what it was like to be attacked by fellow Republicans. We were definitely on the same team when it came to fighting big government.

On Monday, June 22, stories began to surface that Sanford was missing. No one seemed to know where he was. On Tuesday his staff said he was hiking alone on the Appalachian Trail. Sanford could be eccentric, I knew, but this was beginning to sound suspicious. Even his wife, Jenny, said she didn't know where he was. A husband, father, and chief executive of a state should always be reachable in case of an emergency.

Tuesday afternoon I was on Glenn Beck's TV show discussing ObamaCare and the massive growth in government spending. At the end of the interview, Beck asked me about Sanford's mysterious disappearance.

He was a supporter of Sanford's tough stands on fiscal issues, but like many other Sanford supporters, Beck was beginning to get worried. He asked me, "Can you vouch for Sanford's character?"

A month earlier I would have immediately answered yes. Sanford was principled to the point of absurdity. I could not imagine him doing anything morally wrong. Once when I visited his home, he handed me a Bible and asked me to read his boys a bedtime story. Sanford had a wonderful wife and four young sons who idolized him. But after the stunning revelations about Ensign, I told Beck, "I cannot vouch for anyone's character but my own." And I remember thinking, *I hope I will always be able to vouch for that!*

On Wednesday, Sanford appeared at a hastily arranged press conference in the state capitol building in Columbia, South Carolina. It was a disaster. He confessed he was in Argentina having an affair with his "soul mate." Instead of remorse he gave excuses for his infidelity. He rambled on and on, and every word was more insulting and embarrassing to his wife and family.

I could hardly watch as another friend and conservative stalwart crashed and burned on national television. Many conservatives seriously considered Sanford as the best Republican presidential candidate for 2012, and his national prominence as a principled conservative leader was steadily growing. But now it was all over.

I could not believe what I was seeing and hearing. It was too painful to watch.

I turned off the television in my office and tried to get back to work, but my mind was a blur. The press was eager to get my reaction to the Sanford debacle. They wanted to know if I was going to call for his resignation. I didn't know what to say, so I just said, "I am very disappointed and believe Governor Sanford will do the right thing." I thought Sanford would be more likely to resign if people gave him some room to make his own decision.

When I got back to South Carolina, I went to see Sanford at the governor's mansion in Columbia. Jenny had taken their children and gone to stay with her parents in Florida. I encouraged Sanford to take a temporary leave of absence as governor and spend a few months trying to save his marriage. Our state constitution allows the governor to temporarily leave office and then reclaim the position.

Sanford was being attacked from all directions—from friends (many Republicans called for his resignation) as well as enemies (he had a lot of enemies, and they were more than happy about his fall)—and there was no way he could focus on his marriage and family in this environment. Nor was there any way he could effectively lead the state. When I left the governor's mansion, I thought he would take my advice and focus all his efforts on saving his marriage.

Later that week Sanford and I reconnected by phone. He said he had discussed the idea of a leave of absence with Jenny, but she told him not to take my advice. I wasn't convinced he was telling me the truth, but there was nothing else I could do. Sanford stayed in office and gave another in-depth interview with a reporter who made him look even more like a fool. The embarrassments for Jenny continued, and it wasn't long before she announced she would seek a divorce.

The Bible often reminds us we are in a spiritual battle. This is especially true in politics and in Washington, D.C. That's why the most comforting thing I hear from fellow citizens is, "We're praying for you." And thankfully I hear it a lot.

Because like everyone else, I need it, and I know it.

The Freedom Tour

On June 24, the same day of Sanford's disastrous press conference, President Obama signed an emergency war-funding bill stuffed with wasteful and reckless spending wholly unrelated to the war, including $108 billion additional credit line for the International Monetary Fund and another $1 billion for the failed "Cash for Clunkers" program to help sell new cars.

This bill was a prime example of the cynical strategy used by Democrats to force Republicans to vote for bad legislation and wasteful spending. If I voted against the bill because of all the wasteful spending, I would also be voting against essential funding for our troops. This is how they make thirty-second campaign commercials on the floor of the Senate. But I couldn't betray my principles or common sense, so I voted against the bill, despite knowing South Carolinians would be told, "DeMint voted against the troops."

On June 29, Congress left Washington for our Fourth of July break, and I headed to New York to begin my book promotion tour. *Saving Freedom* debuted, appropriately, on Independence Day. I appeared on numerous television and national radio shows to talk about my favorite subject: the principles of freedom. The book gave me a platform to talk about the differences between socialism and freedom and the opportunity to challenge Americans to stand up, speak out, and stop the insanity in Washington.

Continuing our Freedom Tour back in South Carolina, my publisher, B&H Publishing Group, wrapped a motor home with my book cover for a trip around the state. On July 4, we arranged book signings at tea party rallies in Charleston and Columbia. Hundreds of people stood in line waiting for me to sign a copy of the book. As I signed their books, they shared their concerns about the direction of our country and encouraged me to keep fighting.

From the bus I called into tea parties and radio talk shows around the country to promote freedom and the book. I even used teleconferencing to appear at a tea party in Texas while riding across South Carolina. The whole experience was exciting and encouraging. I could not have asked for a better Fourth of July celebration.

Waterloo

Back in Washington after the Fourth of July break, the Treasury Department announced it would use $30 billion of the TARP bailout money to buy toxic securities. A few days later Obama announced a new "Cash for Caulkers" program that used $300 million in stimulus money to offer rebates to people who bought qualified appliances and insulation. I feverishly called conservative media and bloggers trying to inform and engage the American people against the avalanche of new programs, spending and borrowing.

On the evening of July 17, I joined a national conference call sponsored by Conservatives for Patients' Rights to encourage grassroots activists all over the country to keep fighting against ObamaCare. One caller after another expressed frustration at the sheer volume of new government programs, bailouts, and takeovers. How could Republicans with a weak minority in the House and Senate stop all of Obama's initiatives?

We couldn't, that's how. Our best chance of making a difference from our current position was to focus on stopping the centerpiece of Obama's agenda: the socialization of America's health-care system. So I encouraged the participants on the call to direct all their energy in this direction. If we could stop Obama's top priority initiative, we could hopefully break his momentum on the multitude of other new government programs he was promoting. Then perhaps he would slow down and listen to the American people.

This is where I (not so deliberately) inserted the word "Waterloo" into the national debate on the government takeover of health care. Searching for an analogy to simplify my strategy, I said, "If we are able to stop Obama on this, it will be his Waterloo. It will break him, and we will show that we can, along with the American people, begin to push those freedom solutions that work in every area of our society."

It didn't occur to me that *Waterloo* would ignite a media explosion and serve as a "call to arms" for Americans who were ready to fight against socialized medicine. But soon enough my quote was all over the media— at least part of it. I never heard my whole statement with the "freedom solutions" part, only the words, "it will be his Waterloo; it will break him."

At first I was embarrassed. My words sounded mean and sinister. Then President Obama began to criticize my quote and used my name in speeches across the country. Several of my Republican colleagues chastised me for making all Republicans look like obstructionists.

I was, once again, the skunk at the party in Republican Conference meetings.

What to do now? I had to decide whether to apologize for my statement or try to ride out the storm. Apologizing would put me and other opponents of socialized medicine on the defensive. It would be like pouring blood into a pool full of sharks. Instead I decided to use *Waterloo* as the battle cry for the freedom movement standing in defiance of the Obama/Pelosi/Reid agenda.

The bare facts are, I only used the word *Waterloo* once on a conference call. It was Obama and his surrogates who made it a national issue. Once again he had lowered himself beneath the office of the presidency by personally attacking a junior senator by name. As usual he overreached. Yet on July 25, 2009, *The Washington Post* published a cartoon depicting me as an assassin. They, along with most of the liberal media, were trying to portray President Obama as a victim of mean-spirited attacks.

Well, I don't mind taking a punch in a fight worth being in, and I've been around long enough to know the media can blow anything out of proportion they want to. But they would soon learn the opposition to ObamaCare and the entire progressive Democrat agenda was not restricted to a few so-called right-wing radicals. Much of America was ready to do battle—at Waterloo or wherever the true proponents of radical, socialized government wanted to meet.

Chapter 5

The Summer of Discontent

August 1, 2009–September 9, 2009

Congress traditionally takes recess during the month of August. Congressmen and senators typically use this time to meet with constituents, visit local businesses, and hold town hall meetings in their state.

Because there was so much interest in Obama's controversial health-care takeover, Americans made a point to attend town hall meetings that summer. Democrats in the Senate were united behind it. And while most Republicans opposed the plan, the usual moderate suspects were expressing a willingness to cut a deal with the Democrats.

But this wasn't just a matter of negotiating for compromise and tweaking the language. The whole premise of ObamaCare was flawed, having been built on the socialist platform of government control. Compromise can only work when two parties share common goals. And no matter how you slice it, dice it, or spin it into a sound bite, there is no commonality between socialism and freedom. Despite his dismissive claims to the contrary, Obama's vision (as he was caught on camera saying) was to eventually replace private insurance plans with a single-payer, government-run, health-care system.

Well, that's impossible. Creating a competitive and efficient health-care system wholly controlled by the government simply cannot be done. Attempts to compromise with Obama and the Democrat majority were all in vain because they would not allow any free-market principles in their plan.

Some Republicans did offer alternatives to socialized medicine I supported, such as reducing costs associated with frivolous lawsuits, allowing small business pooling for insurance discounts, providing tax credits for individuals to buy health insurance, allowing patients to buy health insurance across state lines, expanding health savings accounts, and encouraging state insurance pools for patients with preexisting conditions. Our goal was for every American to have access to an affordable health insurance plan they could own and keep from job to job and even into retirement.

But all ideas to make the current health system work better and cost less were rejected by Obama and the Democrats because any improvements would destroy the whole premise for their plan. They would accept no alternative proposals that didn't begin with the assumption America's health-care system was irreparably broken and must be taken over—completely—by the federal government.

Town Hall Uprisings

Freshly minted Democrat Arlen Specter was the first victim of the 2009 August town halls. He brought along Obama's Secretary of Health and Human Services Kathleen Sebelius to explain the benefits of ObamaCare to the crowd. When Specter arrogantly told the audience they didn't understand what was good for them, they didn't take it well. A FOX News story reported the reaction of one member of the audience: "I look at this health care plan and I see nothing that is about health or about care. What I see is a bureaucratic nightmare, Senator. Medicaid is broke, Medicare is broke, Social Security is broke; and you want us to believe that a government that can't even run a 'Cash for Clunkers' program is going to run one-sixth of our U.S. economy? No sir, no," she said.

The crowd erupted, and for Specter it all went downhill from there. The confrontation was captured on personal cell phone video cameras and posted on YouTube. The video of Specter and Sebelius being shouted down by dozens of citizens went viral on the Internet with millions of views. This set the tone for the August break and inspired many more Americans to show up at town halls across the country.

The next day the Democratic National Committee, the official fund-raising arm for the Democrat Party, blasted tea party activists attending town halls, calling them "the mob." On August 4, the DNC Communications Director Brad Woodhouse released a harshly worded statement denouncing town hall attendees:

> The Republicans and their allied groups—desperate after losing two consecutive elections and every major policy fight on Capitol Hill—are inciting angry mobs of a small number of rabid right wing extremists funded by K Street lobbyists to disrupt thoughtful discussions about the future of health care in America taking place in Congressional Districts across the country.
>
> However, much like we saw at the McCain-Palin rallies last year where crowds were baited with cries of "socialist," "communist," and where the birthers' movement was born—these mobs of extremists are not interested in having a thoughtful discussion about the issues—but like some Republican leaders have said—they are interested in "breakin" the President and destroying his Presidency.
>
> These mobs are bussed in by well-funded, highly organized groups run by Republican operatives and funded by the special interests who are desperately trying to stop the agenda for change the President was elected to bring to Washington. Despite the head-line grabbing nature of these angry mobs and their disruptions of events, they are not reflective of where the American people are on the issues—or the hundreds of thousands of thoughtful discussions taking place around kitchen tables, water coolers and in homes.
>
> The right wing extremists' use of things like devil horns on pictures of our elected officials, hanging members of Congress in effigy, breathlessly questioning the President's citizenship and the use of Nazi SS symbols and the like just shows how outside of the mainstream the Republican Party and their allies are. This type

of anger and discord did not serve Republicans well in 2008—and it is bound to backfire again.[8]

The Democrats had officially lost it. They convinced themselves—or at least were hoping—the growing grassroots opposition to their agenda was a calculated, Republican-driven conspiracy. Their theories, however, could easily be declared null and void because Republicans, too, who voted for the bailouts and were willing to "compromise" on the health-care bill were also being shouted down in town halls across the country. Americans had little affinity or patience with establishment Democrats or Republicans.

The DNC press continued to use my "breaking" the president statement to elicit sympathy for Obama and to portray him as the victim. But no matter how they chose to skew reality, it didn't change the fact the steadily increasing volume of public outcry against Obama's policies was not coming from an organized movement. It was a real awakening in the hearts and souls of Americans who were genuinely worried about the future of their country.

Yet sadly, and irresponsibly, most of the national press continued taking their cues from the DNC. On August 4 a *San Francisco Chronicle* blog said:

> Congressfolk have been getting heckled when they hold town meetings back in their home districts. Looks like the work of the Tea Party crew—combined with Obama health care haters like the Conservatives for Patients' Rights. There's even a memo about how to heckle a meeting. So we asked Speaker Pelosi—after her finely-manicured photo op Thursday at San Francisco General Hospital—if she thought that those protests were a sign of genuine grass roots opposition to the Obama health care plan. "I think they're Astroturf," Pelosi said Tuesday.[9]

The White House eagerly jumped into the fray. That same day the President's press secretary Robert Gibbs told reporters during an off-camera session: "I hope people will take a jaundiced eye to what is clearly the Astroturf nature of grass roots lobbying. This is manufactured anger."[10]

But despite the best efforts of the White House press machine and every other influencer who was intent on lacquering over the truth, opposition to the president's agenda and tactics was spinning out of control. Later the

White House posted a blog asking citizens to report "fishy" information about the administration or Obama's health-care bill to an electronic tip box—flag@whitehouse.gov. The president seemed to be asking citizens to snitch on their neighbors if they caught them opposing any part of Obama's agenda. Within a week public outcry against Obama's citizen informants program forced the White House to shut down their tattletale Web site.

And yet the mainstream media turned a deaf ear, continuing the deceptive assault on the tea party, its adherents, and their motives. On August 7, *New York Times* columnist Paul Krugman took his turn smearing the tea party in a piece titled, "The Town Hall Mob." In it he claimed, "Cynical political operators are exploiting that anxiety to further the economic interests of their backers." And the hits against citizen activism kept coming. On August 21, *Politico* published an article with the headline. "The Summer of Astroturf," claiming Washington was "paved with Astroturf"—the label liberals used to brand the tea party as "fake grass roots."

Most members of the media couldn't accept the reality of a genuine and growing group of Americans who were actively opposing the irresponsible spending, debt, and government takeovers by the Washington elite. They were so used to political operatives manufacturing protests and demonstrations for leftist causes (but of course rarely reporting them as such), they immediately assumed this same sort of top-down strategy was driving both the tea party rallies and town hall protests. But there was no group even remotely capable of initiating, organizing, and staging the thousands of demonstrations now happening around the country. This was a real American awakening! Like it or not.

During this time I did as much media as I could schedule to talk about the importance of Americans going to town halls and letting their representatives know their concerns. Talk show hosts had more questions than there was time to answer. They wanted to know what Americans could do to stop the continuing bailouts, the stimulus, ObamaCare, Obama's czars, and Cash for Clunkers.

Cash for Clunkers, the billion-dollar federal program designed to sell fuel-efficient cars and to destroy older cars (clunkers), ran out of money after one week. It was supposed to be a program to sell cars through fall. Before leaving town in August, the House and Senate quickly passed a bailout for Cash for Clunkers costing another $2 billion. President Obama signed the clunker bailout bill on August 7. Within a few weeks the program was bankrupt again. Clunkers became symbolic of the federal government's inability to manage anything effectively.

Cash for Clunkers was another "straw" breaking the back of any remaining credibility of the Obama administration and the Democrat majority. Sadly, this program and its bailout passed through Congress with a significant number of Republican votes. Neither party seemed willing to carry the mantle of fiscal responsibility. There were still too few of us willing to say no to more spending and debt.

The Spoils of Battle

While Democrats and many Republicans were facing the wrath of voters across the country, I was relieved to get a warm welcome when I came back to South Carolina for recess. In Washington my battles against amnesty, cap and trade, and for the lifting of the moratorium on drilling for oil and natural gas often got me into trouble. But I've always been fortunate to find friends at home who supported me.

My role as the leading opponent of ObamaCare, highlighted by my call to make it the president's "Waterloo," convinced my fellow South Carolinians I was speaking for them in Washington once again. "They're not listening!" or "They must think we're stupid!" were common phrases I heard from voters throughout the state. And with almost every handshake, I was told, "Thank you for fighting." Once they saw I was willing to stand against my own party, South Carolinians knew I was on their side.

My recess travels began in Greenville with a breakfast at Tommy's Ham House, famous for ham biscuits, grits, and sweet iced tea. This was where, only a few days before, my friend Congressman Bob Inglis was skewered for his support of the bailouts and the energy tax called "cap and trade." In front of an already impatient crowd, he also tried to make a case for compromise on the health-care bill and criticized "angry" Republicans who were just following the "mob." Inglis even told the audience to stop listening to their hero Glenn Beck!

When I arrived, I wasn't sure what to expect. This was my annual review, and it was time to see if my bosses were happy with my performance. Thankfully, they were happy to see me. The praise from the people I served was all I needed to keep up the fight. Their thank-yous were the spoils of battle.

I spent an hour listening to their concerns and answering their questions as best I could. Their knowledge of the issues was truly amazing, especially when it came to ObamaCare. One woman held up part of the health-care legislation she printed from the Internet, cited a specific section, and confidently announced the president was not telling the truth about what was in the bill. No one could argue with her because she was holding the legislation in her hand. She had read more of the bill than most members of Congress.

News coverage of my first town halls in the Upstate helped grow the crowds for my town halls along the coast. When I arrived in Myrtle Beach, it seemed everyone in town was expecting me.

We held the Myrtle Beach town hall at Rioz, a large restaurant in the downtown area of this legendary summer vacation destination. Growing up in South Carolina, Myrtle Beach was synonymous with the "first week of summer." Like most high school and college students in the state, my highest goal each year was to spend the first week of June in Myrtle Beach playing in the sun on one of the nation's most beautiful beaches.

Before driving to the town hall, I toured South Carolina's most popular tourist destination, Ripley's Aquarium of Myrtle Beach. I've found visiting major employers and innovative new businesses is a good way to keep in touch with local economies around the state. The aquarium is a fascinating combination of flashy retail merchandising and millions of dollars' worth of high-tech equipment operated by scientists and marine biologists.

As we left the aquarium for my town hall, a cell phone call from our advance team warned me Rioz's was already completely full, with as many as a thousand people stuffed inside and dozens more who were standing outside unable to get in. Joining them were maybe ten or fifteen protesters the local Democrat Party had managed to organize, positioned out front with signs supporting ObamaCare. My staff advised me to enter through the kitchen at the rear of the building.

As we approached the restaurant, the streets were partially blocked with police cars, protesters, and people trying to get inside. It looked more like a rock concert than a town hall. In the past it was sometimes difficult to find two dozen people to attend one of my town halls. But this year Americans had an urgent message they wanted me to take back to Washington.

The crowd was pushing in from all sides as I made my way to the center of the room. But most were just trying to encourage me with a familiar refrain: "Thanks for fighting." "We pray for you every day." "What can we do?"

The local Republican Party president introduced me to the roaring crowd. They weren't just cheering for *me*. They were cheering for themselves and reveling in the sense of power emanating from the collective force of hundreds of citizens standing together for a common cause. I spoke while standing in the middle of the crowd literally elbow to elbow with people standing all around me.

The mood was electric. So exciting, you could feel it and see it everywhere you looked, in everyone's face. We were all on the same team, and everybody knew it, even though in one way it seemed wrong to me they felt required to be here—to get up and leave their homes to demand their government stop destroying America's economic system and bankrupting our nation—to do what we're supposed to do. But we needed their help, and they seemed to understand better than Washington politicians the dangers America now faced because of irresponsible governance.

I took questions and comments for more than an hour. One woman shared the difficult problems she was having with health insurance. She was a small business owner with several preexisting health conditions. Her insurance costs were over $1,000 a month. She concluded, "Nevertheless, I do not think the federal government should control our health-care system, and I do not support ObamaCare." The crowd cheered and applauded with respect and admiration.

I responded to this courageous woman by reviewing the policy ideas Republicans were promoting to lower the cost of health insurance and to make affordable health insurance available to everyone, including those with preexisting conditions. Several in the crowd, including a group of physicians, offered their own solutions to help the millions of uninsured Americans.

Others spoke at length about education, the financial crisis, the bailouts, the failing economic stimulus, and the apparently insatiable spending agenda of President Obama. Again I was amazed at the depth of knowledge and understanding by the people in the audience.

For weeks I continued to travel the state of South Carolina visiting businesses, meeting with local economic development officials, holding town halls, and calling into radio talk shows around the country from my car. Speaking with talk-show callers in other states confirmed what I was experiencing in South Carolina: Congressmen and senators who were speaking against government spending, bailouts, takeovers, and ObamaCare were being affirmed by the voters. On the other hand, those who were defending federal action and making excuses for their votes were feeling the wrath of the voters.

The difference was becoming crystal clear.

To Run or Not to Run

My first six-year term in the Senate would be complete in 2010. I didn't want to spend another six years in Washington, but I didn't want to give up either. Every time I considered announcing my retirement from the Senate, a picture flashed in my mind that haunted me: the soldiers I visited at Walter Reed Hospital who lost their arms and legs fighting against terrorism and tyranny in Iraq and Afghanistan. I also thought of all the Americans who lost their lives defending freedom since the signing of the Declaration of Independence.

How could I vote to send men and women to give their lives for freedom if I wasn't willing to fight for it here at home? The pain and loneliness I felt was small compared to that of a widow with three children facing the future without a husband or father. Elected office is not the only way civilians can fight for freedom, but God must have put me in the Senate for a purpose.

My friends, supporters, and staff encouraged me for months to announce my reelection early to deter potential Republican and Democrat opponents. But it was hard for me to justify putting Debbie, our children, and myself through another tortuous campaign. As a high-profile opponent of the Obama/Pelosi/Reid agenda, we knew there would be millions of dollars of negative advertising spent against me by the Democrats. And, since I was a thorn in the side of the Republican leadership, I was unlikely to receive a lot of support and sympathy from my own party.

My first campaign for the Senate had been a difficult two years that included a six-way Republican primary, a runoff with a former governor to win the nomination, and a negative general election campaign. Debbie had become afraid to turn on the television for several months because of all the negative commercials aired against me. I raised and spent over $10 million to win my Senate seat, and my opponents spent three times that much against me. I also spent most of those two years on the road away from home with little sleep and little contact with my family. But the chance to make a big difference in Washington with Bush in the White House and big majorities of Republicans in both the House and the Senate kept me going through a long and difficult campaign.

Six years later I was no longer sure it was worth it. Republicans, controlled by big-spending senior members, betrayed the principles of limited government, lost the confidence of the American people, and finally lost control of Congress and the White House. Now, with a minority so small we could hardly apply any brakes or resistance to the Obama agenda, I was looking outside the Senate to continue my fight for freedom.

There were not even enough bold conservatives in the Senate to field a basketball team. Even those senators who agreed with me in principle were not willing to rock the boat with our leadership and the appropriators on key issues like banning self-serving, wasteful, pork-barrel earmarks. The absence of enough comrades in arms in the Senate led me to believe I might be more effective fighting for freedom outside politics rather than from the center of the federal government.

I promised my staff before the August break I would talk with my family and give them my decision when I returned to Washington in September. When I was first elected to the House, we had two children in middle school and two in high school. None of us wanted to move to Washington so I commuted every week. Since then, all four had finished college and married. And we had two grandsons. Even though I flew home every weekend, I missed a lot during those twelve years.

Debbie and I struggled with the decision through the month of August and finally settled on postponing a final decision. I told my staff and campaign team to proceed as if I was going to run again, but I would not make an official announcement until the first of the year.

You Lie!

Congress returned to Washington the second week of September, following an August that had been a bad month for Obama and his Democrat accomplices. Support for ObamaCare was significantly declining, and Obama's favorability was now below 50 percent in some polls.

To save his sinking ship, President Obama called a joint session of Congress for September 9. He wanted to make a televised speech to the nation to sell his health-care plan. I admit, I was not looking forward to attending. Frankly, it was getting harder and harder for me to listen to President Obama. I called him "the world's best salesman of socialism" because he seemed to believe every problem could be solved with another government program. But there was no substance behind his rhetoric. Never. It was tough to sit through.

I spent the day in Washington before Obama's speech doing interviews and holding a press conference with Representative Mike Pence to accept tens of thousands of "Free Our Health Care Now" petitions from a grassroots group, Americans for Prosperity. But night finally arrived. And with it, more of what I already expected. Obama's speech included the obligatory tales of woe about Americans without health insurance and assurances his plan would solve everyone's health-care problems. He continued to sell the idea America was in the middle of a health-care crisis requiring immediate intervention. He never mentioned that the large majority of Americans were happy with their health insurance and health care.

Obama often claimed, "Forty million Americans are without health care." The fact is, all Americans and residents (legal or illegal) have access to health care. Hospital emergency rooms are required to take all comers whether they can pay or not. Approximately ten million of Obama's uninsured were illegal immigrants. Another twenty million of America's so-called uninsured were workers who had access to health insurance but chose not to take it, low-income Americans who qualified for Medicaid but hadn't signed up, or people who were temporarily without insurance because they were between jobs.

There were probably fewer than ten million American citizens who did not have insurance either because of preexisting conditions or low income. And while this is indeed a problem—an issue well worth addressing—it does not constitute a crisis requiring a government takeover of one-sixth of our economy. There were many ways to make health insurance more affordable and to work with states to offer affordable plans for Americans with preexisting conditions.

And ObamaCare wasn't it!

Actually, guaranteeing affordable private health insurance for all Americans was never the goal of Obama and the Democrat Congress. The goal was essentially this: to allow the federal government to take control of the health-care system. The Democrats avoided every proposal to make private health insurance and the delivery of health care less expensive. All of their efforts were focused on moving decisions from patients and doctors to government bureaucrats.

The president's speech to the American people and the Congress was full of misrepresentations about what his plan would accomplish. The House version of the president's bill would spend more than $1 trillion, create a federal commission to ration health care for seniors, create a "public option" government health insurance plan to compete with private plans, move millions of the uninsured onto the already bankrupt state Medicaid plans, and provide coverage for illegal immigrants.

When the president specifically said in his speech his plan would not cover illegal immigrants, someone shouted from behind me, "You lie!" The House chamber became silent as the president looked in my direction. He seemed to look straight at me. And after a month of quoting me about "Waterloo," he probably was. But no matter how insistently Democrats denied their plan would provide health insurance to illegal aliens, their party had continually rebuffed efforts by Republicans to require those who applied for benefits to produce photo identification. The Congressional Research Service confirmed the health exchanges established under ObamaCare did not contain any restrictions on noncitizens participating in the program.

I later found out the "You lie" culprit was my House colleague from South Carolina, Republican Joe Wilson. Joe is the quintessential southern gentleman, and his outburst was both out of character and out of place. He called the White House that night to apologize, but the media would attempt to destroy him over the coming weeks.

I called Wilson the next day to encourage him as the media attacks increased. He told me the first thing he did when he got home from Obama's speech was call his wife. Her first question was, "Who was the idiot who shouted, 'You lie'?"

Wilson quickly became an unintentional hero to those who wanted to see more fight from their representatives in Congress. Millions of frustrated Americans who were tired of hearing Republicans refer to the enemies of freedom as "my good friend and colleague" found in his reflexive rebuttal a bit of gut-level honesty they wished they heard more of from their elected officials. It's the kind of thing they might like to say themselves to Obama and his subordinates if given the chance—the kind of thing they already shouted at the television nearly every night when the news reported another development in the takeover of American liberty.

But while this incident would help Wilson raise millions of dollars for his reelection campaign, his Democrat opponent became a hero of the left and raised his own millions from liberals and progressives. The battle lines were drawn. I knew this much, however, from what I'd seen over the course of the last few months: millions who still yearned for freedom and common sense weren't about to take Obama's lies "lying down."

Chapter 6

America Comes Knocking

September 10, 2009—October 2, 2009

Americans quickly changed their minds about President Obama's agenda after being subjected to seven months of unrestrained spending, debt, and government expansion under the Democrat majority in Congress. When Obama was inaugurated in January 2009, an ABC/*Washington Post* poll found 51 percent of Americans supported increased government spending to help the economy, even if it increased the national debt. By August 2009, a Rasmussen poll found 70 percent of likely voters favored a government that offered fewer services and lower taxes rather than more services and higher taxes.

Obama's approval ratings were sinking as well. A Gallup poll in August showed congressional approval ratings at 31 percent and Obama at 50 percent (down from 67 percent in January). On September 1, after the tumultuous town halls in August, Gallup reported Obama's approval ratings had fallen to 45 percent.

Americans were increasingly alarmed at the rate of government spending and the corresponding expansion of debt and government control over their lives. So throughout the summer, tea party activists, radio talk show hosts,

Glenn Beck, FreedomWorks, and a myriad of grassroots groups called for a march on Washington on Saturday, September 12, 2009.

9/12 was here. In a big way.

Hundreds of thousands of Americans (as I described earlier in the book) came to Washington to protest the destructive actions of their government and to be with like-minded citizens. These were humble and thoughtful people concerned and fearful about the future of their country. And they were exceedingly grateful for the few congressmen and senators who were willing to stand with them.

FreedomWorks assisted the disparate organizers from hundreds of communities in every state by arranging permits for the march and by renting a stage and massive public-address system. They also invited some of the speakers. I was honored when FreedomWorks Chairman and former Republican House Majority Leader Dick Armey invited me to participate; I was the only senator who spoke at the tea party. Armey insisted the march on Washington would be a pivotal event in the fight to save America. As one of the few senators fighting against the Washington establishment, Armey believed it was essential for me to be there. That was all I needed to hear.

Some of the grassroots groups organized mini-rallies and panel discussions around Washington for early arrivals. I joined several congressmen and conservative journalists on Thursday for a panel discussion at the D.C. Armory a few miles from the Capitol. The crowd was enthusiastic but serious. These people were in Washington to take care of business. They were here as citizens and stockholders, not tourists.

And they wanted to know why the president and Democrat Congress kept spending. Were they intent on bankrupting the nation? Did they think voters were stupid? How did they think the federal government could run our health-care system when it couldn't run Cash for Clunkers for one week without running out of money? What were they thinking?

The Senate finished votes for the week on Thursday night, so only a few senators were in their offices on Friday. As one of the only senators available and the only one participating in the Saturday march, I had a lot of visitors. People from all across the country spent Friday roaming the halls of the House and Senate office buildings looking for someone who would listen.

I was more than happy to listen because what these Americans were saying was music to my ears.

They were here to take back their country.

September 12 March on Washington

Saturday, September 12, 2009, began early for me. I was up at 5:30 a.m. getting ready for a live 6:45 a.m. appearance on ABC's *Good Morning America*. They wanted to talk about the march on Washington, and I was anxious to add a positive spin to the smears being lodged by establishment politicians and liberal journalists.

To my surprise the hosts allowed me to cast the protest as a genuine expression of concern by a large and diverse group of Americans. Other commentators attempted to minimize the size and importance of the gathering, so I was thankful for the opportunity to present a positive perspective of the event. The march was to begin in downtown Washington about a mile from the Capitol—a real march down Pennsylvania Avenue to the steps of "the People's House."

My publisher set up a table stacked with volumes of *Saving Freedom* in front of a coffee shop where people were gathering. I arrived about 9:00 a.m. to sign books and mingle with the crowd. At first I was embarrassed about using the occasion to sell books. But signing books turned out to be a great entrée to talk to hundreds of people who love America and believe in the principles of freedom. For more than two hours, they encouraged me, and I tried to encourage them. They were Democrats, Republicans, Independents, and many who had never been involved in politics. They possessed little, if any, loyalty to a political party. They were ready to throw all the bums out!

These were also people of faith. I knew this because, "We're praying for you" was the phrase I heard most often throughout the day. Although these individuals were united by fiscal issues of spending, debt, and government takeovers, they were clearly motivated by a sense of civic responsibility. They believed their government was trampling on their God-given unalienable right to freedom.

The marchers were an interesting mix of people. I was surprised many times when these men and women holding signs and wearing shorts and

T-shirts emblazoned with patriotic messages introduced themselves as owners of small businesses, lawyers, or teachers. They were not political activists. They were patriotic people afraid Washington politicians were bankrupting America.

I made my way slowly through the crowd to the speakers' area, finding it fenced and guarded. Only those with badges were allowed inside. Not even my congressional pin would get me automatic access here. And since I didn't have an official event badge, the guards kept me standing at the gate for several minutes before confirming with someone on the other end of their radios that I could come in.

The fenced area was full of reporters and television cameras from around the country. I talked with dozens of reporters, but the noise from the crowd and the speakers was so loud it was almost impossible to hear the questions. The atmosphere was electric. I had never been in a situation where there was such a pervasive sense of urgency.

The media was in a frenzy. They couldn't understand what could have motivated all these people to come to Washington. Their questions searched for self-serving reasons for the protesters to be there, but most participants just wanted the government to get its hand out of their pockets and leave them alone. They didn't want free health care or someone to pay their mortgage. They simply wanted elected officials to keep their oath of office to protect and defend the Constitution.

My turn to speak came around 1:00 p.m. When I walked up the steps to the stage and saw the size of the crowd, I was overwhelmed. From such a high vantage point, I saw people jammed together not only in front of me on the National Mall but as far as I could see to my left and right. Roads and parking lots were full of proud, cheering, yet upset Americans. It looked like a million people were there! This was by far the largest crowd I had ever addressed.

Instead of being nervous (which still happens to me regularly), I felt a personal connection with the marchers after spending the morning talking to hundreds of them. It was like speaking to friends at a pressing neighborhood meeting about a developer who was trying to use eminent domain to take our homes and build a shopping center where we lived.

"Welcome to Waterloo!" were the first words out of my mouth. The crowd erupted with cheers. Hands and signs were waving as far as I could see. My speech was short. I reminded my fellow Americans our country was in trouble and the power to change our course was in their hands. I thanked them for coming. For me they were the cavalry coming to the country's rescue—and to mine.

Despite attempts to vilify the marchers, the Capitol Police and National Park officials responsible for the care of the Mall reported the crowd was the best-behaved group they'd ever seen in Washington. The marchers even picked up their own litter! The best of America had come knocking at Washington's door.

The question remained: who would answer?

On Monday, September 14, I flew to New York to speak to students at King's College, a Christian school located in the Empire State Building. I came at the invitation of Marvin Olasky, the best-selling author of several books about the socioeconomic problems in America caused by perverse federal government incentives. Olasky was provost of King's College and editor of *World Magazine*.

Before my noon appointment at the college, I stopped by FOX News to appear on their *Happening Now* morning show. I didn't miss a single opportunity anymore to talk about the great awakening happening across the nation. The march on Washington had been a great success—a sure sign the awakening was real—but FOX was the only network giving it the attention it deserved.

I hadn't been in the Empire State Building for almost fifty years. When I was about ten years old, my grandfather brought my brother, cousin, and me to New York to see the Yankees play in the World Series. While in New York we went to the Empire State Building because it was the tallest building in the world. I still remember standing on the top and looking with disbelief across the street at the Rockefeller Center. The buildings were swaying! I couldn't understand how steel and concrete could safely sway. I still don't.

Near the ground floor I sat with Olasky in front of 175 students. Olasky is a Christian intellectual, and he inspires his students vigorously to question unsubstantiated dogma in all areas of life, including political, economic, and spiritual matters. He interviewed me for a half hour focusing mostly on sections of my book dealing with the principles of freedom. Then he opened the discussion for questions from his students.

These were bright students from all over the country who had made their own decision to deepen their faith through debate and questioning and to apply the things they believed to all areas of their lives and careers. I was awed by their understanding of the complex issues and their ability to frame questions in a way that discouraged nonspecific, political answers. America's greatest generations may still be in front of us.

On the way back to LaGuardia Airport, I called into Judge Andrew Napolitano's radio show to discuss President Obama's speech to Wall Street bankers and stock traders earlier that morning. Obama was in New York on the one-year anniversary of Lehman Brothers' collapse to take credit for saving American's financial system. He blamed the collapse on a lack of regulations instead of the real culprit: bad government policies and a lack of congressional oversight of federal agencies and government-sponsored enterprises Fannie Mae and Freddie Mac.

"It is important to note," Obama said, "that the very absence of commonsense regulations able to keep up with a fast-paced financial sector is what created the need for that extraordinary intervention. The lack of sensible rules of the road, so often opposed by those who claim to speak for the free market, led to a rescue far more intrusive than anything any of us, Democrat or Republican, progressive or conservative, would have proposed or predicted."

Baloney.

Napolitano is a constitutional expert and a strong proponent of free-market economics, and he knew full well not to buy what Obama was selling in New York that morning. The interview was easy. All I had to do was agree with the Judge. Napolitano believed Obama was creating a clear-cut contrast between two views of the American economic system. He asked, "Which is better at providing high quality goods and services at the best possible prices: the free market or the government?" He pointed out that every program the federal government manages is inefficient and most are bankrupt.

Napolitano said Obama had come to Wall Street to argue for more government ownership, more government management, more taxpayer subsidies, and the takeover of one-sixth of America's economy—

the health-care industry. The judge and I agreed: government only consumes wealth; it doesn't create it. Expanding government control will only make America poorer and deeper in debt.

Congressional Chaos

Many believed, after the public outcry against the health-care bill in August, President Obama would shelve the idea or at least try to work with Republicans on a compromise. Instead the president began a full-court press on Democrats to pass the legislation without Republican support.

Dubious Democrats were subjected to appeals by former President Bill Clinton who told them this was their chance to make history. Even if the vote for government health care cost them their seats in Congress, the next generation of Americans would thank them for their vision and courage just as grateful citizens had lauded the Democrats who voted to create the Medicare program fifty years earlier.

Grassroots activists around the country were incredulous the president was ignoring the pleas of millions of Americans who were asking him to fix rather than replace the best health-care system in the world. And the more the president ignored them, the angrier Americans became—enough that Democrat leaders encouraged their members to avoid town halls and constituent meetings during the fall break because they didn't want a repeat of the August town hall meetings.

For my part I *increased* the number of media interviews to expand public opposition to Obama's health-care takeover, and I continued to interview good candidates who needed support from the SCF. Candidates from all over the country saw how SCF had assisted Pat Toomey and Marco Rubio. Underdog Republicans, who were being ignored or opposed in primaries by the NRSC, came to Washington to ask me to help them join the fight against the establishment.

This was truly rewarding. I had always been assured this strategy would result in making a significant difference in the way government is viewed and practiced—or at least it had the potential to. But I'd be exaggerating to say I had the foresight to see just how quickly and intensely the need for such a fund-raising channel would be. This wasn't a slow build-up requiring years to take root and establish a presence. The weight of its beliefs and influence was bearing immediate fruit, attracting high-quality candidates and creative, conservative ideas into a very fixed governmental orbit. I will always be grateful—and gratified—by what I see SCF accomplishing. And believe me, we're just getting started!

On Tuesday morning, September 15, I took a time-out from domestic issues to give a speech at the Heritage Foundation about the pitfalls of the U.S. signing the New START Treaty with Russia. I was trying to keep my focus on stopping Obama's health-care takeover and electing new Republicans to the Senate, but I could not ignore absurdities in our foreign policy. President Obama was advocating for a treaty with Russia to reduce the number of long-range nuclear missiles held by both countries. He would need great support from Congress to do it; the Constitution requires two-thirds of the Senate to ratify a treaty. But I could not support it. New START was another promise with no substance. I believed it would increase nuclear proliferation and make the world more dangerous.

New START was built on the assumption the U.S. and Russia should maintain nuclear parity. But our two countries have different roles in the world. The U.S. is the protector of many and a threat to none; Russia is a threat to many and a protector of none. More than thirty U.S. allies count on the U.S. nuclear umbrella for protection. If the U.S. reduces its capabilities to match the Russians, more countries will be compelled to develop their own nuclear arsenals.

New START also assumes a continuation of the now-outdated Cold War strategy of mutually assured destruction with Russia. In the treaty the U.S. agrees not to attempt to develop a missile defense system capable of defending American citizens against a Russian missile attack. But bottom line, it would render the U.S. incapable of defending itself against *any* country capable of firing multiple nuclear missiles.

The Constitution charges the federal government with the primary responsibility of defending the people of the United States. New START, in my opinion, would be an abrogation of our constitutional responsibility. My speech against it was my first attempt to focus public attention on a bad treaty. It would be months before this issue stirred any public debate.

I left the Heritage Foundation to speak to the American Association of Christian Schools (AACS). Back-to-back speeches on different subjects are a regular part of my Washington routine, and it is sometimes challenging to keep my facts straight on so many issues. But the privilege of addressing such a fine group of citizens as this organization represents is well worth the effort of "doing my homework."

The AACS visits Washington every year to remind legislators how education built on the Judeo-Christian values of our founders has proven superior to secular education when it comes to producing students with the character and skills to succeed in our free society. Not many in Congress like to be reminded of this. I told the Christian school advocates we must transform America's secular government education system into a system of choices serving the education needs of the public. Quality education for the public cannot be achieved through government schools.

From there I was off to the weekly Republican Policy lunch—the first since the September 12 march on Washington the previous Saturday. I've told you already that I fully expected a lively discussion about what the magnitude and volume of this event meant for our party and how we could harness the energy of the tea party movement to advance Republican principles.

But no one even mentioned September 12—no one. I was so disappointed it was difficult to speak. As one marcher had said with exasperation on Saturday, "I'm outraged out!" That's exactly how I felt.

I raised my hand at the end of the meeting, knowing no one in the room wanted to hear what I had to say. Trying to break the ice, I began by saying, "Former friends and colleagues . . ." There were a few smiles but mostly deadpan stares. Forging ahead, I reminded them of their appeals to build a big-tent Republican Party. I told them the big tent we were waiting to find had found our front door last weekend and was inviting us to join them. Hundreds of thousands of Americans had come to Washington to ask Congress for everything Republicans say we believe: less government, less spending, and less taxes. But they weren't going to join us until we joined *them*. How could we ignore such an obvious opportunity to advance the cause of freedom?

None of my colleagues responded. The room was silent, and I felt like a fool.

This was one of those key moments when the institutional inertia of the Senate hit me squarely over the head. This institution was clearly more important to most senators than either the cause or the party. It really was more like a fraternity or club. The hierarchy, the seniority system, and the personal relationships are sacrosanct. I was little more than an irritant, but the tea party movement was becoming a real threat to the club.

Meanwhile, Democrats were frantically working on a health-care bill that could pass the House and get unanimous Democrat support in the Senate. A tall order. In fact, several Democrat senators—Ben Nelson (Nebraska), Bill Nelson (Florida), and Mary Landrieu (Louisiana)—publicly expressed reservations about aspects of the legislation.

As behind-the-scenes negotiations on the health-care bill continued, news began to leak that Senate Democrats were making backroom deals to win the votes of these reticent senators. Ben Nelson received a special waiver from new Medicaid costs, dubbed by the media dubbed as the "Cornhusker Kickback." Bill Nelson of Florida received a waiver to maintain Medicare Advantage policies for his state. His buy off became known as "Gatoraid." Mary Landrieu's vote was bought with what the media called the "Louisiana Purchase."

While all this was happening, hearings were being held on a myriad of subjects in every committee, and the appropriators were working to ball up all the spending bills into a huge omnibus bill with thousands of earmarks. On the floor of the Senate, Republicans were bashing ObamaCare and the president's big-government agenda while the Democrats were screaming about Republican obstructionism.

Democrats were looking hard for some successes as they completed their third year controlling both chambers of Congress and their first year in control of the White House. Their attempts to blame President Bush were no longer getting traction with the American people. Their economic stimulus plan was failing. Their health-care bill was increasingly unpopular. Yet the progressive forces that got them elected would not allow them to moderate their positions and work with Republicans. Like lemmings running over a cliff, they seemed driven by a force beyond their control. Obama convinced them if they passed the health-care takeover, Americans would forget their objections and realize it was a historic accomplishment by the 2010 elections.

We'd see about that.

Stoking the Flames of the Awakening

On September 16, I met with Dr. Rand Paul, an ophthalmologist from Kentucky who was running for the Senate to replace retiring Senator Jim Bunning. Paul is the son of Congressman and former presidential candidate Ron Paul. Paul was not the choice of the other Kentucky senator, Mitch McConnell, or the NRSC.

Paul had never run for public office, but he was as knowledgeable about national issues as anyone currently serving in the Senate. He embraced the ideals and energy of the tea party movement and planned to give them a voice in Washington. He was laser focused on reducing the national debt and stopping earmarks. But Paul was the underdog in the Republican primary running behind McConnell's handpicked choice, Attorney General Trey Grayson.

The key to helping Paul was getting the support of Republican Senator Jim Bunning, the state's senior senator. Bunning was bitter at McConnell for forcing him to retire by threatening to support a Republican opponent in his reelection. So Bunning had no interest in being replaced by McConnell's handpicked candidate.

I encouraged Bunning to meet with Paul. Paul had not been active in the Republican Party in Kentucky so Bunning was not inclined to throw his support behind someone he didn't know or trust. I continued to bring up Paul to Bunning whenever we talked, hoping he would endorse him.

The day after my first meeting with Rand Paul, I met with Sue Lowden who was running for the Senate in Nevada hoping to replace Majority Leader Harry Reid. But Lowden first had to beat Republicans Danny Tarkanian and Sharron Angle in a primary before facing Reid in the general election. The NRSC picked Sue Lowden as their favorite because she was a poised, former television commentator, with experience in the Nevada Republican Party. They believed she had the best chance to beat Reid.

Lowden was polling well ahead of her two Republican opponents, but grassroots activists and tea party groups were gravitating toward Angle and Tarkanian. While I was impressed with Lowden, she lost my support when she later accused Reid of not bringing home enough money to Nevada.

Not this one.

That's when I shifted my attention in Nevada to Angle and Tarkanian. My friend, Senator John Ensign from Nevada, told me not to get involved in the Nevada Republican primary. He didn't know enough about Tarkanian, and he didn't think Angle had any chance to win the primary or the general election. So I decided to watch the Nevada race a little longer before getting involved.

Over the next two weeks I did more radio and television interviews about stopping ObamaCare and the reckless Democratic agenda than I could count. Public concern continued to grow about actions from the Congress, the administration, and the regulatory agencies under Obama's control. I used some of the more absurd (but very true) examples in my media interviews to stoke the flames of activism among Americans.

One of these absurdities was the John Murtha Airport in Pennsylvania. Congressman John Murtha (now deceased), a senior Democrat appropriator in the House, had directed millions of taxpayer dollars over his years in Congress to a small rural airport that served his district. Taxpayers heavily subsidized regular flights to Washington, D.C. rarely used by anyone except Murtha. I introduced an amendment to an appropriation bill to eliminate any future earmarks or subsidies to Murtha's airport. One television network did a special in which the reporter actually traveled on a plane from the Murtha airport to D.C. He was one of three people on the plane. While the Democrats and some Republican appropriators voted down my amendment, it helped connect the dots for Americans who wanted answers about our dysfunctional and wasteful government.

Another absurdity I could not resist giving some media attention was how the Environmental Protection Agency was killing jobs and crops in the Central Valley of California. The EPA cut off the water supply to thousands of farmers to protect an elusive, supposedly endangered fish on the California coast. I introduced an amendment to force them to turn the water back on.

· This was no small matter. The Central Valley of California produces over half of the vegetables for the United States and employs tens of thousands of workers. The EPA's actions led to unemployment as high as 40 percent in some areas of the Valley.

The two California Democrat Senators, Barbara Boxer and Diane Feinstein, told me to mind my own business. But the nation's food supply is everyone's business. Their votes against my amendment created a negative backlash for both of them in California. Feinstein went to work immediately after the vote to try to solve the problem for thousands of farmers in her state, and I received dozens of calls from farmers in California thanking me for forcing the issue.

On October 1, I picked another fight with the administration. When I met with Obama's nominee to be director of the Transportation Security Administration, Erroll Southers, he wouldn't agree not to unionize America's airport security officers. President Bush and Congress had agreed when the TSA was originally created that collective bargaining and union work rules were inconsistent with the constantly changing requirements of transportation security. We couldn't just have these people off the job for any period of time because of a labor dispute or stoppage. But Obama promised the unions during his campaign he would guarantee collective bargaining for airport security personnel.

Consequently, I did not give my consent for Southers to be confirmed without a full floor debate and a recorded vote. In the Senate, when you don't allow a nominee to be confirmed by unanimous consent, it's called a "hold." Obama had already delayed his nomination for the head of TSA for more than seven months, so I didn't think it was unreasonable for me to ask for a few more days to debate Southers's plan to unionize security workers. I also asked for all the records of his past employment. These records would ultimately lead to Southers's undoing.

Such battles—New START, education, health care, out-of-touch nominees—are very hard work, full of rancor and serious opposition. But this is what the people elected me to do: to fight for our shared principles, to fight for our future, to fight for our right to live in peace and safety as families and citizens.

To fight for freedom.

But I felt like a man with all ten fingers in a leaking dam while trying to build a new dam with my feet. I was doing everything I could do to stop Obama's liberal agenda while trying to elect some new Republicans who would help reverse the damage done. I was picking more fights than I could win, but I couldn't watch bad things happen without at least trying to stop them.

Honduras

The administration was also mishandling the constitutional crisis in Honduras. On June 28, the Honduran Congress and Supreme Court removed President Manuel Zelaya from office for trying to change a constitutional provision limiting his time in office. Eliminating term limits for democratically elected leaders undermines democracies all over the world. And our nation should not be in the habit of sanctioning such practices by other nations and their governments. These kinds of policies and leadership decisions don't stay contained within foreign borders but have a way of rippling around the globe—today more than ever, *faster* than ever.

Hugo Chavez, for example, successfully made the same change in Venezuela and installed himself as the permanent "president." He is really a dictator. Nobody denies that. And without question he was heavily involved with President Zelaya's attempt to join the ranks of other permanent presidents such as Fidel Castro and Manuel Ortega in the region. Increasingly, democratic elections were being used by tyrants to legitimize their power grabs.

After warning Zelaya to cease his attempts to force a national referendum to change the Honduran constitution, their Supreme Court ordered the military to arrest him. The military obeyed the order. Then to avoid civil unrest and danger to Zelaya, they transported him out of the country to Costa Rica.

The Obama administration immediately announced Zelaya was removed from office by an illegal military coup. The Organization of American States and the European Union quickly joined the condemnation of the "coup leaders." But recognizing that something just wasn't passing the smell test, my staff went to work to investigate what was really happening in Honduras.

I met with several representatives of the interim government there before the administration revoked their visas, even though no one in the Obama administration would meet with representatives from Honduras to hear their side of the story. I was even able to verify through documents from the Honduran Congress and Supreme Court that Zelaya had clearly broken the law and ignored warnings to cease his attempts to violate presidential term limits.

I also asked the legal arm of the Library of Congress to review all of the documentation. They concluded the Honduran government acted according to their constitution, with the exception of removing Zelaya from the country. Had they put him in jail instead of taking him to Costa Rica, there could be no legal case against them at all.

Nevertheless, the Obama administration would not relent. They cut off aid to Honduras and revoked travel visas to Honduras.

This was a knee-jerk reaction at best. The U.S. was Honduras's most important ally and trading partner. And yet the administration was attempting to strangle the interim government until they agreed to put Zelaya back in office, without fully investigating to see what was going on.

Surprisingly, the Hondurans said no. They believed it would destroy their constitutional government if they ignored their own laws. But the administration would still not listen.

So I found a way to get their attention.

Obama had nominated the current assistant secretary of state for Western hemisphere affairs, Tom Shannon, to be ambassador to Brazil. Obama also nominated Arturo Valenzuela to replace Shannon as assistant secretary. Both nominees insisted Hondurans had illegally replaced Zelaya. Secretary of State Hillary Clinton added to the chorus by saying the U.S. would not recognize the upcoming elections for a new president in Honduras.

I put a hold on the nominations of Shannon and Valenzuela until the administration was willing to look at the evidence about what really happened in Honduras. Their complaints against my hold helped publicize the issue and get some media coverage. But I needed to do more to focus attention on what the administration was doing to Honduras.

I had to go to Honduras to see for myself.

On Thursday, October 1, the same day I put a hold on Obama's TSA nominee, I decided to travel to Honduras. As a member of the Foreign Relations Committee, I was allowed to ask for military transportation when visiting a foreign country. My trip only required a courtesy sign-off from the chairman of the committee, Democrat Senator John Kerry of Massachusetts. But when I visited the Democrat cloakroom to ask Kerry for his approval, he said he wouldn't give it unless I released my holds on the two Obama nominees. This kind of overt *quid pro quo* was poor form, even in the Senate. But Kerry wouldn't budge.

I contacted Leader McConnell to ask for his help. To his credit and despite our disagreements, he used his leadership position to bypass Kerry. At 6:30 a.m. the next morning, two congressmen and I left Reagan National Airport on a military jet for Honduras. The notice was too short to get another senator to go with me, but Republican Congressmen Doug Lamborn (Colorado) and Aaron Schock (Illinois) were more than ready for a road trip. They are both serious legislators, and I was grateful for their help.

We landed in the Honduras capital of Tegucigalpa a few hours later. Some staff from the American embassy met us, but we were snubbed by the ambassador. The Democrats in Congress, we later learned, had sent advance notice to our embassy and to the Honduran government that we were not representatives of the U.S. government.

A driver took our "illegitimate" delegation to the U.S. Embassy, where we met briefly with the U.S. ambassador to Honduras, Hugo Llorens—and where it became immediately apparent why the Obama administration thought there had been a military coup in Honduras. Ambassador Llorens *told* them it was a coup. He was heavily invested in President Zelaya, and he continued to insist Zelaya was removed illegally.

Since the U.S. cut off diplomatic relations with Honduras, no one from the embassy went with us to meet with Honduran government officials. When we arrived at the government complex, a few military personnel were guarding the gate, but that was the last we saw of the military. They were obviously not in charge of the government, as had been claimed. We met with Interim President Roberto Micheletti. He was no coup leader and had no designs on keeping the presidency. His goal was to protect the fragile

Honduran constitutional democracy in the face of opposition from Hugo Chavez, Fidel Castro, Daniel Ortega, and other dictators in the region. Unfortunately, their democracy was also being threatened by another close neighbor: the Obama administration.

We met with members of the president's cabinet, members of congress, and the entire Supreme Court. We also met with a number of Americans who lived and worked in Honduras. They were all in agreement that Zelaya was on a course to undermine the Honduran constitutional democracy. His removal had been a good thing, a healthy guard against corruption, and above all, an upholding of constitutional law.

We left Honduras with a strong conviction there had been no coup and with enough evidence to conclude the government acted properly to protect its constitution. When we returned to Washington, *The Wall Street Journal* agreed to publish my report on the trip titled, "What I Heard in Honduras." In it I wrote:

> When I asked Ambassador Llorens why the U.S. government insists on labeling what appears to the entire country to be the constitutional removal of Mr. Zelaya a "coup," he urged me to read the legal opinion drafted by the State Department's top lawyer, Harold Koh. As it happens, I have asked to see Mr. Koh's report before and since my trip, but all requests to publicly disclose it have been denied.
>
> On the other hand, the only thorough examination of the facts to date—conducted by a senior analyst at the Law Library of Congress—confirms the legality and constitutionality of Mr. Zelaya's ouster.
>
> Unlike the Obama administration's snap decision after June 28, the Law Library report is grounded in the facts of the case and the intricacies of Honduran constitutional law. So persuasive is the report that after its release, the *New Republic*'s James Kirchick concluded in an Oct. 3 article that President Obama's hastily decided Honduras policy is now "a mistake in search of a rationale."[11]

The national media coverage about what really happened in Honduras ultimately forced the Obama administration to soften its position. Secretary Clinton agreed to reestablish relations with the Honduran government and to recognize the upcoming elections for a new president if I would agree to release my holds on their two nominees.

And that was that. It was rewarding to make a real difference on an important international issue, and many in Honduras expressed their appreciation. I even received an anonymous thank-you note from an employee of the American Embassy in Honduras. But my work had come with a price. The Obama administration's curious lack of comprehension and insight had forced me to invest an inordinate amount of time on an issue about which few Americans were even aware, while the Democrats were advancing on so many fronts, it was impossible to stop them without more help. I could only hope the SCF, along with the millions of people who were part of the American awakening, could provide the manpower and resources to elect a few new Republicans who were willing to fight against the onslaught of socialist economic policies and the Democrats' destructive progressive agenda.

When I was first elected to the U.S. House, a seasoned congressman told me I would be tempted to involve myself with every issue coming through the Congress. But after a few years, he said, most members of Congress ultimately chose to focus on one or two issues. Granted, there is a lot of wisdom in specializing in a few areas where you can be most effective, but the result of this approach in Congress has been that few members ever really consider the big picture—what is happening to our country. Individual members of Congress are all straightening the chairs in their section on the deck of the *Titanic*. They're not even concerned about the deck chairs outside of their area, much less that the ship is sinking. They all still believe America is unsinkable.

They need a great awakening.

Chapter 7

Government Health Care
for Christmas

October 3, 2009—December 31, 2009

After returning from Honduras I spoke at the third annual Defending the American Dream Summit. This was another opportunity to be a cheerleader for grass roots activists who were trying to save America.

Americans for Prosperity (AFP) organized the event. AFP, one of the largest and most effective conservative grassroots organizations in America, had been instrumental in informing and activating hundreds of thousands of voters against ObamaCare and the out-of-control Pelosi-Reid agenda in Congress. Without organizations like AFP, my work against the status-quo Washington establishment would have been dead in the water.

The conference was attended by thousands of AFP financial supporters and grassroots leaders from all over the country. The large meeting venue included an entire room filled with bloggers and radio talk show hosts in booths broadcasting live to hundreds of thousands of listeners in media markets from New York to California. I spent about two hours talking to hosts and their listeners. The message from Americans was consistent:

"What are they thinking? Why are they continuing to cram this stuff down our throats? Can't they hear us?"

David Koch, chairman of the board of the AFP Foundation, introduced me and presented me with an award for defending the American dream. Koch said the annual award was given to an individual "who has contributed in a powerful and unique way to defending our economic freedoms." He added: "Sometimes there's more to being a political leader than simply saying no to a bad idea or even presenting your proactive solutions. There are times when a true leader has to be willing to take an action, on principle, that angers all of his colleagues. Jim DeMint is always prepared to do just that."

Awareness was growing in conservative circles that party leaders had declared war on me for my efforts to undermine the power of appropriators by eliminating earmarks. While I continued publicly to express support for the Republican leadership team in the Senate, some of them, as well as their "anonymous leadership aides," had become increasingly critical of me in the press. And I'm sure they would have crushed me, permanently extinguishing my relevance and effectiveness in the Senate, except for one thing: *millions of voters were on my side.* Americans had my back! Senior Republicans were aware that any attack on me by party leaders would be viewed as an attack on the tea party movement. SCF members were watching their every move.

The month of October turned into a blur of radio and television interviews. The press was still interested in Honduras, and I was anxious to put more pressure on the administration to normalize relations with our Central American ally. The media was also beginning to show some interest in the upcoming gubernatorial elections in Virginia and New Jersey, as well as a few special elections for the House.

On Tuesday, October 6, I was scheduled to be on Greta Van Susteren's show *On the Record* on FOX News at 10:00 p.m. Van Susteren is one of my favorite hosts. She is a tough investigative reporter and lawyer but not one of those "gotcha" hosts who is always trying to make themselves look good at their guests' expense. The only problem I have with doing the show is I am usually tired and half asleep by 10:00 p.m. She is always sharp and quick, and even with a strong cup of coffee before her show, it's hard to keep up.

Van Susteren wanted to talk about Honduras. She had taken the time to look at the legal review produced by the Library of Congress and had come to the same conclusion I had: the Hondurans were trying to do the right thing. Her advocacy for constitutional government in Honduras made it hard for the Obama administration to continue calling the removal of their president a "coup." Van Susteren, the whole FOX News team, and *The Wall Street Journal* deserve credit for saving constitutional government in Honduras by reporting the truth.

November Election Surprises

The upcoming gubernatorial elections dominated the political atmosphere over the next few weeks. Everyone was watching to see if the tea party movement would put Republicans over the edge in Virginia and New Jersey.

Polls in Virginia showed Republican Bob McDonnell pulling ahead in the governor's race by attacking his Democrat opponent to Obama. Democrats claimed their poor showing in the polls in Virginia was only because they had a weak candidate, not because of Obama. They pointed as evidence to their candidate in New Jersey, Governor Jon Corzine, who was running on his support of the Obama agenda and doing fine against Republican Chris Christie. Or so they thought. The Democrats underestimated Christie's tenaciousness.

World Magazine published an article by Edward Lee Pitts on October 24, 2009, saying what most political observers knew was true: the off-year elections in Virginia and New Jersey were the first test for Obama's agenda and would provide the first indicators of a potential GOP revival in 2010. Pitts concluded: "The early success of both McDonnell and Christie suggests that their strategy of embracing their conservative bona fides has tapped into the grassroots energy that has been unleashed in the growing Tea Party movement, which favors the limited-government views of Republicans."

For their part, President Obama and the Democrats in Congress played down the upcoming elections and kept their focus on passing their health-care bill. But the pressure from voters was obviously getting to them. When a CNS News reporter asked Speaker Nancy Pelosi where the Constitution authorized Congress to order Americans to buy health insurance, Pelosi dismissed the question by saying, "Are you serious?" She treated it as a joke.

Her spokesperson later said the constitutionality of the health-care bill was "not a serious question." Pelosi's laughing at the relevancy of the Constitution only added fuel to the fire of discontent among voters.

Criticism from conservative media was also getting to Obama. On October 11, the Obama administration declared that FOX News—and its owner, reporters, and commentators—were shills for the president's Republican opponents. "Let's not pretend they're a news network," White House Communications Director Anita Dunn said on CNN's Sunday program *Reliable Sources*. "FOX News often operates almost as either the research arm or the communications arm of the Republican Party. What I think is fair to say about FOX, and certainly the way we view it, is that it really is more a wing of the Republican Party."

And the way I viewed it, the Democrats were starting to sound desperate.

As the November elections neared, another race began to dominate media coverage. A special election for New York's 23rd Congressional District seat was a three-way race between Democrat Bill Owen, Republican Dede Scozzafava, and Conservative Party nominee Doug Hoffman. The 23rd district had for years been one of the few Republican strongholds in New York. But Republican Party bosses in New York nominated the pro-choice, pro-union, liberal state Assemblywoman Scozzafava to carry the Republican banner.

Early polls showed Scozzafava with a large lead. But tea party activists and conservative Republicans rebelled against the Republican establishment and supported the Conservative Party nominee Hoffman. As Election Day approached, Hoffman moved ahead in the polls—so far ahead, in fact, Scozzafava decided to drop out of the race.

Hoffman looked like the sure winner until Scozzafava endorsed Democrat Bill Owens. *Politico* reported on November 1, "Scozzafava's husband Ron McDougall, a leading labor official in upstate New York who works closely with New York Democrats, sent an e-mail out Saturday night offering enthusiastic support for Owens' candidacy." Like many moderates and liberals in the Republican Party, Scozzafava would rather have a Democrat elected to Congress than a conservative.

When Hoffman ultimately lost the election to his Democrat opponent, many Beltway Republicans blamed conservatives and tea party activists for costing Republicans a House seat. But New York's 23rd district results actually said more about Republican moderates than conservatives.

It revealed a truth that had been obvious to me for years. It's this: conservatives are not the purists in the Republican Party, the ones who don't have room for those whose views don't match their own. Republican moderates are the ones who don't have room in their "big tent" for conservatives. Moderates are much more aligned with big-spending, big-government Democrats than they are with conservative Republicans. We may have our differences of opinion on nominees at primary time, but when the general election rolls around, conservative Republicans can be counted on to support their party candidate. Not so, the other way around. When pressed, so-called moderates would rather have another Democrat in Congress than another conservative Republican. The race in New York proved this truth again. Republicans lost a House seat in New York trying to run against the tea party movement. It's that simple.

But in Virginia and New Jersey, Republicans upset their Democrat gubernatorial opponents by embracing the energy of tea party activists and running as conservatives. McDonnell won big in the Virginia governor's race, and Christie—running on a platform of less government, less spending, and less taxes—stunned the entire country by defeating a liberal incumbent Democrat in New Jersey, one of the most solidly Democrat states in America.

The Republican victories in Virginia and New Jersey were bittersweet. They proved the political awakening in America was real and already strong enough to elect a Republican, even in New Jersey. But it was discouraging to think we had to wait another year to get the reinforcements we needed in Congress to stop the Obama agenda. Obama, Pelosi, and Reid had their sights set on socializing America's health-care system, and they were threatening to keep Congress in session until Christmas to get their legislation passed.

Recruiting Reinforcements

While the news from Virginia and New Jersey was beginning to trickle in, the SCF held a conference call to talk to our members about the 2010 elections.

I invited SCF supporters to participate in the call, cohosted by the editor of the conservative blog Redstate.com, Erick Erickson, in an e-mail sent out earlier that day. I wanted to get their opinion on upcoming races and give them a way to vote on the candidates they liked best.

I also had a major announcement to give: SCF was ready to endorse conservative Chuck DeVore in the California Republican Senate primary. DeVore was the least known candidate in the Republican primary competing for the right to take on ultraliberal Democrat Senator Barbara Boxer. I was the only senator to support DeVore. Guess I was just getting used to it.

The NRSC and most Senate Republicans were encouraging Carly Fiorina, the former Hewlett-Packard executive, to enter the primary. Fiorina entered the race later, along with California Congressman Tom Campbell. But DeVore was the proven conservative. He opposed the stimulus, opposed the Wall Street and auto bailouts, opposed earmarks, and is 100 percent pro-life. As a state assemblyman, he took on the big spenders in both parties. We needed people with courage and convictions like DeVore in the U.S. Senate.

I knew DeVore was considered a long shot by those who were waiting for Fiorina to announce her candidacy. California is bigger than many countries, and he would need tens of millions of dollars to get his message out across the entire state. Fiorina is a multimillionaire who could put millions into her own campaign. And Campbell already had significant name identification and many fund-raising allies from his days in Congress. The odds were long for DeVore, but I determined he was worth fighting for. If I could help a person win an election with his kind of principles and convictions, great. If he didn't win, I still wanted to be on his side.

When I created the SCF, I decided that winning was not as important as winning with the right people. SCF was not going to support candidates just because they were most likely to win. I wanted to find the right candidates and then do everything I could do to help them win. DeVore was the right candidate in the California Senate race, even though I knew California would be a hard state to win.

Another opportunity to recruit a new conservative Republican was in Texas. Incumbent Senator Kay Bailey Hutchinson was running for governor, and she had pledged to resign her Senate seat after the Republican gubernatorial primary in March 2010. Governor Rick Perry would appoint a replacement for Senator Hutchinson when she resigned. Then, there would be a special election in November 2010 to elect a senator to complete Hutchinson's remaining term.

Texas Railroad Commissioner Michael Williams had already announced his candidacy for the special election. He hoped Governor Perry would appoint him senator when Hutchinson resigned. Williams is an African-American who distinguished himself as a Texas Railroad commissioner. In Texas, railroad commissioners have broad authority over the oil and gas industry, making them among the most powerful elected officials in the state.

Williams had a reputation as an outspoken, free-market conservative. He was opposed to earmarks, supported a balanced budget, spoke passionately against ObamaCare, and believed in term limits. He was a good friend of Perry, so there was a real chance he could be appointed senator within a few months. I was extremely excited about the possibility of Williams becoming a conservative ally in the Senate.

But before endorsing Williams, I wanted to be sure Hutchinson was serious about resigning after her primary against Perry, which was only a few months away. I caught up with her on the way into a Republican Policy lunch in early December. Our relationship was strained because she was an appropriator and a consummate earmarker. We battled against each other in 2006, over whether to pass a pork-filled omnibus appropriations bill that contained more than ten thousand earmarks. At the time she was chairman of an appropriations subcommittee and a major proponent of the bill. Oklahoma Republican Senator Tom Coburn and I were successful in stopping it during the final days of the Republican majority.

I asked Hutchinson if she was sure she was going to resign from the Senate after her primary for governor in March. She confirmed she would resign regardless of the outcome of the primary. The next day the SCF formally endorsed Williams. He flew to Washington and spent two days in Washington with me holding press conferences and conference calls with the media. Our work generated good press coverage back in Texas, and I was hopeful the media attention would put Williams on the top of Perry's list to replace Hutchinson.

As it turned out, Hutchinson's commitment to resign the Senate was not kept.

House Democrats Pass ObamaCare

On Thursday, November 5, 2009, more than ten thousand Americans came to Washington to protest ObamaCare. But this time they came at the invitation of House Republicans. Finally Republicans were embracing the movement that could reshape our party and restore our majority.

That's what a great American awakening can do!

Representative Michele Bachmann, a Minnesota Republican, was a leading proponent of the rally, asking Americans to come to Washington to visit their congressmen and senators to voice their concerns about socialized medicine. "They're going to listen," Bachmann told the crowd. "The biggest voice in the United States is *your* voice."

Actor Jon Voight and Family Research Council President Tony Perkins were among the speakers, along with Mark Levin, one of the most popular conservative radio talk show hosts in America. The speakers encouraged attendees to demand that Congress stop the government takeover of health care. "Kill the bill! Kill the bill!" the crowd chanted.

Meanwhile, Speaker Pelosi kept the House in session over the weekend to hotbox fellow Democrats into voting for the health-care bill. President Obama came to the Capitol before the vote to further pressure undecided Democrats. By holding the vote over the weekend, Democrat leaders could escape the criticism that would surely come on the weekday nightly news programs. Most major media outlets do not carry weekend news programming. And few Americans watch C-SPAN on Saturday night for live coverage of congressional action.

Then suddenly . . . a tragic diversion.

When the news of the Fort Hood massacre hit the airwaves on Thursday afternoon, any hope of using media pressure to dissuade a few Democrats faded. An army psychiatrist had opened fire at Fort Hood, Texas, killing twelve people and wounding thirty-one others. The gunman, identified as Major Nidal Malik Hasan, was wounded but captured alive and was hospitalized in stable condition.

The nation's attention quickly shifted from health care to questions about how a Muslim army officer who supported radical jihadists had been allowed to continue as an officer. Had political correctness and fears of racial or religious profiling resulted in the deaths of a dozen people on a secure military base? Were politics undermining the safety of our troops?

With the weekend news focused almost entirely on the Fort Hood shootings, the Obama-Pelosi team was able to continue working beneath the smoke screen, making deals to pass the health-care bill with little media scrutiny. Many of the "Blue Dog" Democrats, who claimed to be fiscal conservatives, were bought with the flimsy promise ObamaCare would save money in the long run.

On Saturday, November 7, House Democrats passed their health-care takeover by a vote of 220 to 215. Razor thin. Only one Republican voted for the bill. The big question remaining: could Senate Democrats pass the bill before Christmas? Senate Majority Leader Harry Reid was insisting the Senate vote on the bill before the Christmas break. He did not want his members to spend a month back home with their constituents before voting on an increasingly unpopular bill. He knew what a good, solid dose of down-home American opinion could do to the strength of his voting bloc. This wasn't about what America wanted. It was about what *he* wanted.

A Cold, Blue Christmas

December was one of the coldest months on record in D.C. It snowed several times, and a blizzard on December 19 shut down the city. But it did not stop the Senate from debating and voting on amendments to the health-care bill. I trudged through the snow numerous times to cast what felt like meaningless votes. Republicans offered many amendments to improve the bill and stop it from making cuts to Medicare. But under Senate rules, the Democrats only needed forty-one votes to stop every Republican amendment.

When Senate Democrats needed sixty votes to pass one of their own amendments, they were forced to transport the infirm and aged Senator Robert Byrd, West Virginia Democrat, through the snow from his home to give them the deciding vote. The Democrats stuck together, and all of those who hedged their votes to receive a special provision in the bill got what they needed in return for their vote on the final bill.

This was the first time in my thirty-six years of marriage I wasn't home to put up the Christmas decorations around our house. It was depressing being around all the snow in Washington with no Christmas spirit.

Almost half of the senators live in D.C., so the schedule wasn't as much of a problem for them. But for those of us who were away from home and family for the holidays, the seemingly pointless votes on the health-care bill were maddening. We knew the Democrats were going to pass a bill they hadn't read. It really didn't matter what was in it.

While I was trapped in Washington, participating in the national health-care debate, Debbie was going through a lonely personal drama back home. In November she had a regular mammogram checkup. Her doctor saw something that concerned him and asked her to come back for another mammogram on December 2. I needed to be at home with her, but she wanted me to stay in Washington to try to stop the passage of the health-care bill.

The doctor told her there might have been an issue with the X-ray film and there was nothing to be worried about. But the second X-ray showed the same problem. So the next week Debbie was back at her doctor's office for lab work, more tests, and finally a biopsy on December 10. On Friday, December 11, she called me in Washington to tell me the news.

She had breast cancer.

That's a mind-numbing statement to hear even in the most favorable conditions, no matter how it's delivered. But to hear it through the impersonal distance of a telephone receiver, without the immediate opportunity to reach out and hold my wife who was having to bear this somber development alone—it hurt more than words can say. My world seemed to go dark, and the cold around me penetrated my soul. Debbie shouldn't have been alone at a time like this.

I immediately caught the next flight home.

Debbie and I had a quiet dinner at home Friday night. Her doctor believed they had caught the cancer early but still wanted to schedule surgery immediately. He had arranged a meeting with a surgeon the next Wednesday. But Debbie was insistent the surgery would have to wait until after Christmas and the holiday season. Nothing was going to interfere with her family time.

We bought a Christmas tree on Saturday, positioned it in the traditional place in front of the bay window in our living room, and began adding the decorations. Later we cooked steaks on the grill and built a big, warm fire in the fireplace.

Sitting there with my wife that night, contemplating our mortality—that's how God sometimes helps bring some clarity to your thinking. Debbie and I had worked hard and raised four wonderful children together. It didn't seem right at this point in our lives to be spending so much time apart. I told her I was frustrated and did not want to spend another six years in the Senate. If she was in agreement, I was ready to look for another way to serve the country.

Knowing that her mind was naturally occupied with heavier thoughts, I knew this admission of mine would bring her some measure of Christmas hope and cheer. Debbie had never wanted me to run for elected office in the first place, and she did not enjoy public life. The constant media attacks violated our private lives and made things harder for our children. She could not stand the thought of enduring another negative campaign in the upcoming year. I was sure she would jump at the slightest hint I might be ready to get out of it. But something made her hesitate—which surprised me. She suggested we wait until after Christmas to make a final decision.

I returned to Washington on Sunday without finishing the Christmas decorations. Our home was the only one on our street without lights.

The next week, while the health-care debate in the Senate moved toward a conclusion, my daughter Ginger came home to accompany Debbie as she met with the surgeon, had more lab work done, and underwent an MRI. That weekend my son-in-law joined them and helped put up our Christmas lights. My system of storing our Christmas decorations in our attic was organized chaos at best. I couldn't imagine how they could figure it out, but somehow they did.

On Christmas Eve 2009, sixty Democrat senators voted to pass a bill essentially nationalizing America's health-care system. All forty Republicans held together and voted no. It was discouraging to watch the Democrats celebrate this massive expansion of government, but I was proud of every Republican senator who listened to their constituents and voted against this breach of constitutional government.

We had lost. For now. But the millions of Americans I had seen and heard from over the past year could be sure of one thing: their voices had been heard. And though none of us were exactly sure how or in what form their sentiments were going to come into play as we battled through what remained of this laborious process, no one expected their passion and anger to go away. As for me, I was going to do everything I could do to make sure this great American awakening of ours wasn't put to sleep.

Home for the Holidays

I made it home for dinner on Christmas Eve and was more than ready to forget politics for a while. When I drove into my driveway, our house was bright with Christmas lights. It never looked better. All four of our married children, their spouses, and our two grandsons were scheduled to come home at various times over the next few days. My only job was to cook the largest turkey I could find.

Christmas is my favorite time of year: lots of family around, big fires in the fireplace, football on television, and a spirit of thankfulness for all God's blessings. The birth of our Savior Jesus Christ and the reflection on His life, death, and resurrection always helps put our lives in perspective.

The holiday cheer was dampened by reports of an attempt by the "Christmas Day bomber" to blow up an airplane carrying passengers from Europe to the U.S. Fortunately his bomb failed and the plane landed safely. But the incident quickly put me back in the news.

Controversy doesn't take holidays.

This near tragedy was obviously an indication of a massive security failure, and President Obama wanted to blame me because I had held up his nominee to head the Transportation Security Administration, Erroll Southers. The first thing I wanted to say was that there had been more than ample time to bring Southers's confirmation to the floor of the Senate for a vote during those long, endless days we were stuck in D.C. in December. But the administration did not want his record up for public debate.

I didn't intend to do any media interviews during the holidays, but the administration and their surrogates were absurdly blaming me for the

Christmas Day bomber, and their claims were getting traction. I appeared on CBS's *The Early Show* on December 30 to go on the offense.

As I said, my initial concern about Southers was that he was not forthcoming about whether he would give union bosses control of airport security, which is one of the most important decisions he could make as the head of TSA. His unwillingness to take any kind of position for or against collective bargaining seriously called his judgment into question. Unionization weakens security and had already been rejected by other arms of the government tasked with major security duties—the CIA, the FBI, the Coast Guard, as well as every previous TSA administrator. Furthermore, we knew Southers had misled Congress in sworn testimony about accessing confidential records, and the White House never responded to requests for more information relating to his false testimony.

During my interview on CBS, I pointed out that Obama was sacrificing the security of Americans to fulfill his campaign promise to unions. I reminded viewers that Obama had waited seven months to nominate a chief for TSA and that the President did not even try to get a vote for him on the Senate floor.

Further details about Southers's record were now coming to light, and the administration was even less interested than before in a public debate. It was discovered that Southers had previously misled Congress about accessing confidential records at the FBI to spy on his then-estranged wife's new boyfriend. This information, when combined with questions surrounding the unionization of America's transportation security officers, led others to question whether he was the most qualified person for the job,

The CBS interview—as interruptive as it was to my Christmas mood and my family's needs—proved to be just the turn we needed in the Southers debate. The criticism soon shifted away from me and toward Southers and Obama. Before the dust settled, Southers withdrew from the nomination process.

Settling back into the holiday festivities, it seemed everywhere Debbie and I went during the week between Christmas and New Year's Day, people stopped to thank us for fighting for common sense in the Senate. They especially thanked Debbie for the sacrifices she was making for me to be in Washington. No one knew she was just diagnosed with cancer because we had not told anyone, but they knew my job made life much more difficult for her.

To my amazement, Debbie said we couldn't quit. She thought I should run again and stay in the fight. So we spent those special moments at the end of the year praying and asking God to help us through the next year of campaigning.

We had no idea He would answer that prayer in such a clear and wonderful way.

Chapter 8

Senator Tea Party

January 1, 2010—April 25, 2010

The year 2009 was just a prelude to what would prove to be a historic reshaping of American politics in 2010. Neither the public backlash against the Obama agenda during the August 2009 town halls nor the surprise Republican victories in the Virginia and New Jersey gubernatorial elections deterred the Democrats' big-government agenda. President Obama had inexplicably closed out 2009 by raising the U.S. debt limit to $12.4 trillion and guaranteeing Fannie Mae and Freddie Mac unlimited access to the federal coffers.

With heavy hearts, Debbie and I opened 2010 with her cancer surgery. On January 5, we arrived at the hospital at 7:00 a.m. for pre-op work. Since the cancer was small, the surgeon only had to remove the lump. It was a long day, but the report was good. The surgeon reported the cancer was contained and the surrounding tissue looked clear. We would have to wait several days for a biopsy report, but we left the hospital feeling optimistic about her complete recovery.

My schedule was mostly clear for the next two weeks so I stayed at home to help Debbie get back on her feet. I continued to call in to dozens of radio talk shows around the country and track the news from home. It was interesting to watch the national news from the perspective of a private citizen. President Obama was still ignoring the outcries from the American people, but a few Democrats were beginning to get the message and see the writing on the wall.

On January 6, senior Democrat Senator Chris Dodd, Connecticut, announced he would not seek reelection. Dodd had served thirty years in the Senate, but faltering poll numbers indicated he could not win a sixth term. On the same day another senior Democrat senator, Byron Dorgan, North Dakota, announced he would not seek reelection.

More changes came fast. Days later voters in the true-blue state of Massachusetts elected a Republican in their special election for the late Democrat Ted Kennedy's Senate seat. Senator Kennedy had died of brain cancer in August 2009 and was replaced temporarily by Paul Kirk. Democrat Martha Coakley seemed the overwhelming favorite to claim the seat in the special election scheduled for January to fill Kennedy's unexpired term. But in the last weeks before the election, tea party activists and conservative radio talk shows began to create momentum for Republican Scott Brown. When I realized there was an outside chance for Brown to win in Massachusetts, I began calling into national radio talk shows encouraging Americans to go to Brown's Web site to contribute to his campaign. I also used my e-mail list to encourage my supporters to get behind Brown.

Brown campaigned as a conservative, and his election sent shock waves through Washington. If a Republican could win Kennedy's Senate seat, a Republican could win anywhere in the country. With Brown as the critical forty-first vote against ObamaCare and other parts of the Obama agenda, media pundits predicted Obama and the Democratic leadership in Congress would pivot away from their increasingly unpopular agenda.

Was change truly on the horizon?

Still Not Listening

But Democrats were still not listening to anyone except their ultraliberal financiers. And too many Republicans were still not speaking up. When Congress returned to session on Wednesday, January 20, Speaker Pelosi and Leader Reid immediately began to talk about how they could circumvent the regular congressional process to pass ObamaCare without the necessary sixty votes in the Senate. People couldn't believe what they were hearing from the Democrats. The phones in all of my offices were ringing off the hook with calls from outraged citizens. They wanted to see Republicans fight back.

The House and Senate passed different versions of the health-care bill so the next step normally would be to produce a conference bill agreed to by representatives from the House and the Senate. But again, this process would require sixty votes to pass a final conference bill in the Senate. Brown was the forty-first Republican vote against ObamaCare, which meant Democrats only had fifty-nine.

Pelosi and Reid, grasping at straws, claimed they could use an arcane loophole from the budget process to circumvent regular parliamentary rules. How did they think Americans would react to that? Did they expect to influence favorable public opinion by resorting to sleight-of-hand technicalities to push through monumental legislation? Twisting nuances of procedural language to justify a tectonic shift in the nation's health-care laws? But the Democrats didn't seem to care. Before they finally crammed ObamaCare through the Congress, Representative Alcee Hastings, Florida Democrat, spoke for many Democrats in Congress when he revealed his disdain for the traditional rules of Congress while speaking at a committee hearing broadcast on C-SPAN: "There ain't no rules here, we're trying to accomplish something. . . . All this talk about rules. . . . When the deal goes down . . . we make 'em up as we go along."

Lord, help us.

On February 1, 2010, President Obama unveiled his proposed budget for 2011, doubling the national debt in five years and tripling it in ten years. But even this huge projected increase in our national debt was likely understated because the White House was using overly optimistic projections of economic growth. On February 12, Obama signed another law raising the national debt limit from $12.4 trillion to $14.3 trillion. The roller coaster just kept on rolling downhill, and the Democrats didn't seem to care how far or how fast it went.

Only adding to the free fall, Obama announced plans on February 19 to spend $1.5 billion of the bank bailout funds, known as TARP, to help pay the mortgages of people living in Arizona, California, Michigan, and Nevada.

He dubbed this bailout the "Hardest Hit Fund," as if people in other states who were losing their homes were not equally hard hit. On March 4, Obama signed the Travel Promotion Act, creating a new federal agency to promote tourism. He said it would be paid for by raising taxes on tourists.

Then on March 24, 2010 . . . the big one. The Obama Administration and Congressional Democrats officially passed ObamaCare. But not without some high drama and painful arm-twisting.

Pro-life Democrats in the House, led by Bart Stupak of Michigan, represented the last bastion of Democrat resistance. Obama had said, in trying to swing their votes his direction, the health-care bill would not use taxpayer money to pay for abortions. But the language in the final bill explicitly allowed subsidies to insurance plans that paid for abortions. Proabortion Democrats, of course, would not allow the language to be changed, but Stupak had enough votes to kill the bill if they didn't. Obama appeared to have a problem.

The pressure on Stupak was extraordinary. He received death threats. Liberal groups and family planning advocates excoriated him in the press for pushing a pro-life agenda, while pro-life groups prayed he would not yield.

Ultimately, he did.

Obama invited Stupak to the White House on Friday before the final vote and promised to issue an Executive Order prohibiting taxpayer-funded abortions in the health-care bill. Stupak is an honest and principled man, but unfortunately he saw this as a way to escape the terrible pressure he was under. The only problem: presidential executive orders cannot overrule the law. Once the health-care bill was passed into law, its language would supersede the president's order. Stupak got a raw deal and so did America.

Within a few weeks after the passage of the health-care bill, Stupak announced he would not seek reelection in November. He joined a growing list of Democrats who had voted for ObamaCare and other parts of the Obama agenda but did not want to defend their unpopular votes in the upcoming election. Obama's popularity was falling, and Democrats realized his charisma would not spare them from a brutal campaign.

Unfazed or perhaps just feeling unstoppable, Obama would not slow down his rampage of government interventions. Two days after the passage of his health-care takeover, Obama announced he would spend another

$50 billion in TARP funds to expand mortgage assistance through his Home Affordable Modification Program. Then on March 29, he promised to spend another $600 million of taxpayer money on his "Hardest Hit Fund."

It seemed no matter what Americans said—and no matter how many of them said it—their voices of reason were being ignored and overrun, one blank-check bill of legislation at a time. There just had to be a way to stop this free-bleeding of money from taxpayers' wallets into whatever government program happened to have a hand out.

Election Day 2010 couldn't get here soon enough.

Senator Tea Party

As Obama and the Democrats continued to push their socialist agenda, my national profile and, by some accounts infamy, continued to grow.

On February 24, the *National Review* published an article officially dubbing me "Senator Tea Party." This article was one of the first to suggest my actions were more than an internal irritant to dusty old Senate traditions. The author of the article, John Miller, predicted I was part of something much bigger:

> If DeMint once looked like a crotchety conservative who was satis-
> fied to serve in a dwindling and disgruntled minority, he now appears
> more like the prophet of a coming resurgence. Until recently, many
> Republicans would have been content to pick up a mere handful of
> Senate seats in the midterm elections this year. With Scott Brown's
> startling special-election victory in Massachusetts, however, there is
> talk of sweeping gains not just for the GOP in general, but specifi-
> cally for the conservatives within it.[12]

My attempts to be a voice for disgruntled Americans in the Senate came at a steep personal price. Relationships with fellow Republicans were increasingly strained. Many of my colleagues were not willing to listen or change, and they hoped "those tea party nuts" would just go away. On March 12, 2010, *Politico* published an article titled "Jim DeMint's Bid to Embrace Tea Party Irks Senate GOP Colleagues." It described my "poor form":

Examples of his senatorial poor form keep growing. DeMint has refused to endorse some of his fellow Republican senators facing intraparty challenges from the right. He openly backs some candidates opposed by his party's Senate leadership. And he is unabashed in announcing that the best way to win influence in the Senate is not by making friends and patiently massaging the legislative process but by exerting public pressure from activists and the media to bear on his colleagues.

Not surprisingly, his colleagues don't especially like it. Many GOP senators privately scoff at DeMint as a showboating opportunist and a pain in certain parts of the anatomy. Even in on-the-record interviews, some Republican senators said that DeMint does not appreciate the need for a successful party to widen its ideological and geographic base beyond the deeply conservative Southern state he represents.

DeMint said he is unapologetic about rocking the boat. "I've found that most of the people in the Congress are here to get money for their states or their congressional districts—they think that's what their role is," he lamented in an interview. "The reforms we have to make to save our country—like getting rid of earmarks, balancing the budget, tax reform or fixing Social Security or Medicare—you can't get these folks to sign up for a bill."

Of his own place of employment, DeMint said: "I've just found that the Senate is going to be the last place to change, and if I wait for them to act, America will be in a ditch."[13]

Well, it's hard to be graceful when you're blasting rock.

Changing the most powerful and stagnant club in the world was not going to be easy. And the guardians of the status quo would not give up without a fight. Senate leaders had the power to muzzle me inside the Capitol, and that's clearly what they intended to do.

But the grass roots awakening across America and the constant oversight of conservative media meant the old Republican guard couldn't muzzle me. Not anymore. Not without serious repercussions. Their only option was to isolate me by portraying me as an ineffective wing nut. They couldn't openly criticize me for trying to stop earmarks, wasteful spending, and the growing national debt because that's what the majority of Americans expected Congress to do.

The "Senator Tea Party" title suggested I was one of the top leaders of America's political awakening, but let's be honest: the tea parties and the growing national grassroots activism did not have leaders at the top of a hierarchy. Some called it a leaderless organization, but it was actually a movement with millions of leaders. The tea party movement was a picture of how freedom works—millions of people making their own decisions about what they value and what they want to do.

On April 14, the SCF endorsed another antiestablishment conservative in Colorado. Ken Buck was a decided underdog running in the primary for the Senate against the Republican establishment pick, former Lieutenant Governor Jane Norton. He was a great candidate with a commendable record. As Weld County District Attorney, Buck didn't just talk about enforcing immigration law. He actually did it. He assisted in the 2006 sweep of the Swift & Co. plants, which led to the arrest of thirteen hundred illegal immigrants nationwide. During his tenure crime in Weld County went down by 50 percent. And before becoming Weld County district attorney, Buck had worked on the Iran-Contra Investigation and as a prosecutor with the U.S. Department of Justice.

He advocated a balanced budget amendment, a ban on earmarks, term limits for office holders, and the full repeal of Obama's health-care takeover. He had also gained an impressive following among grassroots activists in Colorado for his straight talk on the issues. Buck was the right candidate to support, even though endorsing him was another unpopular move among my Republican colleagues. He was such a long shot, however, no one viewed my endorsement as much of a threat.

Obama's Gulf

Tax day, April 15, 2010, saw another nationwide explosion of tea party protests, just like the year before. The media generally downplayed the continued growth in the tea party movement, and many pundits predicted their energy would fizzle before the November elections. But a Rasussen poll found the number of people who said they were a part of the tea party grew from 16 percent in March to 24 percent in April.

Former Republican vice presidential candidate Sarah Palin became a hero to the tea party. She traveled the country encouraging Americans to stand up and take back their country. In Boston on the eve of the April 15 tax day protests, she sent a message via the media to the White House, "We'll keep clinging to our Constitution, our guns, and our religion, and you can keep the change!" This was a reference to then-presidential candidate Obama's comments in 2008 that working-class Americans "cling to guns and religion" during times of economic uncertainly. Palin's courage was contagious for citizens and politicians in every state.

Emboldened to act, the Arizona legislature passed a tough new law on April 19, 2010, to enforce federal policies against illegal immigration, requiring law enforcement officers to check the immigration status of people who were stopped or arrested for other reasons. Critics, including President Obama, immediately claimed the new law would lead to racial profiling. Some California politicians called for a boycott of Arizona, but many Americans wanted their states to pass similar, Arizona-style immigration laws. President Obama further diminished his faltering popularity by threatening to sue the state of Arizona for enforcing federal immigration policy.

This course of action by the Obama administration really riled the majority of Americans who were cheering for Arizona, not only by ordering his Justice Department to begin legal proceedings against the state, but also by consistently misrepresenting the content of the law. Secretary of Homeland Security Janet Napolitano, after giving a speech condemning the Arizona law, even admitted she hadn't read it.

Then on April 20, Obama mishandled another major issue. An oil rig operated by BP exploded in the Gulf of Mexico. Several workers were killed, and the entire platform sank after thousands of gallons of water were pumped onto the rig to extinguish the fire. Oil began gushing into the pristine waters of the Gulf.

Obama responded by shutting down dozens of American oil rigs in the Gulf of Mexico. Thousands of jobs were lost. While the president tried to vilify BP and appear to be in control of the situation, his actions led to public outcries from unemployed workers in the oil and tourist industries along the Gulf Coast. The oil would continue to gush into the Gulf for months.

Back in Washington, congressional Democrats continued to distance themselves from the American people. Representative Frank and Senator Dodd were finishing the Democrat's new financial regulation bill giving the federal government broad control over America's financial system. They claimed this new expansion of federal power was needed to prevent another financial meltdown, but the bill did not even address the major culprits of the financial crisis: subprime mortgage giants Fannie Mae and Freddie Mac.

The Democrats claimed their financial regulation bill would shake up Wall Street, but reports were rampant that Wall Street executives actually helped write the bill. Americans knew the fix was in when the people Obama called "fat cat bankers on Wall Street" expressed public support for the financial regulatory overhaul.

The binge of government spending and takeovers continued unabated in Washington. When Americans expressed their outrage, President Obama dismissed them as irresponsible or worse. Speaking at a commencement on May 1 at the University of Michigan, Obama said "over the top rhetoric" was becoming more common in American politics and undermining "democratic deliberation." He specifically criticized those who used the word *socialist* to describe his administration: "Throwing around phrases like 'socialist' and 'Soviet-style takeover;' 'fascist,' and 'right-wing nut' may grab headlines, but it also has the effect of comparing our government, or our political opponents, to authoritarian, and even murderous regimes."

The president's increasing defensiveness toward his critics was symptomatic of the growing distance between himself and the American people. And his problems were not just with conservatives. Obama's approval ratings were declining significantly with Independent voters as well.

But Obama's tone remained more defiant than conciliatory. He seemed completely unable to yield on any part of his agenda or even to soften his disagreements with voters by demonstrating an ability to empathize with their concerns. The president implied through all of his actions that he knew what was best for America. Other opinions were unwelcome.

My Mountaintop Experience

On Tuesday night, April 20, I made another tough endorsement decision. Marlin Stutzman, a young farmer and businessman, was running for the U.S. Senate in Indiana. And his opponents in the Republican primary, former Senator Dan Coats and former Congressman John Hostettler, were both friends of mine.

A few months earlier Stutzman and his wife, Christy, came to see me in Washington to ask for my help. Stutzman told me he'd made a decision to become politically active when his first child was only a few weeks old and terrorists attacked America on September 11, 2001. "What good is building a business for the future if you don't even have a country to pass on to your children?" he said.

In 2002, he was elected to the Indiana House of Representatives, beating a well-funded incumbent. His conservative platform focused on cutting spending and taxes, safeguarding schools, and improving Indiana's economy. While in office he took unpopular but necessary positions. He even opposed the "Lifetime Health-care Benefits" that the Indiana legislature gave themselves. "As the youngest member of this body at twenty-eight years of age, on the present plan I alone would cost this state over $1 million if I lived to be eighty," he said. "No Hoosier I know in the private sector has such a benefit, and it is wrong for public servants to have it at the taxpayer's expense."

It was clear to me Stutzman was another young and genuine candidate who stood for the principles of limited government and could help restore the integrity of the Republican Party. My heart told me to get behind Stutzman, but I hesitated to get involved because of my friendship with Coats and Hostettler.

After watching Stutzman struggling to gain traction against the other high-profile candidates, I decided to follow my heart and support his campaign. Stutzman was well behind in the polls, running a distant third to his better-known opponents

It was painful—no less painful than ever—but I called Coats on Tuesday evening to tell him of my decision to support Stutzman. Coats was well ahead in the polls, but he didn't want the distraction of another variable in his race. He wasn't happy with me, of course, and I couldn't blame him.

But Coats is a gentleman and a class act. We agreed we would make up after the primary.

On Wednesday, April 21, I spoke to a group of about one hundred pastors at the Library of Congress who were in Washington as part of a WallBuilders conference. David Barton, the president of WallBuilders, regularly invites pastors to Washington to remind them of the importance of Judeo-Christian values in the founding of America.

Barton's tours of the Capitol astound visitors who have been taught America was founded by deists who believed religious values should be separate from public policy. During his tours of the Capitol, Barton stands in front of the huge paintings in the giant rotunda and uses a laser pointer to tell the real story of America's religious foundations. He identifies our founding leaders while reading from original documents containing their quotes. Barton proves beyond any doubt the men who founded America considered faith and morality as indispensable for a prosperous and free society.

I encouraged the pastors to take strong, public moral stands and not be intimidated by those in the media who eschew any moral limits. We can't expect Americans to take strong stands on moral issues if their pastors are afraid to back them up.

These pastors seemed to agree. I left their meeting grateful for their commitment to engage the culture and for Barton's organization. His work informing and activating pastors was more important than anything I was doing in the political world. The American awakening would fade and die without moral leadership. Spending some time with these pastors lifted my spirits, and their encouragement was just a foretaste of another profound experience in store for me soon.

I left Washington the next day, Thursday, April 22, for what turned out to be a spiritual and political mountaintop adventure in, of all places, California. The Orange County Republican Party asked me to be the speaker for their annual Lincoln Day Dinner on Thursday night. I wouldn't have traveled across the country for one event, but David Horowitz asked me to speak at a Friday dinner as part of his annual Restoration Weekend in Santa Barbara. The trip also gave me an opportunity to help promote Chuck Devore for the U.S. Senate.

The Orange County Republicans were every bit as conservative as Republicans in South Carolina. Pundits often tell me other states are not as conservative as South Carolina. That may be true in part, but commonsense conservatives are active in every state, even California. Several hundred people attended the dinner, and much like Americans I'd addressed all over the country, they were ready to take their country back from professional, self-serving politicians.

The warm reception I received in Orange County gave me hope that even California would be a part of the American awakening. After the Lincoln Day Dinner, I flew to Santa Barbara where the Horowitz Restoration Weekend was being held. My speech wasn't until Friday night so I planned to spend the day at Young America's Foundation headquarters in Santa Barbara.

Young America's Foundation (YAF) is committed to ensuring that more young Americans understand and are inspired by the ideas of individual freedom, a strong national defense, free enterprise, and traditional values. As part of its mission, the organization manages the Reagan Ranch Center in Santa Barbara as well as the Reagan Ranch located high atop a nearby mountain.

YAF stepped in to save President Reagan's Western White House, Rancho del Cielo, "The Ranch in the Sky," in the spring of 1998 to preserve it as a living monument to Ronald Reagan and to use it to inspire future generations with Reagan's ideas and character. President Reagan committed himself to reaching young people with his ideas—a goal central to the YAF's mission. Preserving the ranch and passing on Reagan's lasting accomplishments is YAF's way of thanking Ronald Reagan for all he did for his country and the world. His beloved ranch is a place of learning, encouragement, and inspiration for generations to come. YAF describes the Reagan Ranch as a "schoolhouse for Reaganism."

YAF arranged for me to address a large group of students from nearby colleges at a breakfast held at the Reagan Ranch Center. Most of these students were attending liberal colleges where conservative ideas are not welcome. I enjoyed hearing their stories of how they stood up for their beliefs when liberal ideas were presented in their classrooms.

After the breakfast we toured the center and met with their staff. A lunch was arranged with supporters of the Foundation to discuss the status of Reagan's ideas in Washington. President Reagan's son and national radio talk show host, Michael Reagan, attended the lunch. I had been on his show many times, and it was fun to spend some time with him in person. Michael's stories of his father warmed our hearts and entertained everyone.

Many of us left the lunch in a caravan to make the hour-long drive to Reagan's Ranch in the Sky. The YAF director provided commentary all the way to the top of the mountain. The long, winding road up to the Ranch was now paved, but he remembered it as a bumpy dirt road when Reagan was president. His staff was always amazed how Reagan could nap during the rough ride to the top while his wife Nancy held on for dear life. The Secret Service finally convinced Reagan to allow the road to be paved for security reasons.

When our caravan stopped at the ranch house, I thought we'd arrived at the guardhouse. The house was about the size of a double-wide mobile home. Remembering the news reports of Soviet Prime Minister Mikhail Gorbachev at the "Western White House" and Queen Elizabeth visiting the Reagan Ranch, I always assumed it was some huge palatial estate.

It *was* a "white" house—stucco exterior and a Spanish tile roof—with a small covered porch. But it was hardly a mansion. About one hundred feet from the side of the house was a small lake, Lake Lucky, with a dock Reagan built with his own hands. A canoe Reagan named *Tru Luv* lay in the grass next to the dock. It was a gift from Nancy on their twenty-fifth wedding anniversary in 1977. Our guide said Reagan was occasionally able to coax Nancy into the canoe for a romantic paddle around Lake Lucky.

Nancy didn't particularly like coming to the ranch, and who could blame her? The house wasn't even heated. They relied on the fireplace to keep warm. The kitchen was small, and the Reagans slept on two single beds pushed together in a tiny bedroom. But Nancy encouraged Reagan to come to the ranch because she loved being alone with him.

Inside the small house it was as if the Reagans were still living there. There were no velvet ropes to keep visitors from walking around and touching the furniture. Reagan's clothes and boots were still in the small closet in his bedroom. Except for the presidential seal on the old rock fireplace, there was little evidence a person of stature lived there.

From the porch the view of the mountains was breathtaking. Next to the house was a large grazing pasture extending about half a mile up a hill before disappearing over the horizon. Reagan built the split-rail fence surrounding the pasture himself. A few horses grazed near the house. And as if on cue for visitors, a family of deer ran across the pasture about halfway up the hill.

Life at the ranch was centered around horses and the tack barn only a hundred feet from the house. Entering the tack barn, I walked back more than forty years into one of my fondest dreams. I grew up riding horses and still dream of having a place where I can have horses again. The tack barn had all the horse paraphernalia I loved and much more. It also had the toys, tools, and equipment to make my dream complete.

Reagan's old red Willys Jeep was the first toy that caught my eye. Reagan used it to get around the rugged trails on the ranch where he often cleared brush. His tools included several rows of axes and chain saws. Nearby sat an old Montgomery Ward riding lawn mower with a presidential seal on its hood.

Reagan began every day at the ranch with a long ride on his horse "Old Duke." Nancy would sometimes join him on her horse "No Strings." When Nancy was riding, Reagan would walk to the tack barn in the morning and saddle both horses. Then he would ring an old railroad locomotive bell to tell Nancy it was time to ride.

Wow, what a place. What a day.

What a man.

Ronald Reagan is one the political figures I most admire and respect. I regret never meeting him. But after spending a few hours at his Ranch in the Sky, I now feel like I have. We enjoy many of the same things. He saw God in the beauty around him, and he genuinely loved people. He loved his country and was passionate about freedom. And he loved being alone with his wife.

One of the visitors with me at Reagan's ranch was John Barletta, a former Secret Service agent who accompanied Reagan on horseback at the ranch after he became president. Barletta signed a copy of his book for me,

Riding with Reagan. Reading Barletta's book on the plane back to South Carolina was like spending another day at the Ranch in the Sky with Reagan.

The longer I live, the more I believe there are no great men, only average men who occasionally do great things. Reagan's love for his ranch in the mountains revealed a simple, good, and common man. The accomplishments of this common man, however, suggest how strong character matched with bold ideas can transform a common man into a great one.

We could sure use a lot more like him.

Chapter 9

Washington Establishment Crumbles

April 26, 2010—May 20, 2010

When I arrived in Washington on Monday, April 26, Democrats on the Banking Committee, led by Senator Dodd, had finalized their legislation to overhaul the nation's financial system. On Tuesday they began holding hearings with officials from Goldman Sachs and other financial institutions to figure out what had caused the financial crisis. Most rational people would investigate the causes of a problem *before* they developed the solution but not in Washington.

The last week of April was scheduled full of radio talk shows for me as the media began to focus on upcoming Republican primaries. By Thursday, rumors abounded that Florida Governor Crist, now trailing Marco Rubio by double digits in the polls, would leave the Republican primary and run as an Independent. FOX News called asking if I'd appear on *Your World* with Neil Cavuto that afternoon to discuss the implications of a Crist defection.

Cavuto is an astute television commentators, and he knew all about how I'd gone against my party's leaders to endorse Rubio early in the Florida Senate race. The polls showed Rubio would win the Republican primary and easily defeat a Democrat opponent in the general election. But the polls also showed Rubio could lose in a three-way general election against Crist and a Democrat candidate. The often-quoted "unnamed leadership aides" were already suggesting I may have cost Republicans two Senate seats because of my endorsements of Toomey in Pennsylvania and now Rubio in Florida. Cavuto wanted to know if I was doing more harm than good.

It was a good question. In my opinion Republicans needed to show voters we had changed *before* we asked them to trust us again with the majority. Americans were concerned and angry about the direction of their country. If Republicans presented people like Specter and Crist as the new faces of the Republican Party, voters had no reason to vote for us.

Toomey and Rubio believed in constitutionally limited government, and they reflected the growing awakening of the American people. They were the kind of new Republicans we needed to reshape the party, restore the trust of the American people, and save our country.

On Friday, May 1, Crist formally announced he was leaving the Republican Party and would continue his campaign for Senate as an Independent, expecting to attract Democrat and moderate Republican voters. The Crist and Specter defections from the Republican Party helped make a point to my Republican colleagues: when the Republican Party is more interested in numbers than principles, we shouldn't be surprised when our candidates are not loyal to either party *or* principles.

More Endorsements and More Tension

We finished votes for the week on Thursday night, but I stayed in Washington to speak at a fund-raising reception for Representative Mike Pence on Friday night. Pence was a good friend when we served together in the House and had become a prominent national conservative leader. I was glad to help him with his event.

I made the most of my time on Friday by making fund-raising calls for my own campaign and recording several video messages for my campaign Web site and for the SCF site. I also recorded a video that was sure to get me in more hot water with my Republican colleagues—an endorsement of Mike Lee to be played at the Republican convention in Utah if Senator Bob Bennett was eliminated from the nomination in the early rounds of voting.

Senator Bob Bennett, a senior member of the Senate Republican leadership team and one of the strongest proponents of earmarks, was locked in a heated three-way Republican contest in Utah. In Utah, Republicans use a two-step process to choose their candidates. The first step is conducted during a statewide nominating convention. Unless a candidate gets 60 percent of the vote, the top two vote getters move on from the convention to a primary.

Based on polls, it was unlikely Bennett would place in the top two slots, which would effectively end his Senate reelection campaign. Bennett had alienated conservatives in his state by voting for the Wall Street bailouts and supporting a health-care bill requiring every American to buy government-approved health insurance. Bennett's campaign was built on his ability to use his seniority to bring home the bacon. But Republican voters weren't buying that message anymore.

One of Bennett's opponents was Lee, a strong constitutional conservative who was passionate about limited government and opposed to earmarks. Lee was just the kind of ally I needed in the Senate. That's why I prepared an endorsement video for him in the event Bennett was eliminated.

I knew my colleagues would be miffed at me for getting involved in another primary—against another incumbent—even if I didn't get involved until after Bennett was defeated. But Lee's primary opponent, Tim Bridgewater, would not be an ally in my fight against wasteful, parochial earmarks. Utah was another opportunity for me to help elect a new Republican to the Senate who would fight for real reform. Sitting on the sidelines was not an option with someone as good as Lee on the ticket.

I flew home Saturday, May 1, amid news that a man had attempted to detonate a car bomb in Times Square. Fortunately, even though he was trained at bomb-making by terrorists in Yemen, the bomb failed to go off. The incident reminded New Yorkers and all Americans that nothing had changed since 9/11; terrorists were still at war with us.

The next week in D.C. was a time of high drama. Rubio flew in on Tuesday for a fund-raising lunch sponsored by the SCF. Crist's defection made Rubio the de facto Republican nominee, and everyone who supported Crist were now eating crow. We needed all Republicans behind Rubio, but it was hard to get some of the senators excited about him as our candidate.

This was also the week I had to make a final decision in the Kentucky primary between Leader McConnell's pick, Trey Grayson, and the real conservative in the race, Rand Paul. I had not endorsed in the Kentucky primary out of deference to McConnell, but he formally announced his endorsement of Grayson on Tuesday. McConnell's endorsement made it hard for me to stay quiet. Our party leaders seemed unwilling to give conservatives a fair chance in primaries. Something had to be done to balance the scales.

On Tuesday afternoon, May 4, Senator Bunning called asking for my endorsement of Paul. Bunning had endorsed Paul a few weeks before after becoming frustrated by the overwhelming support for Grayson from the Washington lobbying establishment.

After talking with Bunning, I called Paul to ask him if he thought my endorsement would be helpful. He knew I had been talking him up for months to conservative groups and blogs. But I was afraid an official endorsement could distract from his campaign if the media turned it into a competition between McConnell and me. The primary was only two weeks away, and I didn't want to do anything to hurt his chances.

Paul said my endorsement would help create a sense of momentum for his campaign in the closing weeks. He needed to counter McConnell's public support for Grayson with an endorsement for his campaign by a visible antiestablishment stalwart. And he needed some last-minute fund-raising support from the SCF. I asked Paul to give me twenty-four hours to think and pray about it.

Just before dinner with some friends that evening, I received an e-mail notifying me Stutzman had lost the Republican Senate primary in Indiana to Coats. While I was disappointed, Stutzman exceeded expectations and finished a strong second after winning the hearts of many Indiana voters. He was young and would find another place to serve. I was sure of that.

At dinner I brought up my dilemma about whether to endorse Paul or not. My Senate colleagues would view my endorsement of Paul as a public insult to McConnell. It would be a deliberate "poke in McConnell's eye" and an unforgiveable act of insubordination. But I knew in my heart Paul was just the kind of senator our country needed to save us from economic disaster. He would help restore integrity to the Republican Party. And he was someone I could count on to stand on principle.

I knew what I had to do. After dinner I e-mailed NRSC Chairman Cornyn to let him know I would be endorsing Paul on Wednesday. He forwarded the e-mail to McConnell who quickly e-mailed me asking for a meeting. We agreed to meet the next morning.

Wednesday morning, one of my staffers picked me up for an early speech at the Leadership Institute, an organization that trains young conservative leaders all over the country. It was a large breakfast with more than one hundred institute students, alumni, staff, and donors. I spoke about the importance of the upcoming election and explained why I was working to elect conservative senators in several races.

The students had a lot of questions, and many encouraged me to keep up the fight. But one student challenged me, "If you're supporting conservative candidates against establishment Republicans, why haven't you endorsed Rand Paul in Kentucky?" The audience erupted in cheers for Paul.

Talk about perfect timing. I told them to expect an announcement later that morning. The question and response from the audience helped confirm my decision to endorse Paul.

My meeting with McConnell was at 10:30 a.m. I knew what to expect, but *didn't* know what to expect—all at the same time. The leaders of both parties have large offices in the Capitol near the Senate floor. For my first few years in the Senate, I was always excited to be called to Leader Bill Frist's and later Mitch McConnell's office. They both had asked me to serve on various task forces or to help them with particular projects. Frist often solicited my help with communications since my professional background was advertising and marketing.

But recently most of my meetings with McConnell were contentious. I forced votes on some measures our moderate members didn't want to vote on. On numerous occasions I would not give my consent to pass spending bills without debate and a public vote. And my assault on the practice of earmarking had most of our senior members fuming.

Today's meeting promised to be another difficult discussion. As soon as we sat down, I spoke first to head off any argument about whether I was going to endorse Paul. I told McConnell my decision was final, but I also tried to give him assurance he had my full support as Leader and I was not trying to embarrass him.

"Mitch," I said, "I do not want to be president or leader; I just want a few more Republicans who will help us stop pork-barrel earmarks, wasteful spending, debt, and government takeovers. I support you as leader, and I will state that clearly in my press release announcing my endorsement of Rand Paul." After that McConnell seemed to relax, and a lot of the tension in the room evaporated. We shook hands; I left McConnell's office and quickly released a press statement endorsing Paul . . . *and* supporting McConnell.

I was glad I'd done it.

On the way to my next meeting, I received a breaking-news e-mail reporting Democrat House Appropriations Chairman David Obey had just announced he would not seek reelection. *Another Democrat unwilling to face the music*, I thought. Before putting my BlackBerry back in its holster, another newsbreak appeared on the screen. Freddie Mac had just reported another $8 billion in losses and asked the federal government for another bailout of $10.6 billion. *Incredible.* Our nation was in trouble, and the people who caused the problem were bailing out.

Later Wednesday afternoon I appeared on CNBC's nighttime program hosted by Larry Kudlow with Vermont senator and avowed socialist Bernie Sanders. Sanders and I were the ultimate odd couple. He is about as far left as you can go, and I am pretty far to the right. But we agreed on one thing: Congress needed to conduct an audit of the Federal Reserve to find out what they were doing. I was a cosponsor with Sanders on the legislation to audit the Federal Reserve, and our agreement on the issue helped attract the media attention needed to pass our bill.

It was all stacking up to be an interesting spring. *Very* interesting.

Prayers and Thankfulness

Thursday, May 6, was the National Day of Prayer. The president issued a proclamation, which is required by law, but he did not set aside the day to meet with religious leaders and pray as had previous presidents.

This bothered me. I'll tell you why.

President Abraham Lincoln signed the original proclamation declaring a national day of prayer beginning with the words: "Whereas, the Senate of the United States, devoutly recognizing the Supreme Authority and just

Government of Almighty God, in all the affairs of men and of nations, has, by a resolution, requested the President to designate and set apart a day for National prayer and humiliation."

In Obama's proclamation, he referred to the "Golden Rule" but not the Bible. He wrote: "As we observe this day of prayer, we remember the one law that binds all great religions together: the Golden Rule, and its call to love one another; to understand one another; and to treat with dignity and respect those with whom we share a brief moment on this Earth."

Lincoln's proclamation mentioned God five times and emphasized God's sovereignty over America, along with the need for people to repent and be attentive to the Bible: "And whereas it is the duty of nations as well as of men, to own their dependence upon the overruling power of God, to confess their sins and transgressions, in humble sorrow, yet with assured hope that genuine repentance will lead to mercy and pardon; and to recognize the sublime truth, announced in the Holy Scriptures and proven by all history, that those nations only are blessed whose God is the Lord."

In comparing the two proclamations, I was disheartened at how reluctant our modern-day president was to discuss God and the Bible. We all know we live in a pluralistic society, an intermingling of people with different faiths and nonfaiths. This brand of diversity is one of the distinguishing marks of our nation, our free society. Not every country is secure enough in its principles to allow such disparate views and backgrounds to share space as citizens. But it is a misunderstanding of history at best, and a religious put-down at worst, to downplay our nation's rich heritage of faith and trust in the one Almighty God or to minimize the importance of Holy Scripture in the fabric of our founding tenets and standards. As an American, I can't force anyone to believe or worship a certain way. But the American president has no need to run and hide from our religious legacy in order to placate any particular people group who might be offended—or whatever would motivate him to make such a glaring, unprecedented omission.

I didn't like it. I'll *never* like it.

We finished votes for the week on Thursday afternoon, and I caught the last flight out of D.C. for South Carolina. Debbie and I had a big weekend planned. Both of our sons were being awarded master's degrees on Friday, and we would be driving most of the day to see both ceremonies.

My oldest son was thirty-three years old and, after graduating from Clemson University with a degree in architecture, had worked various jobs in construction, building, and design for ten years. He is married with two young sons who, at the time, were ages three and one. After deciding he wanted to be a licensed architect, he moved his family to Clemson to earn the master's degree required to be licensed.

Going to school full time with a wife and two children meant a lot of sacrifices. They were able to get by with part-time work and frugal living. Now after two years he was receiving his degree. He was given the highest award of his graduating class and was offered a job with a good architectural firm in Charleston. This was quite an achievement in an economy where little design work and construction were underway.

My younger son was twenty-seven years old and graduated from Clemson five years before with a degree in business. He is married and was working for a good company in Columbia that had so far managed to survive the recession. He worked full time and went to classes at night for more than two years. It was a heavy load, but today he was being awarded a master's of business administration degree from the University of South Carolina, one of the best business schools in the nation.

Debbie and I were beaming as we set out for Clemson on Friday morning. We knew what they had gone through. Debbie and I shared their experiences of balancing family, education, and work. Knowing how challenging this was to achieve made us especially proud of what our sons had accomplished.

The Clemson commencement ceremonies began at 9:30 a.m. When my oldest son, Jake, walked across the stage and accepted his diploma, Debbie and I slipped out to begin the drive to Columbia where my other son would receive his diploma at 3:30 a.m.

As we made the two-and-a-half-hour drive to Columbia, it struck me that our sons and daughters were working hard and sacrificing in hopes of one day becoming the "rich" our government treated like enemies. They would spend the next twenty years building their careers, raising responsible and educated children, volunteering in their churches and community organizations, and giving to charities. If they were fortunate enough to make a high income, government would penalize them by taking more than half their earnings. And likely take another half when they died. These thoughts made me sad and angry about what politicians had done and were doing to our country.

My younger son received his MBA degree with students from around the world. We were proud of him and the stellar reputation the business school at USC had achieved. Debbie and I had an early dinner with him and his wife before driving back to Greenville.

All in all, it was a momentous day for Debbie, our sons, their wives, and me. The experience was also a good reminder of the work and sacrifice required by millions of Americans to build strong families and a great nation, and that our government should not discourage and penalize the hard work required to make individuals and our nation prosperous.

Republican Primaries Shake the Establishment

The Utah Republican nominating convention was held the next day on Saturday morning. I kept busy around the house with various projects until news began to come in from the early voting.

At the Utah Nominating Convention, there are three consecutive rounds of balloting. The first two rounds narrow the field to the top two candidates. In the final round, if either of those candidates receives 60 percent of the convention vote, he is the nominee. If not, a primary is held between the top two candidates.

Bennett made it past the first round of votes but was eliminated after placing third in the second round of voting. It was a sad end to a long career of public service for Bennett. After finishing third on the first ballot, he told the delegates, "Don't take a chance on a newcomer. . . . There's too much at stake." He was then heckled by some in the audience who yelled, "TARP! TARP!"

Before the third round of voting, the two remaining candidates, Bridgewater and Lee, were allowed one minute to speak. Instead of speaking, Lee played my video endorsement.

In the video I said:

> I'm thrilled to join you as you cast an important vote that will impact Utah and the nation. First, let me extend my thanks to

Senator Bob Bennett for his service to our country. He's a friend and he's made a real difference. There is much to be done in the U.S. Senate to protect our freedoms. We need a senator who is committed to balanced budgets, constitutional limits, and individual liberty. I believe that person is Mike Lee.

For Mike, the Constitution is not an abstract idea or a campaign slogan. He knows it is the road map for changing the course of our country. If Mike is nominated today, he will add his voice to the growing number of new Republicans who understand that protecting and defending the Constitution will restore the greatness of America. I'm not here to tell you how to vote. I'm here to ask for your help. Please send Mike Lee to the Senate so he can join me in the fight for our future. Change in Washington really can begin in Utah. Thank you.

I was gratified to read the press reports saying the room erupted in cheers when the video was played.

Apparently Lee needed my support more than I knew. Turns out, an anonymous mailer had been sent to delegates just before the convention, appearing to come from Lee and containing statements offensive to Mormons, who comprised a large portion of the delegates. The Utah press later speculated the negative fallout from the mailer prevented Lee from achieving the required 60 percent of the delegate votes to win the nomination outright. In fact, Lee finished a distant second and came within one percentage point of being eliminated altogether by Bridgewater. But since neither candidate received 60 percent of the vote, Bridgewater and Lee would face each other in a statewide primary election on June 22.

Bennett's loss was a wake-up call to other senators who had lost touch with their voters. Within a few days Bennett's fellow Utah senator, Orrin Hatch, cosponsored my bill to ban earmarks. Hatch always encouraged me to keep fighting even though he often disagreed with me. He was a vocal opponent of the moratorium on earmarks, but he was up for reelection in 2012. The message from Utah voters was loud and clear, and to his credit Hatch was now ready to listen.

As anticipated, the Washington media reported my endorsement of Lee without mentioning I only extended it after Bennett was eliminated. When I returned to Washington on Tuesday, May 11, the stares from my fellow senators were piercing. At lunch Bennett thanked me for delaying my endorsement until he was eliminated, but word spread I endorsed Lee against Bennett. I was the scourge of the Senate.

On Sunday, May 16, McClatchy newspapers published an article by James Rosen titled, "Jim DeMint Leads Rightward Shift of GOP Candidates Nationwide." The first few paragraphs positioned me versus the Republican leadership in the Senate:

> When voters go to the polls Tuesday for U.S. Senate primary elections in Kentucky and Pennsylvania, they'll write a new act in the ongoing shake-up of the Republican political establishment that's being led by conservative freshman Sen. Jim DeMint of South Carolina.
>
> In Kentucky, GOP voters will choose between Trey Grayson— the handpicked choice of the state's most powerful Republican, Senate Minority Leader Mitch McConnell—and DeMint-backed Rand Paul, son of former Libertarian Party presidential candidate—and current Texas congressman—Ron Paul.
>
> In Pennsylvania, Democrats will select Rep. Joe Sestak or incumbent Sen. Arlen Specter, who bolted the Republican Party last year after DeMint became the first Republican senator to endorse Specter's opponent, former Rep. Pat Toomey, in the GOP primary.[14]

The stage was being set by the media for a mini Super Tuesday for Senate primaries in several states: the Republican primary in Kentucky featuring tea party favorite Rand Paul versus establishment pick Trey Grayson; the Democrat primary in Arkansas with incumbent Blanche Lincoln pitted against union-backed Lieutenant Governor Bill Halter; and the Democrat primary in Pennsylvania between Republican-turned-Democrat Arlen Specter against Representative Joe Sestak.

On Tuesday the Kentucky primary was called for Paul within a few minutes of the polls' closing. Paul won an overwhelming landslide victory garnering 59 percent of the vote to 35 percent for Grayson. In his victory speech Paul drew a thunderous applause when he shouted, "We have come to take our government back!" He later said in an interview: "It's just a tremendous mandate for the tea party. It cannot be overstated that people want something new. They don't want the same old, same old politicians; and I think they think the system is broken and needs new blood."

Specter lost to Sestak, setting up a general election between Sestak and Toomey, now the Republican nominee for the Senate. In Arkansas incumbent Democrat Senator Lincoln was forced into a runoff with her opponent Bill Halter. Incumbents and establishment candidates were taking a beating as tea party activists continued to raise the temperature on business as usual in Washington.

Politico editor Jim VandeHei declared the Tuesday primary "marked the official end of Washington dominance." This was a particularly insightful perspective and reflected what I had been sensing was happening for months: power was slipping out of the hands of Washington politicians and back into the hands of the American people. As Rand Paul said, Americans were taking back their government.

And I couldn't help thinking back to where I saw it all starting.

All the media attention was beginning to make me uncomfortable, but it was helping draw attention to the success of the tea parties and to direct contributors to the SCF. Unfortunately, operating quietly in Congress allows everyone to ignore you. For better or worse, no one was ignoring me now.

Some of the reports were more lighthearted than others. *Time* published an article by Jay Newton-Small on its Web site titled, "Jim DeMint: Moving the Republican Brand to the Right." It said, "Senator Jim DeMint knows when a brand's gone bad and what to do to fix it. The South Carolina Republican spent more than 25 years in advertising before going into politics, and his demeanor—from the pinstripe suit to his salesman pitch delivered with a smile—has a *Mad Men* quality to it, almost as if Don Draper had been thrown forward 50 years and his only client was the Tea Party movement."

The Christian Broadcasting Network's David Brody continued to poke fun at the growing tension between Senator McConnell and me. His article was titled, "Mitch McConnell, Wayne Newton, Jim DeMint, and Justin

Bieber." I could only guess about how angry it must have made McConnell and his staff:

> Here's a GOP analogy for you. Right now, Mitch McConnell is looking a lot like Wayne Newton. Jim DeMint is looking a whole lot like Justin Bieber. You get my drift? Let me explain.
>
> You see, Wayne Newton is still popular with his fans but he's got limited appeal. He plays Vegas and that's about it. McConnell is sort of the same way. He's got his fans, he fights Obama's policies but he feels very 1973. Wayne Newton has been doing the same act for decades.
>
> Jim DeMint on the other hand is the hot new thing just like Justin Bieber. He's freelancing on his own by endorsing candidates with his Senate Conservative PAC fund. DeMint probably can't sing or dance like Bieber but he sure is making McConnell squirm. DeMint is the new act in town. DeMint's Tea Party message is playing to sold out shows across the country.[15]

None of this was endearing me to McConnell or any of my colleagues. Even my friends were starting to suggest I was showboating. *No way.* I was just raising money and promoting conservative candidates. That was all. Nothing fancy. Yet very effective. Ironically, even the constant criticism from "unnamed leadership aides" was only fueling stories that sent more and more people to the SCF Web site to donate money. The more they criticized me, the more the media played me up as a kingmaker, and the more money we raised for candidates. Seasoned political experts were now beginning to recognize the impact SCF was having in primary campaigns. Scott Powers of the *Orlando Sentinel* wrote, "Campaign-finance experts say they've never seen anything like Sen. Jim DeMint's efforts on behalf of Rubio."

No matter how innovative SCF was, however, the political establishment would not give a friendly welcome to the candidates it was supporting. The national press corps was in a frenzy over comments Paul made to NPR regarding the Civil Rights Act of 1964. MSNBC personality Rachel Maddow misrepresented his comments to suggest Paul was against the Civil

Rights Act. That was all the ammunition some politicos needed in order to say, "We told you Paul was too radical to win a general election."

This was the recurring theme: conservatives could win primaries, but they couldn't win in general elections in Pennsylvania, Florida, or even Kentucky. Reporters were crowding around me all day asking me to disavow Paul's comments. But once I read what he really said, I realized this was the same kind of media hatchet job I'd experienced many times myself. One reporter creates a bogus story, and the rest of the media continue to build it up and further distort it. But Paul stayed cool and eventually quieted the storm by correcting the record. I was convinced he was going to be a good general election candidate.

That week in D.C. had been a hotbed of tense encounters with colleagues and the media. The Republican primaries for the Senate were shaping up in a positive way, and it was gratifying to think I was playing a small role in helping restore the Republican Party to its core principles. But my success came with a price. My words and motives were often misrepresented, and most of my friendships with colleagues were now cold and distant.

At this point our work had helped to make Toomey, Rubio, and Paul the Republican nominees for the Senate. This was a great improvement from Specter, Crist, and Grayson. Now we had to get busy to make sure our nominees had the resources to win the general election. The SCF also needed to raise a lot of money to help Lee win his primary in Utah. Senator Bennett endorsed his opponent Bridgewater, and most of the Washington establishment was supporting Bridgewater as well. Lee's opposition to earmarks attracted a large group of Washington earmark lobbyists to oppose him.

We still had a lot of work to do.

Chapter 10

Tea Parties Grow
as Democrats Destruct

May 21, 2010—August 8, 2010

n late May the Senate voted to pass its version of the financial regulation bill. It passed the Senate with four Republicans crossing party lines to vote for it: Chuck Grassley, Scott Brown, Olympia Snowe, and Susan Collins. The legislation represented a massive expansion of the federal government and gave regulators virtual control over most of the nation's credit and financial systems.

The list of misguided, budget-busting legislation produced by Obama and the Pelosi Congress was getting longer and longer. The so-called financial reform bill would prove to be another expensive boondoggle making it harder to run a business and create jobs in America. This bill, endorsed by President Barack Obama, was Sarbanes-Oxley on steroids. Like the costly and largely ineffective Sarbanes-Oxley financial regulation of 2002, this new bill was reactionary legislation. Regulation, not reform.

America's financial crisis had been caused primarily by too many home mortgages being given to people who were not capable of making their payments. These mistakes had then been magnified when the banks repackaged those mortgages and sold them to other banks, destabilizing the financial system.

Some banks, however, didn't engage in these poor lending practices. But the bill the Senate had just passed didn't distinguish between the good banks and bad banks. Instead, it would severely restrict banks' ability to lend and manage their balance sheets, further freezing credit markets.

It would also expand the Federal Reserve's reach by creating a consumer protection bureau inside it. This office would be given sweeping authority to regulate most anything considered to be financial activity including car dealerships offering financing, retailers like Old Navy and Sears offering credit cards, and software companies selling programs to help people manage money.

This was sure to limit the choices of credit and financial products available for consumers. And it meant people and businesses who had nothing to do with the crisis would face new federal laws on top of existing regulations. Unleashing a new army of federal regulators to further complicate the lives of small-business owners would only hurt consumers, kill jobs, and discourage investment. Most insulting of all, the Democrats were leaving many bad government actors untouched, like Freddie Mac and Fannie Mae.

Watching this happening right in front of me was maddening. Bewildering. Infuriating. All of it.

Monday, May 24, we were back in D.C. for afternoon votes. Afterward I joined a few colleagues to watch the series finale of 24. Several of us had been watching the adventures of Jack Bauer whenever we were in D.C. for Monday night votes. This final season of the hit television show was particularly interesting to us because it was set in Washington. The subplots of greed and corruption were uncomfortably real.

On Tuesday, I found myself in a showdown on the floor of the Senate with Democrat Senator Ron Wyden from Oregon. He introduced a bill to end "secret holds" on legislation, and he was upset I would not give unanimous consent for the bill to pass without going through the regular process of debate and a recorded vote. I argued the problem in the Senate was not members holding bills; the problem was 94 percent of measures approved by the Senate were passed without debate or a public, roll call vote.

Senators were sometimes accused of "holding" a bill if they merely asked for time to read it when another member wanted it passed immediately by unanimous consent. When I took over the Senate Steering Committee, one of the first things I learned was that whenever the Senate adjourned, I should expect a call from my staff while on my way to the airport, telling me dozens of requests had come through in that short period of time to pass bills by unanimous consent (UC). Some of them usually had pretty big price tags on them.

The problem wasn't secret holds; it was passing bills in secret by UC. Many times we don't even know who is requesting the bills. In order to find out what is being jammed through by unanimous consent, my staff must be available at night when the so-called "hotline" phone rings. When it rings, my staffer is asked if they will agree to let the bill pass, even though we haven't read it and don't know what's in it. And if we don't agree to pass it, we are suddenly "holding" the bill.

Nobody sent me up here just to waive through at passing legislation. Yes, I understand the time limitations. I understand the backlogs. And I understand the process. But for crying out loud, is this the way to run a responsible government? By saying yes to practically everything, sight unseen?

After my dustup with Senator Wyden, *The Washington Post* wrote three editorials blasting me with their predictable, convoluted logic; DeMint was insisting Senate business be done in secret, they said, which was the exact opposite of what I was doing. They ignored the fact that holds were rarely secret and over 90 percent of Senate bills passed in secret without even being read by members or the public. *The Post* was particularly agitated because after Wyden attached his bill as an amendment to the financial regulation bill hoping to circumvent regular procedure, I used a parliamentary procedure to attach my "Complete the Fence" amendment to his amendment (called a second-degree amendment).

My "Complete the Fence" bill ordered the administration to finish the seven hundred miles of double-layer fencing along our southern border, a law passed by Congress three years earlier to help stop illegal immigration and drug traffic. Only thirty miles of the required fencing had been completed over the last three years. The Democrats were so opposed to completing the fence, they forced Wyden to withdraw his amendment because a vote for his amendment would also be a vote to complete the fence.

Take that.

Within a few days more than seventeen thousand Americans viewed my floor debate with Senator Wyden about secret bills and secret holds on YouTube. Our office was flooded with e-mails and phone calls thanking me for exposing the fact that 94 percent of measures passed the Senate by unanimous consent without a debate or public vote. Not many people outside Washington knew that. And right-minded citizens shouldn't have to put up with it from their elected representatives. The incessant complaints of gridlock and lack of bipartisanship from the media were just plain false. America didn't get $13 trillion dollars in debt without a whole lot of cooperation and bipartisanship in Congress. And not enough "holds."

Alvin Greene and Other Primary Surprises

When I returned to Washington the next week, *The Hill's Congress Blog* posted a story June 2 by Jack Bass titled, "Sen. DeMint Less than a Shoo-in for Reelection." This story, like others back in South Carolina, was attempting to buoy the potential of Vic Rawls, the presumed winner of the South Carolina Democrat primary for Senate to be held the following week. Rawls had the backing of the state's Democrat establishment and had already raised a quarter of a million dollars. Some of his supporters and sympathetic media figures presented me as a vulnerable incumbent, saying I was more interested in building a national conservative movement than serving South Carolinians.

I also had a primary opponent, but she was a former Democrat who was only running to force me to spend my campaign resources before the general election. I decided to put my faith in the Republican voters and not spend any money on the primary.

Rawls did the same. He had an unknown Democrat opponent, Alvin Greene. And with the support of the entire Democrat Party hierarchy, Rawls put his trust in Democrat voters. He didn't spend any money to let voters know who he was or what he stood for. Everyone in the state assumed the U.S. Senate race would be between Vic Rawls and Jim DeMint.

As I kept an eye on my own reelection in South Carolina, the immigration debate was heating up again in Washington. Arizona Governor

Jan Brewer came to the White House on June 3 to meet with President Obama and discuss her state's new law that permitted officers to check the immigration status of people who were arrested for other crimes. When she emerged from her meeting at the White House, I was gratified to hear her tell the press she wanted the border fence completed to keep her state safe. President Obama responded by saying he wanted "comprehensive immigration reform," the Democrat code phrase meaning amnesty for more than ten million illegal aliens.

Later President Obama tried to change the subject back to the economy by claiming his stimulus bill created 431,000 jobs in May, but the Bureau of Labor statistics reported 411,000 of those jobs were temporary jobs for government census workers. And economist Larry Lindsey estimated as many as 20 percent of the small number of private-sector jobs created over the past two months were related to the clean-up of the BP oil spill. The president was trying to put a positive spin on a still stagnant economy.

Meanwhile, back on the primary front, news from Colorado suggested Ken Buck may actually have a long shot chance of winning the Republican nomination. An AP story by Kristen Wyatt posted on June 4 was titled, "GOP Noticing Ken Buck's Outsider Senate Bid." The story began to give Buck credibility and shake the Republican establishment:

> Buck, a Princeton-educated prosecutor from Greeley, has spent the last year campaigning almost nonstop. Buck works tea party gatherings and shows up at county Republican meetings to shake hands and promote himself as the most conservative in the race. He's selling ideological purity, not compromise, but he pairs his hard-right conservatism with an earnest smile and a folksiness that blunts the sharpness of his message. It's a pitch that has a growing number of Republicans thinking Buck can really win this thing.[16]

Tuesday, June 8, was primary day in South Carolina and in several other states. I voted in Greenville Tuesday morning and then flew to Washington. There was no suspense associated with the Senate primaries, but the Republican primary for governor drew national attention.

Four Republicans were competing for the nomination to replace Mark Sanford as governor. Sanford was term limited by law and could not run again. Early in the race, Attorney General Henry McMaster led the field with Congressman Gresham Barrett and Lieutenant Governor Andre Bauer competing for second place and the chance to be in a runoff with McMaster. In South Carolina, candidates have to receive more than 50 percent of the votes to win the nomination, and in a four-way race no one was expected to reach that threshold on the first ballot.

In fourth place in most polls was State Representative Nikki Haley. A few months before the primary, Haley didn't seem to have much of chance. I, too, assumed there would be a runoff between McMaster and Barrett. Initially I thought Barrett, who is a close friend and conservative member of the U.S. House, would have a great chance of winning the race. But there was one problem: Barrett had voted for the Wall Street bailout.

This put me in an awkward position because we had been close friends for years. I was traveling around the country with a clarion call for voters to "stop the bailouts." A number of conservatives in the House and Senate voted for the bailout, but the overwhelming majority of conservative and independent voters believed the bailouts were a mistake. Unfortunately, Barrett had said flat-out in a campaign video he voted for the bailout, and if he had it to do over, he would vote for it again.

A few weeks before the primary, Haley's conservative profile began to rise sharply. Sarah Palin came to South Carolina and created a media sensation by endorsing her. Tea party activists around the state rallied around her, and polls showed her jumping all the way from fourth to first in the primary.

Haley was also a good friend, and she espoused all the ideals of the candidates I was supporting through the SCF around the country. She was the daughter of Indian immigrants who built a thriving clothing company. Haley did bookkeeping for the family business as a teenager before going to Clemson to earn her accounting degree.

When the results of the primary came in late Tuesday night, Haley received 49.5 percent of the vote. She came within a fraction of a percent of winning the primary outright in a four-way race. Practially unheard of. Barrett was a distant second at 22 percent.

I called Barrett's campaign consultant to find out if he thought Barrett should concede to avoid a divisive runoff. He agreed there was nothing anyone could do to help Barrett overcome the overwhelming support for Haley.

That's when I had to make a difficult call to my good friend.

Barrett had endorsed me in my contentious primary for Senate six years earlier, and I always thought I would be able to help him when he ran for governor. However, the voters chose Haley. She was the epitome of a tea party candidate, and she deserved our support. Friendship aside, I knew I would be going counter to my pattern and principles by not supporting her.

When I connected with Barrett on the phone, he was obviously upset and disappointed by the outcome of the primary. He gave up his seat in the U.S. House to run for governor, and now it looked like all his work and sacrifice were in vain. Barrett is a fine man with a distinguished record of public and military service. I felt terrible when I mentioned the idea of conceding the race. He wanted to think and pray about it overnight. Couldn't argue with that. Barrett thought he should probably continue the race on behalf of his supporters. He was gracious, but I could tell he was disappointed.

There were also shake-ups in the South Carolina congressional primaries. Incumbent 4th Congressional District Representative Bob Inglis finished a distant second to Trey Gowdy. That race was headed for a runoff election in two weeks. Conservative, African-American businessman Tim Scott placed first in his 1st Congressional District race ahead of the sons of legendary politicians Strom Thurmond and Carroll Campbell.

Stunning.

Scott was an exciting candidate. He is a strong conservative with an inspiring story. Raised in a single-parent home, he struggled in school until the owner of a local Chick-fil-A took an interest in young Scott and began mentoring him. Together his mentor and his mother ingrained a deep sense of moral values that have guided his life. He ran for Congress in 2010 because, as he said, he wanted "to renew the American ideals of the free market, the entrepreneurial spirit and limited government." In addition to Scott's victory in the first congressional district, new Republicans prevailed in the second, third, and fifth districts—all with tea party support.

I won my primary easily as expected, but incredibly my presumed Democrat opponent, Rawls, lost his primary by twenty points to Greene. This caught everyone off-guard, including me. Reporters didn't know anything about Greene and scurried to find something to write. He had no Web site, no campaign signs, and did not file any campaign finance reports. Several blogs ran the headline "Who Is Alvin Greene?"

By the end of the night, media discovered Greene was an unemployed Army veteran living with his parents in Manning, South Carolina. No one could explain how he paid the $10,000 filing fee to get his name on the ballot. Liberal writers and commentators immediately began to suggest Greene might be a Republican plant. There was no truth to that, of course. Not at all. But one thing was dead sure: the summer and fall were going to be anything but dull.

The California primary was the same night, and the SCF candidate, Chuck DeVore, came in third behind Tom Campbell and Carly Fiorina. This was disappointing but expected. I really like Fiorina and was pleased she beat Campbell. She still had a long, uphill battle to defeat incumbent Democrat Senator Barbara Boxer, but it looked like she had a chance.

Sharron Angle surprised everyone in Nevada by beating two better-known Republicans in the Senate primary. Pundits immediately began blaming me and the tea party movement for giving Democrat Senate Majority Leader Harry Reid a candidate he could beat. I had not been involved in the Nevada primary, but my critics, including many of my Senate Republican colleagues, would label Angle as a "Palin-DeMint candidate" throughout the campaign. I was convinced Angle could be a good candidate if Republicans got behind her. SCF went to work immediately raising money for her campaign.

When I woke up Wednesday, June 9—the day after the primary—the media had discovered my new Democrat opponent Greene had a pending felony charge for "disseminating, procuring or promoting obscenity." He allegedly confronted a University of South Carolina coed with obscene material and attempted to follow her back to her room. The South Carolina Democrat Party was pleading with Greene to withdraw from the race, but he refused. It looked like my reelection might not be the long, hard, expensive, negative campaign I feared.

Tea Party Power Grows

My first appointment on Wednesday in Washington was a speech to the Young America's Foundation. This was the group that arranged my visit to the Reagan ranch. They were in Washington with twenty of the best and brightest rising young conservative stars in the nation. YAF organized three days of intensive training for these young college students to equip them for communicative combat against liberal ideas and policies. Their seminar was aptly named "Mastering Conservative Rhetoric in the Battle of Ideas."

YAF asked me to speak and share some of the thoughts from the speech I gave to students when I was in California. I reminded them ideas are the weapons conservatives must take into battle. Liberals use government benefits and dependence to entice and control voters. Conservatives must convince Americans the ideals of limited government and personal freedom should be the goals of citizens and elected officials. Despite the liberal promises of nanny state security, people are most secure when they are most free.

On Wednesday afternoon, I met with Elena Kagan, President Obama's second nominee to the Supreme Court. Since the greatest threat to America is the uncontrolled growth of government and debt, I asked Kagan if there were any limits on what the federal government could do. She mentioned an obscure court case but struggled to come up with any limits on federal action.

Well, if the Constitution doesn't limit what the federal government can do, then what was its purpose? Did the Constitution simply structure the three branches of government and tell Congress how to pass legislation? Kagan said she gave a lot of deference to the political process. She insisted most decisions about what the government should and should not do are "decisions for Congress, or states, or the people." Kagan did not seem to believe the Supreme Court had any role in enforcing the enumerated powers listed in the Constitution limiting what the federal government can do. Previous decisions by the High Court essentially removed all limits on the federal government's jurisdiction to intervene in any area of American life. Kagan apparently had no interest in changing existing precedent by reining in the power of the federal government.

She wasn't looking good in my book.

That's because there's just no getting around this fact: it will never be possible to reduce spending, borrowing, debt, or to stop the eventual financial collapse of America if politicians and judges believe the federal government should run our schools, our health-care system, our energy sector, our transportation system, our financial system, our largest auto companies, mortgage companies, and insurance companies. If it is all up to the politicians to decide, Congress will continue to try to solve every problem in America from Washington. We simply must return to a constitutionally limited government, and the high court must play a role in reversing past decisions that have unleashed uncontrolled congressional actions.

I also asked Kagan if she believed unborn children had any rights. CBS News had earlier revealed memos Kagan wrote demonstrating her commitment to abortion. She responded to me, "The courts have never grappled with that issue, and I wouldn't want to grapple with that now." It was clear she was going to dodge any specific questions and was not going to reveal any of her positions on important issues like abortion. I could not support her nomination.

Unfortunately, the majority of senators did not share my concerns.

On the way to the airport that evening, I began getting e-mails about the Utah primary race. Lee's opponent, Bridgewater, had sent out a mailer accusing me of supporting Lee because Lee would help me send nuclear waste from South Carolina to Utah. *Huh?* It reminded me of the old axiom, "If you can't convince them, confuse them." Utah voters were too smart for that kind of nonsense. I was confident the strategy would backfire.

On Friday my staff forwarded me news reports of a Seattle man who was charged with sending suspicious mail to me. He had mailed me an envelope full of white powder, staples, and paper clips. He'd also included a handwritten message: "I hope you choke on your own excrement such as this."

The post office intercepted the envelope before it got to my office. It turned out the powder was harmless, but the episode reminded everyone in my office that many people didn't agree with our limited government agenda.

Meanwhile, the media continued to focus on my Senate race. A front-page story in *The Washington Post* by Manuel Roig-Franzia titled "In

South Carolina, Greene Is Mystery Man Despite Winning Democratic Senate Nod." One paragraph summed up a candidate who already had more national notoriety than I did:

> Things have gotten even stranger since Greene's win. First, the Associated Press reported that he faces felony obscenity charges for allegedly showing pornography to a University of South Carolina student last November. Greene says he's not guilty. Then the state's Democratic Party chairman called on him to withdraw from the general election. House Majority Whip James E. Clyburn (D-S.C.)—who has questioned whether Republicans may have planted Greene in the race—is calling for federal and state investigations. A spokesman for Republican Sen. Jim DeMint (S.C.) called that notion "ridiculous," and Greene dismisses suggestions that he is anyone's pawn.[17]

The liberal media was just not giving up on replacing me. On June 18, Lawrence O'Donnell on MSNBC, after a long interview with the stumbling Greene, still concluded Greene would be the better senator. O'Donnell said, "Jim DeMint's record is so bad, maybe we'd be better off with Alvin Greene in the Senate."

Tuesday, June 22, was another primary day in some states, producing even more surprises and victories for tea party candidates. In Utah, Lee edged out Bridgewater to win the Republican nomination for the Senate. This was a huge victory for SCF. With Utah being one of the most Republican states in the nation, this effectively guaranteed Lee would be elected to the U.S. Senate in November.

The Washington Times ran a front-page article announcing how my influence now extended all the way to Utah. This appeared the same day as a big profile piece on me in the *National Journal*. This only added fuel to the criticism that my efforts were all about self-promotion. The media would not even consider the possibility that a politician might do something because it was the right thing to do.

The same day in South Carolina, tea party activists pushed Nikki Haley to a landslide win in her primary runoff to become governor. Trey Gowdy trounced incumbent Republican Congressman Bob Inglis 71 percent to

29 percent—one of the most lopsided losses ever by an incumbent in a primary. And Tim Scott bested Paul Thurmond.

The next day at the Republican Policy Lunch, NRSC Chairman Cornyn introduced businessman Ron Johnson who had just announced he was going to run for the Senate against incumbent Democrat Russ Feingold in Wisconsin. Johnson was a successful businessman who had decided to use his own money to finance his campaign. No one gave him much of a chance, but everyone appreciated his willingness to take on a popular Democrat incumbent.

I had yet to meet Johnson, but after Cornyn introduced him, Johnson stood up and pointed to me. "I'm going to quote Jim DeMint," he said, "I'm coming here to join the fight not the club." I smiled and wondered if he knew he was speaking to the club. He later told me he was putting the club on notice.

Johnson was relatively new to politics and only became a candidate after gaining an impressive following from the tea party. Regional talk radio hosts replayed his speeches, and others encouraged him to run. As a businessman Johnson owned a plastics manufacturing company; he could attest to the damage being done by the Democrats in Washington. He made the decision to run for the Senate after watching the Democrats pass the health-care takeover in March 2010. "I spent thirty-one years building a business, and now we see politicians spending without constraint, really pushing the United States of America to the brink of bankruptcy. We in the private sector, with some business experience, have a responsibility to step up to the plate and offer some alternatives," Johnson told *National Review*.

Good for him.

The SCF immediately endorsed Johnson and began raising money for his campaign. He intended to use his own money, as I said, but it is always good to have thousands of supporters with their hearts and minds tied to your campaign. This allows people from all over the country to be a part of what seems like an impossible dream.

But increasingly for many conservative candidates across America, the dream was looking more and more like reality. I couldn't have been more thrilled by what I was witnessing, even if many others—even if some of my own friends—didn't see it that way.

On Sunday, July 4, I was on *Fox News Sunday* defending the tea party movement. My fellow senator from South Carolina, Lindsey Graham, said the tea parties would die out. The host of the show, Chris Wallace, wanted to know if I disagreed. In my opinion the energy and influence of the tea parties were just the beginning of a real and lasting American awakening. Tea party activism would not only make historic changes in the 2010 elections; they would also be a powerful force in the 2012 presidential elections.

I really believed that. I *still* believe that.

Hitting the Road for the Cause

After being home several days for an Independence Day break, I took a flight to Denver on Thursday afternoon, July 8, to campaign for Ken Buck. Buck had become one of my favorite candidates because he was so passionate about saving freedom in America. At one point during an event, a large group of his supporters surrounded me to tell me they were praying SCF would get behind Buck. It was truly amazing how many Americans believed they were involved in a spiritual battle to save our country.

The only bad part of the trip was I missed the last connecting flight home in Charlotte. But rather than stay in a hotel another night, I managed to find a rental car company still open with an available car. The drive home took about two hours. With a large cup of coffee and an oldies radio station, I kept myself awake singing along with some of the old songs I used to play in my high school rock-and-roll band. Not one political thought even crossed my mind until I turned into my driveway at 1:30 a.m.

The next week the final House/Senate Dodd-Frank financial regulation bill passed the Senate by only one vote. This bill was written by the two Democrats most responsible for causing the financial crisis, Chris Dodd and Barney Frank. Their liberal housing goals, close ties to the financial industry, and unwillingness to hold Freddie Mac and Fannie Mae accountable had resulted in a catastrophic meltdown of America's financial system. Yet somehow they had deemed themselves experts on how to fix it.

The financial regulation bill created a huge new consumer protection agency as part of an already unaccountable Federal Reserve. It perpetuated the "too big to fail" category of banks while claiming to eliminate them. And it didn't even address Freddie Mac and Fannie Mae.

The bill gave the federal government virtual control over America's financial system. Completely. Scary.

Democrats needed only three Republicans to pass their financial takeover. We knew we would lose Maine Republican Senators Olympia Snowe and Susan Collins. The only other Republican vote in play was Massachusetts Senator Scott Brown who initially indicated he would oppose the bill. But he changed his mind at the last minute and gave Democrats their sixtieth vote to pass the bill.

That surprised me.

But as *The Washington Post* reported on June 29, "Democratic leaders altered the legislation in recent weeks in an effort to secure Brown's support. They included an exemption to allow insurance and mutual fund companies, which are major employers in Massachusetts, to continue trading on their own accounts. Brown also won a concession to allow banks to invest up to 3 percent of their capital in hedge funds and private equity funds."

We needed to make it a lot harder than this for Republicans to pass Democrat legislation. I prayed again that November would give us the opportunity to do that.

The last order of business for the Senate before the August break was the confirmation of Solicitor General Elena Kagan to be the next Supreme Court Justice. The vote was 63–37 with only a few Republicans supporting her confirmation. This was a positive sign Republicans were becoming more united against Obama's progressive "yes we can" judicial philosophy. Her confirmation was also a reminder elections have consequences. Obama and the Democrats now had the votes to stack the courts with liberal progressives for years to come.

As we finished up in Washington and prepared for a month of work in our states and travel around the country during August, John McCain headed for Colorado to raise money for Jane Norton, Arizona Republican Senator Ken Buck's primary opponent. SCF sent an e-mail to our supporters asking them to help balance the scales for Buck with an online fund-raiser. Within two days, we raised an additional $25,000 for Buck. The SCF was working. Like gangbusters.

Before we left D.C., Democratic senators voted against several amendments I offered that would have stopped the large increases in federal taxes scheduled for January 1, 2011. Every member of Congress knew taxes were going up for everyone if Congress didn't take action to extend the current tax rates. So I forced separate votes to prevent all the coming tax increases.

The Democrats voted each of them down. On June 23, I forced a vote to stop hikes on capital gains and dividends paid by seniors and investors. It failed to get the sixty votes needed and was defeated 57–40. On July 21, I forced a vote to stop the government from increasing the death tax to 55 percent. It was defeated 59–39. On August 5, before leaving for recess, I tried again. I forced a vote to stop the increases on all marginal tax rates. It lost 58–42. I tried one more time that day by forcing another vote to stop tax increases on small businesses. That vote failed 58–42.

Anybody spot a trend? Democrats voted four times to approve Obama's massive tax increases and then left town. The Democrat-led Congress would not again take any action to stop the tax increases until the last minute in a lame-duck session that December.

Meanwhile I kept trying to bring attention back to the broken appropriations system. I wrote a piece for the July-August edition of *The American Spectator* magazine taking aim at the self-serving system bankrupting the country.

> Senior appropriators, Republicans and Democrats, effectively control the House and the Senate using the power of the purse. They buy other members of Congress off with earmarks, which makes it difficult for anyone who accepts earmarks to cut overall spending. It would amount to biting the hand that feeds. Appropriators dominate leadership positions in both parties and are chairmen and ranking members of major policy-making committees. They decide how money gets spent, who gets earmarks, how bills get written and who gets shut out of the closed-door negotiations.
>
> Most importantly, they work in harmony to drive up spending, borrowing and debt, with no regard to their party label. Shrinking the federal largesse would diminish their power, so they have a built-in incentive to grow government.[18]

I knew the article would make many of my colleagues angry, but instigating a voter backlash against the status quo was the only way to change the Senate.

Conservatives were fighting two battles. One was to restore the Republican Party to its core principles. This required breaking the stranglehold appropriators had on our party. The second battle for Republicans was to re-earn the trust of the American people. This required us to prove we would fight to restore fiscal sanity in Washington.

Three months before the midterm elections—thanks to the Democrats and the tea parties—we were now making progress on both fronts.

Chapter 11

Countdown to Election 2010

August 9, 2010—September 25, 2010

The congressional August recess marks the official countdown to Election Day. Everything shifts into high gear. The Senate stayed in session through the first week of August so our break didn't actually begin until August 9. But August is no break from work for members of Congress in election years. This is when the work really begins.

And when the media tries to shape the election.

On Monday, August 9, *GQ* published an article titled "GQ Exclusive: Rand Paul's Kooky College Days (Hint: There's a Secret Society Involved)." Cable news picked up the story, and Paul was once again on the defensive. The liberal press was doing everything it could to radicalize conservative candidates in a year the voters were demanding a return to conservative principles. The attacks were painful, but the backlash against these attacks likely helped Paul and other conservatives in the election.

On Tuesday, August 10, I flew to Chicago to speak at an event for Family PAC, a pro-family, antitax political group based in Illinois. A surprising number of former Obama supporters joined our meeting. They were disillusioned by Obama's antibusiness policies, the massive increases in spending, and his continuing efforts to expand the federal government. Even in Obama's hometown, the enthusiasm for his version of change had turned into concern and alarm.

Tuesday evening I joined them for a cruise on Lake Michigan. We cruised about a half mile offshore, cut off the engines, and watched the sunset over the tall buildings of downtown Chicago.

It was a challenging setting for a speech. There was too much wind even to attempt to use notes so I just spoke from my heart. This group understood the connection between faith and freedom, which made it easier to speak without mincing words. They knew the values and principles derived from biblical faith create the foundation for freedom. Without this foundation our culture would continue to decline, and our government would grow to fill the void.

I talked about the connection between social and economic issues. Cultural decline in America has created a huge burden to taxpayers and a drag on our economy. The decline of two-parent families, incentivized by perverse government policies, has contributed to increases in school dropout, crime, drug use, and incarceration. Over 40 percent of American children are now born out of wedlock. A free society and a vibrant, free-market economy will only flourish if millions of people have the character and skills to make constructive decisions about the things they value. As our culture declines, government grows and people become more dependent on government services. The more dependent citizens become, the more they need government. It's a vicious cycle that grows government and destroys freedom.

This group certainly got that. They were *with* us.

After the dinner cruise I returned to my hotel room and turned on the news. Buck had narrowly won the Republican primary for Senate in Colorado—another huge victory for SCF. I knew some of my colleagues who were supporting Norton would be disappointed, and I don't like to offend my friends, but electing more senators who would fight the out-of-control spending in Washington was a goal I wasn't going to compromise.

Another interesting news item caught my attention before I turned off the television—a classic comment from Majority Leader Harry Reid. He said he didn't know "how anyone of Hispanic heritage could be a Republican."

The Democrats, who seemed to believe voters were stupid, were trying to create class, race, and ethnic divides between Republicans and the voters. I was betting the voters were too smart to fall for that junk.

My flight from Chicago on Wednesday left early, and I was home in Greenville by noon. After unloading my bags, I headed to the gym to begin reversing the damage from several months of too much sitting, stress, and food. Running on the treadmill is also a good way to catch up on the news. Marco Rubio was on FOX News blasting Reid for his condemnation of Hispanic Republicans. Rubio said the most important issue for Hispanics was economic empowerment and upward mobility. He reminded Reid that America's free enterprise system was the only economic system in the world where that was possible. Rubio added, "And the reason why Americans of Hispanic descent should be Republicans is because the Democratic leadership is trying to dismantle the American free enterprise system."

Rubio made me proud to be an American . . . and even prouder to be a supporter of his campaign.

On Friday, President Obama hosted a dinner at the White House to celebrate Ramadan, the holiest time of the year for Muslims. In his speech Obama defended the plans to build a mosque at Ground Zero in New York. His defense of the proposed mosque included the following statement: "Ground Zero is, indeed, hallowed ground. But let me be clear: as a citizen and as president, I believe that Muslims have the same right to practice their religion as anyone else in this country. That includes the right to build a place of worship and a community center on private property in lower Manhattan, in accordance with local laws and ordinances."

Republicans like Newt Gingrich and Sarah Palin, along with most conservative groups and media, were adamantly opposed to the mosque, which would be built only two blocks from Ground Zero. Public opinion was strongly against it. A CNN poll found 68 percent of those surveyed did not approve. The president's refusal even to suggest it was unwise to build the mosque further diminished his credibility with many Americans who value our Judeo-Christian heritage.

For the life of me, I just couldn't understand what he couldn't understand.

Traveling South Carolina with an Eye on the Nation

On Tuesday, August 17, Steve Moore of *The Wall Street Journal* flew into Greenville to interview me for a feature story about the SCF and the tea party movement. SCF's success had caught the attention of many reporters.

Part of me was afraid the publicity would distract from the greater cause. This election was about the people, not politicians. But the media coverage was encouraging grassroots activists around the country and helping to convince them their voices were being heard in Washington. So I considered anything I could do to sustain the momentum a good use of my time.

Still, the media coverage of me was a double-edged sword, personally. It offended some of my Senate colleagues because it perpetuated the perception I was on an ego trip. But it also served to empower the movement and to encourage grassroots activists by publicizing the successes of tea party candidates and the growing power of the tea party across the country. Media coverage of my work also gave me a layer of protection against reprisals by Washington power brokers. Any public attack on me was answered aggressively by the conservative media and by millions of Americans who were more than ready to throw the bums out.

The American awakening was not about me. I was totally clear on that. In fact, I was a bit player compared to Sarah Palin and a large group of tea party leaders, radio talk-show hosts, bloggers, and other conservative media. But I became a movement ally inside the U.S. Senate and one of the few elected officials willing to break ranks to support tea party candidates. That was my role, and I wanted to be a faithful steward of this position and platform God had given me. Working the media was the best way for me to communicate with Americans who were fighting to restore a government of, for, and by the people.

Other tea party favorites were also making news on that Tuesday. *The Washington Post* was slamming radio and TV host Glenn Beck for planning a rally on August 28 at the Lincoln Memorial, the same date and location as Martin Luther King's "I have a Dream" speech. Beck said he didn't plan it that way, explaining the one-year anniversary of his September 12 rally was on a Sunday that year, and he wasn't going to ask people to attend an event on Sunday. The article quoted many black leaders who were upset with Beck.

The same day, August 17, Dick Armey and Matt Kibbe, the leaders of FreedomWorks and organizers of many tea party rallies, published a joint op-ed in *The Wall Street Journal*. They wrote, "The movement is not seeking a junior partnership with the Republican Party. It is aiming for a hostile takeover." I shared their sentiment; the tea parties needed to force the principles of limited government back into the DNA of the Republican Party.

That was the drumbeat waking me up on Wednesday, August 18, the morning that marked the beginning of my annual tour of South Carolina. This year I planned to mix official activities with campaign work for other Republican candidates in the state. I spent Wednesday in Columbia holding an education roundtable, meeting with CPAs about the onerous new federal regulations on their industry, and talking with businesspeople about the state's economy. We ended the day at a small hotel in Sumter, a short distance from an early morning tea party rally where I would appear with Mick Mulvaney, a Republican candidate for Congress.

Thursday I spent the day with Mulvaney, who was challenging Democrat Congressman John Spratt, chairman of the House Budget Committee. Tea party activists organized rallies in Sumter, Camden, Elgin, Rock Hill, and Lancaster. This was a great opportunity for me to talk with my constituents in rural South Carolina and encourage them to help us take back our country by supporting Mulvaney and other Republicans.

But these Americans didn't need a lot of encouragement. They were fired up. We were swarmed at every event.

While in Clemson a few days later, I received a call from Sharron Angle in Nevada. She called to thank me for my support for her campaign. She also thanked me for $156,000 I sent from my campaign to the Nevada Republican Party for their "get out the vote" efforts. Angle was taking a beating by the media and from millions of dollars of negative campaign ads. Harry Reid and the liberal press were trying to make her look like a kook. I really like Angle and wanted to do everything I could to help her win. She was doing a good job raising money, but I was concerned that the Nevada Republican Party was not organized and equipped well enough to compete on the ground against the well-financed, union-backed Democrat machine.

As I continued my tour of South Carolina, the Democrat National Committee released a three-minute video claiming the Republican tea party candidates were too radical to be elected. The video said: "They are flawed and as far out of the mainstream as you can imagine. And the Republican Party knows it. They didn't want Sharron Angle or Rand Paul or Ken Buck or Rick Scott or Linda McMahon to be their candidates, because they know what will soon be obvious to voters; they are flawed and out of the mainstream."

That's exactly what I expected from the DNC. You just deal with that. But what hurt was the undercurrent of negative comments from some of the Republican elites who were hurting our candidates. A few Republican leaders were even quoted saying some of our nominees were not electable. But I was committed to supporting all Republican nominees, especially those SCF helped win primaries.

Honestly, we didn't need any help badgering our own candidates. Case in point: As part of their attempts to radicalize Republican candidates, the Democrats resorted to playing the race card, accusing tea party activists and candidates of being bigots. Charles Krauthammer fired back in *The Washington Post* on August 27: "What's a liberal to do? Pull out the bigotry charge, the trump that preempts debate and gives no credit to the seriousness and substance of the contrary argument. . . . The Democrats are going to get beaten badly in November. Not just because the economy is ailing. And not just because Obama over-read his mandate in governing too far left. But because a comeuppance is due the arrogant elites whose undisguised contempt for the great unwashed prevents them from conceding a modicum of serious thought to those who dare oppose them."

How thankful I was for such good, smart, cogent responses to these kinds of ridiculous accusations. While the Democrats flailed at Republicans, the nation heard continuing reminders that the Democrat agenda of spending and debt was not only bad policy—it was dangerous. CNN reported on August 27 the Joint Chiefs of Staff Chairman Admiral Michael Mullen said America's debt was the nation's top security threat. Mullen was on a three-day tour across the Midwest encouraging businesses to hire veterans but also reminding all Americans that debt hurts our economy and a bad economy reduces our ability to defend ourselves.

Mullen said, "The most significant threat to our national security is our debt. . . . That's why it's so important that the economy move in the right direction, because the strength and the support and the resources that our military uses are directly related to the health of our economy over time."

Excellent analysis. Such statements proved the point that the protests of tea party activists against spending, borrowing, and debt were not motivated by partisan politics. They knew what Admiral Mullen and most thinking Americans knew: America would not remain a great economic or military power if we didn't change course soon. This fact, more than any other, created the sense of urgency in the hearts of tea party members and all grassroots activists.

Friday, August 27, was another big news day, and I was back at the gym late in the afternoon on the treadmill watching the news. Glenn Beck held an event at the Kennedy Center in Washington as a preview of his Restoring Honor rally, which he said would draw at least 100,000 to the Lincoln Memorial the following day. Beck promised a "great awakening," a phrase I had been using in my speeches and articles for months. He wasn't copying me; he saw the awakening for himself.

FreedomWorks held a Take America Back convention the same day at the Daughters of the American Revolution Constitution Hall in Washington. Speakers included Dick Armey and Senator-to-be Mike Lee from Utah. It was rewarding for me to see Lee, who had never held public office, take the national stage with his "Back to the Constitution" message. I had to smile when I thought about Lee soon making speeches about constitutionally limited government from the floor of the U.S. Senate.

Perhaps the biggest news of the day was from Alaska. Unknown tea party candidate, Joe Miller, had beaten incumbent Senator Lisa Murkowski in the Republican primary. All the polls predicted Murkowski would win by more than twenty points. I was not involved in the Alaska primary, but I knew Miller would be a staunch ally in our fight against spending and debt. Murkowski is a friend, but she was an appropriator who fought every effort to limit earmarks and spending.

Things were shaping up very nicely—not just for conservative Republicans but for America.

Divided Loyalties

SCF immediately endorsed Joe Miller in Alaska and went to work raising money for his campaign. His campaign coffers were empty after spending all his resources on the primary. We had only two months to make sure he had the money and staff to compete in the general election. But Alaska is a Republican state so with a little money and organization Miller would be the next senator from Alaska. Or so I thought.

Murkowski soon reentered the race. Running as a write-in candidate, Murkowski, a moderate, pro-choice Republican, would attract votes from both parties and Independents. But winning a write-in campaign was difficult because voters would not be prompted by a name on the ballot.

That obstacle assumed Alaska would follow its own laws. But a judge ruled write-in ballots could be printed and handed out at all polling places, essentially creating a second ballot that was arguably more visible and intrusive than the official ballot. This changed everything. Miller now had opponents on ballots from both the Democrat *and* Republican side, and he was concerned the National Republican Senatorial Committee would not totally support his campaign, even though he was the Republican nominee.

Murkowski's action represented a worrisome pattern among Republican moderates. Primaries are held to allow voters in both parties to select candidates who best represent their views. Those who win Republican primaries should expect the full support of the party organization. Those who lose should be expected to support the nominee. But this had not been the case in this election year for Republican moderates.

When senior Republican appropriator Arlen Specter fell behind his primary opponent, Pat Toomey, he left the party and attempted to run against Toomey as a Democrat. When moderate Republican Charlie Crist fell behind Marco Rubio in the Senate primary in Florida, Crist left the party and opposed Rubio as an Independent. After her primary victory in Nevada, Sharron Angle only received a tepid endorsement from her Republican opponent, who was heavily supported by the Republican establishment. Ken Buck's primary opponent in Colorado did not support him at all after he won the primary.

The Republican establishment was clearly biased against conservative candidates, and it was undermining the party's ability to win elections. Murkowski's direct attack on Republican nominee Miller took the problem to a new level. It was not a question of Miller's electability; with Republican support he would easily win the election. But Murkowski divided Republican support for our nominee and undermined the primary system established to give Republican voters the right to choose their candidates.

Murkowski held an elected leadership position for Republicans in the Senate; she was the ranking Republican on the Energy Committee on Energy and Natural Resources, and she was an appropriator. If Republicans could not count on our leaders to support our nominees, conservative candidates would be encouraged to run as Independents or third-party candidates instead of attempting to win a competitive Republican primary. Moderate and unprincipled Republicans in Congress were foolishly encouraging conservatives to create a third party.

Later in September, Republican senators made the situation in Alaska much worse. After considerable pressure from conservative groups and media, Republican leaders in the Senate called for a members' conference to strip Murkowski of her ranking position on the energy committee. (I had not asked for Murkowski's removal because it appeared our leadership was serious about doing it themselves.) She was using her position on the energy committee to raise money from energy lobbyists and to convince voters in Alaska she was supported by the Republican Party. Alaska's economy is heavily dependent on the production of oil and natural gas. Allowing Murkowski to keep her leadership position on the energy committee was a huge boost for her write-in campaign against Miller.

But when the member conference convened, it was obviously an orchestrated meeting controlled by Murkowski's fellow appropriators. After five appropriators spoke in favor of Murkowski, appealing to loyalty and friendship, no one was willing to ask for her removal. Not one member of leadership even spoke.

I understand the importance of friendships and the need to support our colleagues, but there was too much at stake for Republicans to provide assistance to someone running against our own nominee. Miller presented his vision and ideas to Republican voters in Alaska, fought against impossible odds, and won the primary. It was inconceivable to me Republicans would now implicitly endorse Murkowski by allowing her to keep her leadership position on the energy committee.

I was incredulous. All the public statements from Republican senators expressed support for Miller. Our leadership called for Murkowski's removal from her leadership positions. But now, behind closed doors, it was business as usual. I knew it was useless to speak, but someone needed to challenge this deliberate attempt to undermine not only Miller but also the future of the Republican Party.

So here I went.

"I hate to be the skunk at the party again," I said, "but . . ." and then proceeded to give all of the arguments for setting aside friendships and doing what was best for our party and our country. No one wanted to hear what I had to say. We moved quickly to a secret ballot vote. Murkowski won, but we were not allowed to know the vote count. We were also admonished not to speak to the press about the meeting.

Fat chance. Reporters surrounded me on my walk back to my office, and I dutifully made no comment about the meeting. But within ten minutes after arriving at my office, reporters were calling my Communications Director with every detail from the meeting and asking for my reaction. They had been told the vote was unanimous in favor of Murkowski and that I was the only one to speak against her. It was like they had been sitting in the room.

By this point I was seriously angry and immediately composed an e-mail to SCF supporters condemning Republican actions and asking for more support for Miller. I said:

> Rather than taking away Murkowski's leadership position on the committee, Senate Republicans decided to let her keep it. One senator after another stood up to argue in favor of protecting her place on the committee—a position she will no doubt use in her campaign against Joe Miller, the conservative Republican nominee.
>
> It was bad enough to watch my colleagues work to support her in the primary after she had built a record of betraying conservatives' principles. But watching them back her after she left the party and

launched a campaign against the Republican nominee was more than I could bear. I spoke out against the motion and I voted against it. But the good ol' boys Senate club, which always protects its own, prevailed. The motion was adopted by secret ballot and the final tally was not disclosed.

As had been the case throughout the election cycle, taking on the establishment inside Congress fired up grassroots activists around the country. The phones in my office lit up with people asking for the names of senators who voted against Miller. Americans wanted someone to fight the clubby system in the Congress, and they were quick to thank anyone willing to take a stand.

I talked with Miller later that day by phone. He was devastated. He had been working hard for months with little sleep to win the primary, and now the media in Alaska was reporting the Republican Party was still supporting Lisa Murkowski. *National Review* was one of the few publications that recognized the potential negative implications of Republicans going against the results of their own primaries. A few paragraphs in the story "Help Joe Miller" captured the growing concern I had for my party:

> This is perverse on several levels. As we noted before, it leaves intact part of Murkowski's campaign message. It sends the message that Senate Republicans expect her to win and are therefore hedging their bets. But, more important, it serves to create conditions over the long term for the potential fracturing of the Republican Party.
>
> It doesn't take a long memory to recall the days when it was considered a possibility that the tea party would run third-party candidates against Republicans and Democrats. Instead, they have invested their energy in a good-faith attempt to win Republican primaries and influence the course of the country through the GOP. They have played by the rules, and often, they have won. That has prompted moderates to go rogue and switch parties, run as Independents, and wage sour-grapes write-in campaigns.
>
> Unless Republicans crack down on this behavior in the toughest manner possible, what incentive do tea-partiers have to play nice when a primary outcome goes against them? Why would they feel

loyalty to a Republican Party that doesn't take its own rules seriously? Jim DeMint is urging people to donate to Joe Miller to boost him against Murkowski, and we urge our readers to contribute to that effort. Not only is Miller a better conservative, his race is an important test for tea partiers around the country. It's too bad more Senate Republicans don't realize that some things are more important than their colleague Lisa Murkowski's feelings.[19]

The Republican Conference vote to support Murkowski started another civil war between party leaders and me. This time it was me going after them. The titles from several articles told the story: from *Hot Air*, "DeMint Rips Senate GOP"; from *Politico*, "DeMint Chides GOP Leadership for Protecting Lisa"; and from AP, "DeMint Scolds Republican Colleagues on Murkowski."

Some of my colleagues were anxious to do whatever they could do to shut me up. An organized effort began to spread rumors I was working against Republican incumbents in the upcoming election and planning an all-out assault on my colleagues in 2012. My good friend and fellow conservative, Oklahoma Senator Tom Coburn, told me a senior Republican asked him to replace me as chairman of the Steering Committee. Fortunately, Coburn was on my side.

The Last Straw: Christine O'Donnell

The war between the Senate Republican Conference and me reached its lowest point in September during the Murkowski fight and after two other endorsements by SCF. I was on my way back to Colorado on Friday, September 10, to speak at a meeting organized by Freedom Congress. While sitting in the Atlanta airport waiting for my connection to Denver, I was reviewing updated reports from the Republican Senate primaries in New Hampshire and Delaware. In New Hampshire, Ovide Lamontagne appeared to be closing a double-digit lead by Kelly Ayotte. In Delaware, Christine O'Donnell also seemed to be gaining traction on Congressman Mike Castle, though still at least ten points behind.

I had stayed out of the New Hampshire primary because conservative grassroots activists were divided. Sarah Palin endorsed Kelly Ayotte, and after meeting Ayotte myself, I believed she was a real conservative. My primary reservation about Ayotte was that she was supported by many incumbent senators and the lobby establishment in Washington. I wasn't sure she would be willing to take a stand against the people who supported her once she became a senator.

Lamontagne is a passionate, articulate conservative. He attracted the attention of tea party activists and conservative talk show hosts in New Hampshire and across America. But because tea party activists were divided between several candidates, Lamontagne was polling about ten points behind Ayotte with only a few days until the primary. Ayotte was one of the most impressive candidates I met in 2010, but it pained me to watch Lamontagne fight against the Washington establishment alone.

In Delaware, Castle appeared to be cruising to an easy victory over political novice Christine O'Donnell. Castle was a friend from my time in the House, but he was one of the most liberal Republican congressmen. As a senator he would likely vote like Arlen Specter, which I believed would further diminish the credibility of the Republican Party.

I had stayed out of the Delaware primary to that point because it didn't appear O'Donnell had a chance. Her platform was consistent with mine and the tea party movement, yet she had been vilified so harshly by a one-two-three combination of the media, Castle, and the Republican establishment that her candidacy seemed hopeless. But after Palin endorsed her and several national radio talk show hosts began to reveal Castle's liberal voting record, O'Donnell actually began to close in the polls.

Although my late endorsement would make little impact, I couldn't stand to see these two underdog candidates fighting against the liberal media and the Washington establishment without one Republican senator on their side. I felt like a coward standing on the sidelines. Sitting in an airplane at the gate, I wrote an e-mail to my SCF director asking him to tweet my endorsement of both O'Donnell and Lamontagne, but I hadn't yet sent it.

The criticism of me would be loud and unrelenting. I knew that. And did I really want to invite more criticism on myself? Didn't I have enough of that already without asking for more? I had to make a decision now, or it would be too late to be credible. My BlackBerry was still on and hidden from the flight attendant under some papers as we pulled away from the gate. The plane turned and accelerated down the runway toward Denver.

As the wheels lifted off the ground, I closed my eyes and pushed "send." Call it the "tweet heard round the world."

As I was in the air, my Twitter account exploded with reactions to the endorsements. SCF followed with an e-mail to our supporters Friday night announcing the Delaware and New Hampshire endorsements. The closing lines of the e-mail warned that these were long odds. "Make no mistake: these two candidates are underdogs. The odds are against them. But we're not going to save freedom in America if we're not willing to take a risk. You've taken many risks with me this year, and I'm so proud to say that many of them have paid off. Let's fight for two more."

The most stinging and painful criticism came the next day from one of my favorite conservative commentators, Charles Krauthammer. He ripped Palin and me for endorsing O'Donnell on FOX News *Special Report w/ Bret Baier* on Saturday, September 13. *Politico* published Krauthammer's remarks:

> Leading conservative commentator Charles Krauthammer has rebuked former Alaska Gov. Sarah Palin and Sen. Jim DeMint (R-S.C.) for making the "irresponsible" choice of endorsing Christine O'Donnell over Rep. Mike Castle in the Delaware GOP Senate primary. "The Palin endorsement, I think, is disruptive and capricious," Krauthammer said Monday night on Fox News' Special Report. "Bill Buckley had a rule that he always supported the most conservative candidate who was electable, otherwise the vote is simply self-indulgence."
>
> Palin has weighed in heavily in the race, cutting robocalls for O'Donnell that have been bombarding the state's GOP voters, who head to the polls Tuesday. "Delaware is not Alaska," Krauthammer said of the state's former Republican governor. "In Alaska you can endorse a Joe Miller, who's going to win anyway though he's more conservative. In Delaware, O'Donnell is going to lose and that could be the difference between Republican and Democratic control of the Senate.

When Fox anchor Bret Baier pointed out that DeMint has also endorsed O'Donnell, Krauthammer branded the senator's move "equally capricious and irresponsible. I'm not sexist on this," the conservative columnist said. "It's a big mistake. Mike Castle is a shoo-in. He wins. O'Donnell is very problematic. She probably will lose."[20]

Dozens of additional news stories savaged me for my stupidity. One anonymous GOP aide told *Politico*: "DeMint may be patting himself on the back tonight. But many Republicans look forward to post-November 2nd, when he has to explain why he helped the Democrats retain the majority for yet another two years."

Another unnamed senior leadership aide told *Hotline On Call* that I had really done it this time: "DeMint took it a step too far here, and I think he has lost the remaining credibility he had, even within the caucus," the aide said. "DeMint is not interested in a majority; he'd rather establish himself as the leader on the fringe."

Few in the media allowed me to give my point of view, but Jon Karl of ABC News wrote an online article in September that at least let me answer the question most pundits were asking: "Your critics say you could have cost Republicans the majority. Do you have any regrets?" My response: "No. I've been in the majority with Republicans who didn't have principles and we embarrassed ourselves and lost credibility in front of the country. Frankly, I'm at a point where I'd rather lose fighting for the right cause than win fighting for the wrong cause."

The following Tuesday, Lamontagne lost a close primary by only a few hundred votes to Ayotte, so close he had the legal right to ask for a recount. Instead, he conceded and pledged his full support for Ayotte. In Delaware, however, there was another tea party stunner. O'Donnell beat Castle by more than six points.

Yet Republicans did anything but line up behind her.

On Tuesday night, Karl Rove was on FOX's *Hannity* trashing O'Donnell: "This was about Mike Castle's bad votes," Rove said. "It does conservatives little good to support candidates who, at the end of the day, while they may be conservative in their public statements, do not evince the characteristics of rectitude and truthfulness and sincerity and character that the voters are looking for. . . . There are just a lot of nutty things she's been saying. . . . We were looking at eight to nine seats in the Senate. Now we're looking at seven to eight, in my opinion. This is not a race we're going to be able to win."

By Wednesday morning the press was reporting that leadership aides at the National Republican Senatorial Committee were saying they were not going to waste any money supporting O'Donnell. Castle refused to endorse O'Donnell, and the press ran stories for several weeks that he was considering a write-in campaign.

In Washington I got all the blame for defeating Castle and handing Republicans an almost certain loss. I could only wish my endorsement had that much power. Nevertheless, I was told by the Republican leadership that O'Donnell was my candidate, and I was responsible for her campaign. That was a challenge I was ready to take, but unfortunately within the previous week Republicans had so damaged O'Donnell she now had almost no chance of winning.

O'Donnell's win marked the end of the contentious 2010 Republican primaries. The full slate of candidates for the U.S. Senate was now finalized, and I was determined to support all of them. My focus would still be on those solid conservatives supported by SCF, but I was enthusiastic about all our candidates.

Chapter 12

Election 2010

September 26, 2010—November 2, 2010

ouse Republicans unveiled their Pledge to America in September. It answered the two most asked questions by millions of Americans, "What will Republicans do if we trust them again with the majority, and will they keep their promises this time?" Unquestionably, Republicans had lost the trust of the American people when we had the majority in Congress and controlled the White House. But Americans now wanted to throw the Democrats out and needed to know they could trust Republicans again.

The Republican pledge, which promised to create more certainty in the markets and control spending, was a good effort to convince Americans they wanted to lead the country in a positive direction. The first section focused on freedom, liberty, and even had the audacity to mention "Creator." Imagine that.

America is more than a country.

America is an idea—an idea that free people can govern themselves, that government's powers are derived from the consent of the governed, that each of us is endowed by their Creator with the unalienable rights to life, liberty, and the pursuit of happiness. America is the belief that any man or woman can—given economic, political, and religious liberty—advance themselves, their families, and the common good.

Senate Republicans generally acquiesced to the pledge but left it to House Republicans to carry the message to the American people. I continued to amplify the voices of the growing American awakening.

I was happy to see an editorial in *The Washington Post* the following Sunday that appeared to be a response to a piece I wrote in *The Post* the week before, titled "Washington Can Hear You Now." My article discussed how Washington politicians ignored the American people until the tea parties and other activists demonstrated they could elect new congressmen and senators. Democrats still seemed deaf; Republicans were now listening.

The Post responded with, "Tea Party has nation's attention, now what?" The editorial was surprisingly insightful:

> Taken together, the many arms of the tea party movement have, in an impressively short time, grown into a potent and disruptive political force. It proved, in a series of stunning victories in Republican primaries across the nation, that it can mobilize volunteers, raise money (at least $60 million this year), end political careers and begin new ones. All without any formal structure or central leadership. Now, with the next test of a general election approaching, the tea party has the nation's attention. The question is whether it is a momentary expression of discontent in an angry election year or the chaotic first efforts of a durable political movement.[21]

With citizen vigilance being a prerequisite for a free and prosperous nation, I planned to do my part to grow the tea party. But much depended on what happened in the 2010 elections, now just over one month away. If Republicans did not meet expectations by retaking the majority in the House, the tea party movement would likely decline as a political force, and Democrats would be emboldened to continue business as usual.

If, on the other hand, 2010 proved to be a historic election, the tea party movement would become an even more powerful force. The polls were still predicting Republicans would take the majority in the House and gain five to seven seats in the Senate. But a month was a long time in politics, and anything could happen.

I was at home on Sunday, September 26, scanning the Internet for news from around the world. No longer did I have to settle for a Sunday newspaper filled mostly with advertising inserts. Even a low-tech baby boomer like me could cruise the Internet. Another article caught my eye, this time from across the Atlantic. *The Telegraph* (UK) proclaimed, "The Tea Party is now more powerful than President Obama." Coming from a nation with experience in the ravages of big government socialism, their analysis was both stunning and sobering:

> The reason for the Tea Party's stunning success and President Obama's equally remarkable decline is relatively simple. A truly popular grassroots movement has captured the fears and concerns of tens of millions of Americans over the relentless rise of Big Government and the growing threat to economic and individual freedom under the Obama administration, while channeling their hopes and aspirations for the future based upon a return to the founding ideals of the Constitution. In contrast, an out of touch presidency that exudes arrogance and elitism at every turn continues to contemptuously spend other people's money with abandon, building up a crippling debt that will ultimately destroy America's long-term prosperity if left unchecked. It is a stark choice that the two sides offer, and it's not surprising that a clear majority of Americans are opting for political revolution rather than the status quo.[22]

A Sunday news story from the *Boston Herald* had Massachusetts Democrat Senator John Kerry demonstrating the "arrogance and elitism" described by the UK *Telegraph*. Remarkably, Kerry claimed Americans were angry because they were uninformed, "We have an electorate that doesn't always pay that much attention to what's going on so people are influenced by a simple slogan rather than the facts or the truth of what's happening."

Democrats were so out of touch they didn't even know when they were insulting the voters.

The New York Times previewed a rally to be held on the National Mall on October 2, sponsored by more than three hundred liberal organizations. It was planned to "get back" at the tea party and Glenn Beck. One union boss said he chartered five hundred buses to get twenty-five thousand bodies there. This is what White House spokesman Robert Gibbs called "the professional left" in action. Or "Astroturf," as Pelosi once said. The liberal groups planning to attend included numerous government unions, the NAACP, the AFL-CIO, the National Council of La Raza, and the National Gay and Lesbian Task Force.

We must have been doing something right to provoke such a reaction from the liberal machine. Showtime was coming up. And the showdown was coming November 2.

More Fights Inside and Outside Washington

Congress would be in recess for the entire month of October to allow members time to campaign for the November elections. As Congress approaches congressional recesses, the "unanimous consent" process really heats up. After discussions with other conservative senators, we agreed to send notice to all the other senators warning them to give us at least three days to review any bills they wanted to pass before we left for the preelection break at the end of the week.

Three days' notice to approve unanimous consent requests was the Steering Committee's standard policy, but senators often ignored us, waiting until the last minute to create a sense of crisis, helping to push their bills through after most members had left town. This time we put it in writing: "The Executive Committee of the Senate Steering Committee has asked the Steering Committee staff to hold all bills that have not been hotlined by close-of-business Tuesday. If there are any bills you would like cleared before we go out, please get them to the Steering Committee staff along with a CBO score (cost), if applicable, by close-of-business on Tuesday."

You might think with the nation screaming at Congress to "read the bills" and to stop drowning America in debt, our request would have been applauded by the press. But on Tuesday the media criticism was brutal. The *Los Angeles Times* published a piece, "Jim DeMint: The Most Undemocratic

Senator?" claiming I was effectively shutting down the Senate. The article stated, "South Carolina Sen. Jim DeMint warned Monday evening that he would block all legislation that has not been cleared by his office in the final days of the pre-election session."

Also on Tuesday, *The Washington Post* published a story headlined, "Did Jim DeMint Just Take Control of the Senate?" Quoting one Senate staffer, *The Post* wrote, "This is really, really, really, really, really, really bad. In a precedent-setting institution like the U.S. Senate, letting one person anoint themselves king is not a good idea."

The Wall Street Journal headlined their story, "DeMint Flexes Muscle." They quoted a spokesman for Majority Leader Harry Reid, "When did he [DeMint] become the arbiter of everything in the Senate? The Senate is set up to be run by consensus, and this is an extraordinary overreach by a senator."

The Wall Street Journal, to their credit, did include a response from one of my staffers: "Americans are sick of Washington ramming through bills that no one reads," said DeMint spokesman Wesley Denton. "Big spenders play a hide-the-bill game at the end of every Congress, hoping to pass secret bills with deficit spending and new regulations without any debate or even a vote."

Based on the telephone calls and e-mails to my office, most Americans agreed with the Steering Committee.

Later on Tuesday, Democrat Senator Specter gave a speech on the Senate floor lambasting me and other conservatives for the way GOP moderates were being treated. Specter would not be coming back after the election and was still bitter about my support of Pat Toomey. *Politico* summarized his speech: "In an oddly timed and strongly-worded speech, Specter took aim at the Republican Party, which he claimed has 'changed the most ideologically' and took not-so-veiled shots at colleague Jim DeMint, who has emerged as the champion of the conservative electorate."

On Wednesday, September 29, *Politico* published another story: "GOP Senators Lash Out at DeMint." The article quoted several Republican leaders criticizing me for publicizing the discussion and vote about Lisa Murkowski in our conference meeting. As I said, I had not uttered a word about the meeting until after all the details were published in several Hill newspapers, obviously leaked by others in the room, not me. But at this point the truth was irrelevant.

As we prepared to recess for the election, rumors continued among my fellow Republican senators that I was planning to recruit and support challengers to my incumbent Republican colleagues who were up for reelection in 2012. *Not true.* I had no plans to oppose any of my colleagues in 2012. The rumors were a coordinated effort to further discredit me with fellow senators. My opponents were afraid to attack me publicly so they had to find more anonymous ways to undermine my efforts to change the Senate. It was ugly. And getting uglier all the time.

And even with skin grown remarkably thick after such a relatively short time in Washington, I was starting to feel the toll this was taking. It's funny, if I could somehow parachute back into my life twenty, thirty years—even as little as ten years ago—and tell myself that I would one day be infuriating people at such a rapid clip, my younger self would never believe it. That's just not the kind of guy I am. Honest. But that's where life in the political bull's-eye had put me, and I'm telling you—being very candid here— the constant criticism was sapping my energy, and the loss of friendships with people I really cared about was painful. But there was no turning back. I was on a mission that required asking forgiveness instead of permission. The traditions and the unwritten seniority rules of the Senate were established to protect those who held power, not those who were working to make a difference. I couldn't change the Senate by following tradition. There would be plenty of time to ask forgiveness after the election.

The Homestretch

I left Washington on Thursday, September 30, flew to New York to speak at a fund-raiser for Ken Buck, and caught a late flight home. At midnight I collapsed into my own bed, never more grateful to be out of Washington.

Back in South Carolina the state media seemed irritated I wasn't having a difficult election, so they determined to put a sinister spin on my efforts to stop earmarks and elect conservative candidates across the country. It seemed like every newspaper in South Carolina bombarded me with criticism for hurting the state's economy by not asking for an earmark to deepen one of our ports. It was the same old yarn: "To heck with America, just send us the money."

Despite all the negative coverage I was getting, my opponent was having an even worse time with reporters. Greene's economic recovery plan made national news: the government should sell action figure dolls of him to generate revenue. Greene was indicted on felony obscenity charges and constantly entertained the national media with his weird antics. I couldn't have asked for a better opponent.

On Saturday, October 2, I flew to Kentucky to campaign for Rand Paul. Paul's father, Congressman and former presidential candidate Ron Paul, joined us on the stage at a large tea party rally in Louisville. The enthusiastic crowd filled a large hotel ballroom. The atmosphere was electric, building my hopes that tea party power would result in dramatic changes on November 2.

Quickly back home again, I continued to travel around South Carolina in October working for Republican candidates. All our candidates appeared to be well positioned to win, even Mick Mulvaney, who continued to run a strong race against powerful Democrat Budget Chairman John Spratt. Nikki Haley held a strong lead in the polls against her Democrat opponent for governor.

The candidates supported by the Senate Conservative Fund were doing well througout the country, though polls were tightening in almost every race. Our candidates were generally outperforming expectations, but the Republican Party organization in many states was weak and underfunded. The Democrat get-out-the-vote organization was still in place from Obama's presidential campaign, and the Republican National Committee was not providing the funding and organizational support necessary for state Republican Parties to be competitive on the ground.

I started to wonder—maybe this was why God had given me such an unusually easy race to run.

So I decided to use my campaign funds to help strengthen Republican state party organizations both in South Carolina and around the country. Election law allows candidates to transfer funds to state party organizations to assist in voter registration, mailers, and get-out-the-vote efforts. My campaign gave away nearly $2 million in ten states. A breakdown is provided below showing how I allocated the money.

South Carolina	$350,000
Colorado	$250,000
Florida	$250,000
Nevada	$156,000
New Hampshire	$100,000
Pennsylvania	$150,000
Kentucky	$150,000
Alaska	$100,000
Washington	$100,000
Delaware	$250,000

My greatest concerns were in Nevada and Colorado. Sharron Angle and Ken Buck were polling ahead of their Democrat opponents, but their state party organizations were no match for the Democrat ground game. In Nevada, Harry Reid had all the resources of big labor and every liberal interest group in the country. In Colorado, the Republican candidate for governor self-destructed, and the state party was in disarray. There wasn't much more I could do but pray.

While I was working to elect new Republicans to the Senate, some of my colleagues and their unnamed aides took one last shot at me before the election. *Roll Call* published a news story by John Stanton on October 13 headlined, "Republicans Take 'No Comment' Approach to DeMint":

> While Sen. Jim DeMint's internecine warfare may rub his fellow Republicans the wrong way, it appears there is little, if anything, they can do to rein him in. No Senate Republicans would discuss the issue on the record, and the few that would talk explained that most in the party think the best course of action is to ignore the irascible South Carolinian, at least for now.
>
> And so, Republicans said, they are essentially left with only one option: ignoring DeMint and hoping the lack of attention is punishment enough. "It's like a piece of fruit. If you leave it on

the counter long enough, it will spoil and go rotten on its own. I feel like that's what's going to happen with Jim DeMint," a GOP aide said.[23]

Fortunately, the criticism from the establishment seemed easier to take when I was outside Washington. Everywhere I went in South Carolina and around the country, people thanked me for fighting. And I thanked them for standing with me.

By Election Day, contributions from the SC and my campaign to Republican candidates for the Senate totaled $7.5 million. We had raised and given far more to Republican Senate candidates and state party organizations than any other senator.

But it wasn't because of me alone. It was due to the thousands of Americans who contributed to the effort to save our country. The average contribution to the SCF was $45. And even my Wade Hampton High School math skills are good enough to know it takes a whole lot of forty-fives to add up to 7.5 million. Collectively, we gave a voice to thousands of Americans who wanted to be part of the fight. It was an honor to go into battle with them.

Election Day

After Debbie and I voted on November 2, we spent most of the day at home preparing for election night. My staff planned a big victory party in a ballroom at an old hotel in downtown Greenville. Most Republican leaders would be in Columbia on election night celebrating Nikki Haley's victory for governor and the election of other statewide Republican candidates. But we were happy to stay in Greenville. Three of our four children, their spouses, and our two grandsons were joining us; and we were all spending the night at the hotel.

I went to the gym in the afternoon to relieve my anxiety about the other Senate races and to watch the news. After watching several pundits pontificate about renewed Democrat confidence in keeping the majority, I switched channels on the treadmill and watched *Andy Griffith*. I admired Andy's wisdom and calm, but if today's election results turned unexpectedly bad—which I knew they still could, even despite our best efforts—I would be Senator Barney Fife.

Debbie and I drove downtown to the Westin Poinsett Hotel about 5:00 p.m. The recently restored hotel was more than eighty years old. We had gone there to attend dances together more than forty years ago in its grand ballrooms when we were dating in middle and high school. Being at the hotel brought back a lot of good memories. We still laugh at a photo from our seventh-grade prom. At that time Debbie was taller than me.

Our sons, daughter, and their spouses joined us in our room until the party started downstairs. The two grandsons distracted us from the seriousness of the day. Just before 7:00 p.m., the Associated Press called the Senate race in Kentucky for Rand Paul. At 7:03 p.m., before any of the votes were counted, the AP called the South Carolina Senate race for me.

We all made our way downstairs on the large service elevator to the ballroom where a DJ was playing the ABBA song "Waterloo" as we entered the room and took the stage. I assumed the lack of suspense about my race would result in a ho-hum response to my victory, but I was wrong. The large ballroom was packed full, the crowd cheered loudly, and the applause lasted so long I was embarrassed. Their appreciation was gratifying and overwhelming.

For all the hard knocks of public life, nights like these—though all too few and far between—are very special. You see them on television. You hear the same post-election speeches. You hear the same old questions from the interviewer and the same old answers from the candidates. You kind of know what to expect. It's an American political tradition. But being with your supporters, surrounded by their gratitude and good wishes, bursting to tell them what their teamwork and sacrifice means to you . . . it's rewarding. It matters. Sharing victories up-close with the ones who really deserve the thanks is an unforgettable experience.

After spending an hour shaking hands, taking pictures, and being buffeted around by the crowd, we went back to our room to watch the election results from around South Carolina and the nation.

- In *South Carolina*, Republicans won the governor's race and five of six congressional races, including Mick Mulvaney's historic win over John Spratt.

- The next U.S Senate race to be called was *Florida*. Marco Rubio would be the new senator from the Sunshine State.
- Another SCF candidate, Ron Johnson, easily won his *Wisconsin* Senate race against incumbent Democrat Russ Feingold.
- The *Pennsylvania* race was close, but Pat Toomey prevailed.
- Mike Lee won easily in *Utah*.
- Other new Republicans were winning as well. Senators-elect Kelly Ayotte (New Hampshire), John Boozman (Arkansas), Roy Blunt (Missouri), John Hoeven (North Dakota), Jerry Moran (Kansas), Mark Kirk (Illinois), Rob Portman (Ohio), and Dan Coats (Indiana).

But Christine O'Donnell lost badly as expected in Delaware, and when the polls closed in the western states, the results were not good. Sharron Angle lost to Harry Reid in Nevada. Carly Fiorina lost badly to Barbara Boxer in California. The races in Colorado, Washington, and Alaska were too close to call, but Ken Buck, Dino Rossi, and Joe Miller would later lose their elections.

All told, Republicans would gain six seats in the Senate and retake the majority in the House with sixty-three new seats. Even with the pockets of disappointment, this was truly a historic election. There had not been a shift of power of this magnitude in Congress for more than fifty years. SCF candidates won in states like Pennsylvania, Florida, and Wisconsin where the experts said conservatives couldn't win. Paul won overwhelmingly in Kentucky where they said he was too conservative to win a general election.

Karl Rove provided a good summary of the election two days later in *The Wall Street Journal*:

> Tuesday's election was epic. Republicans gained over 60 seats in the House and six in the Senate. They'll now occupy eight additional governors' mansions and at least 500 more seats in state legislatures. The GOP picked up more House seats than in any election since 1938, leaving Democrats with the smallest number in the House since 1946. Republican gains in the Senate are roughly twice the post-World War II midterm average. When Mr. Obama took office there were 22 Republican governors: Now there will be at least 29. Fifty incumbent Democratic congressmen lost, including 22

freshmen. An extraordinary nine senior Democrats with 18 years or more of service also went down, including three committee chairs: South Carolina's John Spratt, Missouri's Ike Skelton, and Minnesota's Jim Oberstar. Their offense was to back the Obama-Pelosi agenda.[24]

Five SCF candidates won their elections, but before election night was over, unnamed sources in Washington were accusing me of costing Republicans the majority in the Senate. The polls never suggested Republicans could take the majority in the Senate, but instead of celebrating our great victory, some establishment Republicans were blaming me, Sarah Palin, and the tea parties.

This was a curious analysis, as it was unlikely *any* Republican would have won their election without tea party support. Republicans who think the tea party hurt Republicans in 2010 are completely out of touch. Instead of blaming the tea parties and conservative activists, Republicans should thank and embrace the new grass roots power that can rebuild and sustain the Republican Party and help save our country.

After Democrats won the White House and secured huge majorities in the House and Senate in the 2008 elections, the conventional wisdom in Washington was that Democrats would control government for years to come. Everyone predicted Republicans would lose more seats in 2010, as most of the races would be fought in heavily Democratic states.

Yet even though the class of new Republicans proved all the pundits and columnists wrong, Election Day 2010 was bittersweet for me. While thrilled to be joined by SCF candidates and other new Republicans in the Senate, I was heartbroken we would not be joined by Buck, Miller, and other great conservative candidates who lost their races.

But there was no time to commiserate; I had to prepare for the next battle in Washington: the ban on earmarks. My plan was to force a vote in the Republican Conference when we returned to Washington for the lame-duck session in two weeks. All the new senators would be allowed to vote on the ban, so this year we had a long-shot chance of actually winning.

Finally.

Chapter 13

Real Change and Hope

November 3, 2010—December 23, 2010

Tここ here was no time to celebrate after the election. We had to move quickly to stop the Washington establishment from co-opting the new Republicans before they were sworn in.

On Wednesday morning, November 3, *The Wall Street Journal* published my open letter to new Republicans titled, "Welcome, Senate Conservatives." The letter was another less-than-diplomatic effort to keep a spotlight on the subtle corrupting process that turns passionate conservative candidates into cautious, milquetoast senators. The letter said:

> Congratulations to all the tea party-backed candidates who over-came a determined, partisan opposition to win their elections. The next campaign begins today. Because you must now overcome determined party insiders if this nation is going to be spared from fiscal disaster.
>
> Many of the people who will be welcoming the new class of Senate conservatives to Washington never wanted you here in the first place. The establishment is much more likely to try to buy off your votes than to buy into your limited-government philosophy. Consider what former GOP senator-turned-lobbyist Trent Lott told

The Washington Post earlier this year: "As soon as they get here, we need to co-opt them."

Don't let them. Co-option is coercion. Washington operates on a favor-based economy and for every earmark, committee assignment or fancy title that's given, payback is expected in return. The chits come due when the roll call votes begin. This is how big-spending bills that everyone always decries in public always manage to pass with just enough votes.[25]

My letter warned new Republicans not to allow themselves to be bribed with earmarks, committee assignments, or leadership titles. It also challenged them to surround themselves with conservative staff and to keep their promises to voters instead of focusing on their reelection campaigns. I wrote it to give some pushback to the senators and lobbyists who were determined to maintain the status quo, but it was necessary in order to keep the eyes of the nation on Republicans when we returned to Washington in less than two weeks. All of us behave better when we know people are watching.

Also on Wednesday morning, I had my staff send a briefing notebook to the five SCF senators-elect. The notebook provided information about setting up their offices, hiring staff, and becoming familiar with constituent services operations. I wanted to offer and provide whatever staff assistance they might need. My goal was to organize a team of conservatives, but I knew the nature of the Senate was to divide and isolate individual members. Setting up major offices with forty to fifty staff can overwhelm and distract new senators for months or even years. We needed their full attention immediately for some important initial battles over the next few weeks.

It was time to get busy doing all the right things.

The Buildup to the Vote Against Earmarks

Later that day President Obama held a press conference and admitted the Democrats took a "shellacking" in the election. I was pleasantly surprised when he offered to work with Republicans on earmark reform. Surprised but . . . suspicious.

In the aftermath of the elections, the taxpayers continued to take a shellacking. Freddie Mac announced it had lost another $2.5 billion and was asking for another $100 million bailout. (My goodness.) And the Federal Reserve announced another round of "quantitative easing," a deceptive way of saying they were going to monetize $600 billion of America's debt. Buying federal debt was something Federal Reserve Chairman Ben Bernanke promised he would not do. Other nations were quick to criticize America for undermining our currency.

I knew Congress would never deal with these serious issues until we got our minds off parochial politics. My main focus after the election was to force a vote on an earmark moratorium when the Senate Republican Conference met in Washington on November 16—the same meeting I was embarrassed at in 2008 when I tried to force votes to change conference rules.

Republican House Leader John Boehner, the incoming Speaker of the House, and the entire team of Republican leaders in the House had already pledged to pass a two-year moratorium on earmarks. Senate Republicans needed to do the same.

On Thursday, November 4, Senate Republican Leader Mitch McConnell gave a speech at the Heritage Foundation *defending* earmarks and claiming the elimination of earmarks would not reduce federal spending. He said earmarks are a matter of congressional discretion. According to him, claiming an earmark ban would only give the Obama administration a blank check to direct money to the president's pet projects.

McConnell's speech drew appropriate fire from conservatives around the country. The next day *Washington Examiner* Editorial Page Editor Mark Tapscott wrote, "It is indeed an issue of discretion whether senators should in the form of earmarks give tax dollars to favored spending projects, family members, former aides, or campaign donors. Voters have made clear since before 2005 when the infamous Bridge to Nowhere came to public notice that they want wasteful federal spending stopped, especially when it is used to win votes or reward friends.

The same day *Politico* posted a story headlined, "GOP Senators Fight over Failure." It quoted South Carolina Senator Lindsey Graham and former Mississippi Senator Trent Lott saying conservatives messed up by supporting Christine O'Donnell in Delaware. Leadership aides anonymously blamed the tea parties and me for Senate Republicans not having fifty seats in the next Congress. One of them told FOX News I should be called the "undertaker" instead of "kingmaker."

The more these "leadership aides" criticized me, the more conservative groups and media counterattacked against Senate Republican leadership. Rush Limbaugh devoted much of his show commenting on the *Politico* piece. He said, "You see, this is interesting. Establishment Republicans never lose races. They never lose. It's always somebody else's fault when these losses happen. They never lose."

The Wall Street Journal's James Taranto wrote: "It's a bit odd for the GOP establishment to be blaming the tea party for the outcome of this year's Senate elections. The party did gain six seats, its biggest pickup since 1994. By contrast, the Republicans lost six seats in 2006 and eight in 2008, when the tea party didn't yet exist. True, they picked up four in 2004, but this year they held those and every other seat they carried back then."

Watching this fight from a distance was interesting. In every interview I expressed my support for Leader McConnell and the entire Republican leadership team. I did not made one critical comment about Republican leadership—not one—but their constant carping at me through their staff resulted in a massive backlash against them. Without saying a word, I found myself in a national media showdown with McConnell and the Republican leadership over earmarks and the Republican agenda.

While the media was depicting a war between the Republican leadership and me, I was at home making calls and sending e-mails encouraging Republican colleagues to cosponsor my resolution to ban earmarks. By Tuesday, November 9, we had ten cosponsors, including six newly elected senators—all five SCF senators and Kelly Ayotte. I was really proud of the freshmen senators because they had the courage to take a public stand against appropriators in such a high-stakes war.

We had hoped and prayed for that. But you never know.

It was still an uphill battle. It was open knowledge that leadership was opposing it. *Politico* published a story on Tuesday titled, "McConnell Fights GOP Earmark Ban." The article set the stage for a dramatic showdown the next week. It said: "Senate Minority Leader Mitch McConnell is maneuvering behind the scenes to defeat a conservative plan aimed at restricting earmarks, setting up a high-stakes showdown that pits the GOP leader and his 'Old Bull' allies against Senator Jim DeMint (R-S.C.) and a new breed of conservative senators."

McConnell wasn't the only one who didn't want to give up earmarks. *The Hill* published a story titled, "Senator Inhofe on Warpath Against Earmark Ban." Inhofe is a good friend, but he really likes his earmarks and was firing at me from all directions. In a short span of time, he gave many interviews against the ban and wrote an editorial for the *National Review* headlined, "Eliminating Earmarks Is a Phony Issue."

Over the next few days, Sarah Palin and Mike Huckabee weighed in, supporting the ban on earmarks. Senator John Cornyn was the only member of our elected leadership who cosponsored the resolution. His support emboldened others to join us. By the weekend, we had ten cosponsors with numerous other senators promising to vote with us but preferring not to sign the resolution. If senators voted the way they promised, we would easily win the vote on the following Tuesday. But with a secret ballot vote, I wasn't taking anything for granted.

On Sunday morning I appeared on *Fox News Sunday with Chris Wallace* via satellite from the Greenville airport before flying back to Washington. Wallace is a tough but fair host, and I enjoy being on his show. I talked at length about the positive influence of the tea party movement and my fight against earmarks. After my segment during the roundtable discussion, *Weekly Standard* Editor Bill Kristol predicted conservatives would win our vote to ban earmarks on Tuesday.

Go team.

The Earmark Showdown

Debbie flew back to Washington with me because we were hosting a small dinner for the new SCF senators and their spouses on Sunday night. Sitting at the dinner table with my new colleagues, I felt my eyes unexpectedly well with tears. It had been a long, painful fight, but now the cavalry had arrived. Now we had a chance to change the Senate, to help Republicans re-earn the trust of the American people, and hopefully to turn our country away from a cliff of economic and fiscal disaster.

All the newly elected Republican senators would be able to vote on the earmark ban scheduled for a Republican Conference meeting on Tuesday. The retiring Republican appropriators could not vote. This improved our chances to pass the ban because most of the new Republicans campaigned on banning earmarks.

By Monday, I was confident we had the votes to win the earmark vote. We now had thirteen cosponsors—including me—and at least that many more who promised to vote with us. The initial group of supporters who were brave enough to take a public stand against our appropriators is on the "wall of fame" in my office:

Kelly Ayotte	Jim DeMint	Mike Lee	Pat Toomey
Richard Burr	John Ensign	Rand Paul	
Tom Coburn	Mike Enzi	Marco Rubio	
John Cornyn	Ron Johnson	Jeff Sessions	

While I was optimistic about winning the vote to ban earmarks, I was dreading another unpleasant Republican Conference meeting like the one choreographed to humiliate me two years earlier. It still appeared some of our senior members were going to fight me until the bitter end, and they were not going to lose gracefully.

But Monday afternoon brought a dramatic turn of events.

About 2:15 p.m. one of my staff told me Leader McConnell went to the Senate floor to make a statement about the earmark ban. I turned on the C-SPAN monitor in my office and watched in amazement.

McConnell announced he would be supporting the ban:

> I have thought about these things long and hard over the past few weeks. I've talked with my members. I've listened to them. Above all, I have listened to my constituents. And what I've concluded is that on the issue of congressional earmarks, as the leader of my party in the Senate, I have to lead first by example. Nearly every day that the Senate's been in session for the past two years, I have come down to this spot and said that Democrats are ignoring the wishes of the American people. When it comes to earmarks, I won't be guilty of the same thing. Make no mistake. I know the good

that has come from the projects I have helped support throughout my state. I don't apologize for them. But there is simply no doubt that the abuse of this practice has caused Americans to view it as a symbol of the waste and the out-of-control spending that every Republican in Washington is determined to fight. And unless people like me show the American people that we're willing to follow through on small or even symbolic things, we risk losing them on our broader efforts to cut spending and rein in government. That's why today I am announcing that I will join the Republican Leadership in the House in support of a moratorium on earmarks in the 112th Congress.

I didn't know whether to cheer or cry. Years of work and frustration were suddenly showing results. The Senate that couldn't be changed just moved a few inches in the right direction. This was good news for the millions of Americans who gave Republicans a second chance on Election Day.

The next day many newspapers carried front-page stories about McConnell's abrupt change on the earmark ban. *USA Today* featured an editorial coauthored by Republican Senator-elect Pat Toomey and Missouri's Democrat Senator Claire McCaskill calling on both parties to quit earmarking.

Two Republican Conference meetings were scheduled for Tuesday. This is where we would formally enact the ban. The first meeting was in the morning to hold leadership elections, followed by a second meeting at 4:45 p.m. to consider the earmark ban. All on our leadership team were reelected with no opposition in the morning Conference. As we left that meeting, I appealed to our Conference Chairman, Tennessee Senator Lamar Alexander, to encourage McConnell to pass the earmark ban by voice vote rather than spend an hour with a divisive debate and a fight about whether to have a secret ballot or recorded vote.

Still, when I walked into the second Republican Conference meeting Tuesday afternoon, I didn't know what to expect. We had several speakers ready to go in support of the earmark ban and were prepared for an ugly showdown with appropriators. But none of that was necessary. McConnell opened the meeting with some of the words from his floor speech the day before and asked for a voice vote.

"All in favor, say aye," he said.

Almost everyone responded forcefully, "Aye."

"All opposed, say nay," he said.

There were only a few grumbles.

That was it. I didn't even say a word. The irony of the situation was overwhelming. I had just witnessed one of the leading opponents of the earmark ban lead the effort to pass it.

But there were even more positive surprises to come. Almost every member of the leadership team offered a resolution to cut spending and to stop the expansion of federal power. Cornyn's resolution to balance the federal budget passed with a unanimous voice vote, as did Alexander's resolution to place a moratorium on new unfunded mandates and new entitlement programs. Another resolution returning the government to 2008 spending levels passed with a robust voice vote, as did a resolution to reclaim unspent stimulus money and to freeze the hiring of new federal employees. McConnell put the icing on the cake with a resolution challenging the Democrats to match our ban on earmarks.

The leadership team left the meeting and held a press conference announcing the Republican commitments to ban earmarks and cut spending. At least for the moment, Republican senators seemed united in our commitment to move from parochial interests to the good of the nation.

Finishing Off the Lame Duck

The "lame duck" is the time when Congress is in session after an election before new members take office in January. All retiring and defeated congressmen and senators can vote, but the newly elected members cannot. The weeks between the election and Christmas 2010 were the Democrats' last chance to cram through liberal legislation before Republicans took control of the House. House Speaker Nancy Pelosi and Senate Majority Leader Harry Reid had a full slate of political votes they promised their special interest groups.

In their final days of power, Democrats wanted to overturn "Don't Ask, Don't Tell," the military policy that barred homosexuals from serving in the armed forces. They wanted to pass the DREAM Act, legislation that would give amnesty and citizenship to children of illegal aliens. And they wanted to pass a bill to force unionization and collective bargaining on firefighters and emergency responders. They were also trying to figure out a way to pass another extension of unemployment payments, adding another $56 billion to the deficit.

Republicans had only two agenda items for the lame-duck session. We wanted to extend current tax rates for everyone, stopping the largest tax increase in history scheduled for January 2011. And since the Democrats had yet to pass a bill to fund the operation of the government for the next fiscal year, we needed to pass a stopgap resolution to fund the operation of the government until we came back into session in January.

President Obama had other priorities. He wanted to pass the New START treaty—an arms-control agreement with Russia—before the next Congress was sworn in. The President was seeking a high-profile foreign policy achievement to close the year, but this treaty (as previously discussed) contains major flaws. It restricts our development of a comprehensive missile-defense system, it fails to include a program for modernizing our nuclear arsenal, it has serious verification weaknesses, and it assumes the continuation of the "mutually assured destruction" strategy with Russia.

Big points of concern and question. Lots of problems.

Leader McConnell and Arizona Senator Jon Kyl did a masterful job getting all forty-two Republicans senators to sign a letter to Majority Leader Harry Reid pledging to vote against proceeding to any other legislation until we passed a resolution to fund the government and an extension of current tax rates. That meant Republicans would block "Don't Ask, Don't Tell," the amnesty bill, the unionization of firefighters and emergency first responders, and other miscellaneous political paybacks until the Senate took care of these basic, necessary items.

We knew the Democrats wanted to spend all of the lame-duck session on political votes and the President's New START treaty. If Reid could run out the clock on those items, he could then force a government shutdown showdown the week of Christmas. We expected him to put off the tax extension vote as long as possible, in hopes Republicans would ultimately give in and vote for a tax increase in order to get home for Christmas. The

"42" letter, as it became known, would prove to be a solid backstop against a lot of bad legislation.

Playing Chicken with the Lame Duck

The Democrats were relentless. They were threatening to keep Congress in session until New Year's Day if necessary to pass their long list of legislation. It was a game of chicken, and no one knew which party would blink first.

I believed it was wrong for a Congress that had just been fired by the American people to cram more bad legislation down the throats of the American people before they were thrown out of office. Holding Christmas hostage to pressure Republicans made the Democrat strategy even more callous.

There were no votes on Saturday, December 10, so I caught a flight home on Friday. I was determined to put up my own Christmas decorations this year. Debbie and I bought a Christmas tree, tied it on top of her car, and spent the rest of the day decorating. She had been through a hard year. After her cancer surgery, she'd undergone two months of radiation treatments and started a medication that sapped her energy. She had been an inspiring example of persistence and courage. Now, she was clear of cancer and her prognosis was good. Being home was therapeutic for both of us, renewing our family tradition of putting up Christmas decorations together. Our children were working hard and making us proud. I was, and will always be, a very grateful husband and father.

On Saturday, Debbie went to the mall to do some shopping while I put up the lights on the outside of the house. My daughter and son-in-law, who were now living in Charlotte, appeared at our front door as I was bringing out a box of lights from the attic. They said they just stopped by to help me with the lights again, but it was nearly a two-hour drive from Charlotte, so I knew something was up. They helped me drape the lights around the garland on the front porch banister until Debbie got home. Then they announced they were expecting their first child.

Even with the excitement and energy of the campaigns and rallies, even with the exhilaration of our political triumphs on Election Day and afterward, this was the best news I'd heard all year. Hands down.

While we finished putting up the lights, we celebrated together and talked about their new lives as parents. I felt I was living two completely separate lives. One was a normal life in a middle-class neighborhood, experiencing the joys and sorrows of family life. The other was abnormal among the marble columns in Washington. If those of us working in Washington would just do the jobs we were elected to do, more Americans could live prosperous, normal lives with their families with less interference from government.

Debbie and I said good-bye to my daughter and son-in-law, plugged in all the Christmas lights and had dinner. I did my laundry and packed my bag for another week or two in Washington. We didn't know if I'd be gone two days or two weeks.

When I got back to Washington on Monday, Democrat Leader Reid brought up a trillion dollar, nearly two-thousand-page omnibus spending bill stuffed with more than six thousand earmarks. It was shameless business as usual. The outcry from around America was loud and clear. This was a critical test for Republicans; we could not help the Democrats pass this monstrosity.

Arizona Senator John McCain and I, along with many other Republicans, organized an effort to force the Democrats to read aloud every page of the omnibus bill from the Senate floor, including each and every earmark. We would show the American people what was in this bill. It would take roughly two days of around-the-clock reading, and we had plenty of volunteers to do it. We had to maintain a constant presence on the floor because at any moment the Democrats could ask to stop the reading of the bill if there was not a Republican available to object.

On the evening of Thursday, December 16, we gathered on the Senate floor to begin a two-day vigil to stop any attempt to end the reading of the bill.

Initially, Republican appropriators expressed support for the omnibus spending bill. We had no chance to stop it without their help, so unless they changed their minds, we were just delaying the inevitable by reading the bill. Mitch McConnell, in perhaps his finest hour as Republican Leader, persuaded all of his Republican colleagues on the Appropriations Committee to oppose the bill. When they agreed, Reid was forced to drop it. Instead of staying up all night standing guard on the Senate floor, we held a mini-celebration in the Republican cloakroom before calling it a night.

Ironically, Republican appropriators who had been my nemeses on big spending bills for several years were the heroes who stood with us against the giant spending bill in the lame-duck Congress. They gave up their parochial interests and showed the country we had received the message of the November election.

The next day, all Republican senators met for lunch to discuss ways to cut spending in the next Congress. To tell you the truth, there were many days when I didn't think I'd ever live long enough to sit in on that meeting.

But while we were focusing on spending matters, the Democrats remained committed to passing the DREAM Act, repealing "Don't Ask, Don't Tell," and ratifying the New START treaty. Reid planned votes for Saturday, December 18. He wasn't going to blink.

Republicans ended the lame-duck session with some wins and some losses. We stopped the Democrat tax increases and killed the giant omnibus spending bill. We were also able to defeat the DREAM Act. But enough Republicans bolted to help the Democrats pass the New START treaty and to sanction homosexuality in the military by repealing "Don't Ask, Don't Tell." I fear what this will do to our proud, voluntary armed forces.

The 111th Congress finally wrapped up with a record of creating more debt than the first one hundred congresses combined. We passed a government takeover of health-care and took control of America's financial system. We continued to hobble the economy with interventions, bailouts, and temporary tax policy.

But I am optimistic the 112th Congress will be different. And I am convinced Americans will hold us accountable to do what we promised.

To stay awake.

Reflections

On Wednesday, December 22, my plane left the runway in Washington for the last time in 2010. I watched the Capitol get smaller and smaller as we flew along the Potomac and turned toward South Carolina. Washington was different from two years before—smaller, shaken, and less confident. America was different too—bigger and more confident with millions of Americans discovering their power as citizens and voters. I was different as well—bruised and disliked by many, but now a proven fellow soldier with millions of Americans who were fighting to save their country.

The last two years had fundamentally changed America, Washington, and me. Washington's reckless spending, debt, and government takeovers set off alarms that awakened Americans from their complacency and apathy. Now with the hardest work still ahead of us, I am hoping we won't push the "snooze" button, roll over, and go back to sleep.

The 2010 election did not win the war against big-government socialism; it was only the initial skirmish in the decisive battle we will fight in 2012. Republicans need more commonsense conservative candidates to complete our return of the House and the Senate to the will of America's freedom fighters, and more importantly, we need a presidential candidate who is willing to tell Americans the truth: the federal government has to do less, not more.

I was really looking forward to the next two weeks at home with Debbie for Christmas and New Year's. But for the first time in years, I am actually looking forward to getting back in the fight in January. This time I will have allies. America's refounders sent reinforcements to the House and Senate, and we can now stop President Obama's rampage of spending, debt, and expansion of government.

I am also ready to expand the SCF to challenge the twenty-three Democrat senators who are up for reelection in 2012. Numerous potential conservative candidates from all over the country have already called asking for an interview. Several came to Washington during the lame-duck session to ask for an endorsement.

The long, painful journey is not over, but we are now in a position to change the Senate and harness the power of the American people to save our country. What seemed impossible only two years earlier is now within our grasp. The work and prayers to our Sovereign God of millions of Americans foster a genuine hope we can bring real change to Washington. Americans are awake and ready to take back their country.

So this book is more about the future than the past. It not only recounts how committed individuals came together to change the course of our nation, but reminds us it will take more of the same to keep the healthy change moving forward. There has been a real spiritual and political awakening in America. Some believe this movement will fizzle and die. I believe it will continue to grow.

And I hope this book will inspire more Americans to join this great awakening.

Chapter 14

On to 2012

America's great awakening in 2010 changed Congress and the direction of the country. Republicans are now the majority party in the House, and enough new GOP senators were elected to slow the hemorrhaging of America's freedom. The culture of spending exemplified by self-serving, parochial earmarks has been replaced with debates about how to cut spending and balance the budget. In fact, for the first time in anyone's memory, Congress is now passing bills that actually reduce spending. Republican congressmen and senators are working feverishly to pass a balanced budget amendment to the Constitution, cut more spending, and restore the limited government principles of the GOP.

President Obama, however, has abandoned any pretense of leadership and is on the sidelines taking potshots at Republicans who are trying to save the country from financial disaster. Federal agencies continue to stifle job growth with swarms of new regulations that are smothering the economy. Chaos has erupted in the Middle East, gas prices have skyrocketed, and oil supplies are increasingly threatened. Despite these developments, the President continues to block the development of America's abundant energy supplies. Even as Republican governors fight to save their states from bankruptcy, Obama has lined up with union bosses to support collective bargaining for government workers who already have wages and benefits *far* superior to the taxpayers they are supposed to serve.

As for me, I have one hand in the Senate trying to help my new colleagues balance our budget, and the other hand in the SCF supporting 2012 candidates who will fight for constitutional, limited government. And as we head toward the 2012 elections, the Americans I meet all across the country continue to say to me the same three things: "Keep fighting," "We're praying for you," and "What can I do?"

2012: America's Last Chance?

Here is what we must do to help save our country.

First, we must increase our sense of urgency, motivated by the knowledge that the 2012 elections could be our last chance to rescue America from disaster. This is not hyperbole. Our nation and many of our states are broke. America is dependent on unfriendly foreign countries for the energy and credit we need to run our economy. According to the Heritage Foundation's 2010 Index of Dependence on Government, 64.3 million Americans depend on the government for their daily housing, food, and health-care needs. Americans rely more on the government now for their basic needs than ever before. We are near the tipping point where America and its people could finally become too dependent to live independently and control their own destinies.

Not surprisingly, this appears to be the goal of President Obama and most in the Democrat Party. Almost every one of their policies and actions have grown the federal government and centralized more power in Washington. Interest groups such as government unions, trial lawyers, Wall Street bankers, international corporations, and other such groups that want more money, more benefits, and special treatment from the federal government have been able to get it. And as long as Obama and the Democrat Party control the purse strings and policy decisions in Washington, we can expect more of the same.

Americans who love freedom and want to pass along a free country to the next generation are in for the fight of their lives! Obama will likely have more than a billion dollars to spend on his reelection, and the Democrat "get-out-the-vote machine," led by union bosses and socialist interest groups like those funded by George Soros, will be difficult to beat. Freedom-loving Americans must be energized and well organized to win in 2012.

Second, we must continue to be inspired by our love of God, country, and freedom. Tea Party groups and other conservative citizens must remain passionate and informed. 2012 will not only be a competition between political parties; it will be a decision by Americans to live either in freedom or subjugation—our moment to decide whether future generations of Americans will have the opportunity to work for a better life or be forced to settle for the false promises of government dependency.

Freedom-loving Americans must take a stand, confident in their knowledge that America is and has always been a nation of destiny. Our nation has been blessed and used by God to bless the whole world. Oh, we certainly have our faults and have made our share of mistakes. But there has never been a nation that has done more good in more places than the United States of America. Other nations have tried to duplicate our political and economic systems, as well as our culture of character that has given us such extraordinary levels of success. Even today, people around the world are overthrowing authoritarian regimes in hopes of attaining the level of freedom we have in America.

If we are to save our country, we must seize this moment. We must be urgent. We must be passionate. We must set our sights on nothing less than a "freedom agenda," responding to the great problems (and opportunities) of our time with "freedom solutions."

The Freedom Agenda

Democrats will attempt to frighten Americans by saying Republican budget cuts will result in hardship for everyone, especially children, seniors, and disadvantaged citizens. This is categorically false. In fact, balancing our budget will do just the opposite—ushering in the opportunity of a lifetime to restore America's greatness.

But in order to restore our stability and stature, we must do more than just talk about spending cuts. Republicans must convince Americans that the federal government needs to be restructured, programs reformed and eliminated, and many federal functions returned to the states. This will not only reduce spending and debt but will provide better quality services to taxpayers.

This is not political theory; it is proven economic truth. American manufacturers discovered this truth several decades ago after the Japanese and other foreign manufacturers began to increase their share of American markets with higher quality products at a lower price. Americans figured out that trying to cut costs without reforming processes resulted in lower quality with very little reduction in cost. But when manufacturers decentralized and pushed decision-making down to the workers on the shop floor, processes were much more effectively streamlined, quality was improved, and costs were reduced.

Decentralization is not a new idea for American government; it is *the* idea. It's called federalism. In America's original design, individuals held most of the authority and responsibility in America. From the individual, authority moved to families, churches, and volunteer organizations. Local and state governments provided a framework of law and order, and the federal government was created by the states to provide for the national defense, ensure justice, and to facilitate interstate commerce. But very little of what the federal government does today was ever intended to be functions of a centralized national government.

There are two good reasons why we must restructure the federal government and devolve many federal programs back to the states: (1) we can't afford them, and (2) it has been proven beyond any reasonable doubt that the federal government cannot manage programs effectively or cost-efficiently.

The question Americans should be asking is not what else the federal government should do to solve our problems, but what the federal government must *let go of* to save our nation.

The difficulties we face today are not the result of freedom failing to work; they are the result of politicians failing to *let* freedom work. The 2012 Freedom Agenda is built on the Reagan principle that the federal government is not the solution to our problems; it *is* the problem.

With this in mind, here are some ideas to improve the way government operates and serves the American people.

Education

Since the federal government created the Department of Education in 1979, the quality of American education relative to other industrialized nations has declined. The federal government provides only 7 percent of the funding for public education yet essentially controls our public school system and is responsible for 41 percent of the administrative costs. In addition, dozens of federal programs require matching funds from local school districts that soak up local school budgets.

Freedom Solution: If states were released from federal mandates and programs, they would have more money to spend in the classroom as they see fit. The Department of Education should be eliminated, and federal spending should be phased out, while allowing states to innovate and improve the quality and choices of schools for parents and students.

Energy

The federal government has severely restricted the development of our own natural resources and made us dependent on nations that are not our friends. America possesses some of the largest deposits of oil and natural gas in the world, yet more than half the petroleum consumed by the United States is imported from foreign countries.

In 2010, the Department of Commerce reported that the petroleum-related trade deficit totaled $265 billion and accounted for 42 percent of our total deficit in goods. Millions of jobs have been lost because of America's absurd energy policies. Taxpayer subsidies for ethanol have also resulted in higher food prices as more and more corn is used for fuel rather than food.

Freedom Solution: Release America's private sector to develop all of our oil and natural gas supplies. Millions of jobs will be created, prices will fall, and tax revenues to state and federal governments will reduce deficits. Most importantly, America will be more secure as it becomes less dependent on our enemies for survival.

Transportation

The federal Department of Transportation was created to build the nation's interstate highway system. Today, it regulates and controls the funding and construction of most state and local infrastructure projects, and its federal mandates and requirements significantly increase the cost of construction for roads and bridges in every state. While Americans pay eighteen cents in federal taxes on every gallon of gasoline purchased, most states receive less in federal transportation funding than they send to Washington in gas taxes.

Freedom Solution: Instead of eighteen cents, states should send three cents from every gallon of gasoline to Washington and keep the rest. Dramatically shrink DOT so it only maintains federal roads on federal lands. States should build their own roads and bridges using proven safety standards.

Medicaid

Medicaid has brought many states to the brink of bankruptcy and has become an unsustainable expense at the federal level. Medicaid is now the largest expense of most states, eclipsing the cost of essential state functions.

Adding to the problem, ObamaCare has now forced states to add millions to their Medicaid rolls, and many physicians are refusing to see Medicaid patients because of inadequate reimbursements from the government for services.

One state, Rhode Island, has proven that if states are released from federal mandates, they can deliver better health care to more people at reduced costs. Rhode Island began its innovative program in 2009, and as a result, achieved over $100 million in savings within the first eighteen months.

Freedom Solution: Allow states more flexibility to provide care to the needy by opting out of federal Medicaid programs in return for a capped amount of federal funds.

Welfare

Unwed births and single parent homes are the primary cause of poverty, school dropouts, drug use, crime, and incarceration in America. Instead of reducing poverty, federal welfare programs have only perpetuated it.

Well-intended federal programs to assist the poor have resulted in more poverty, perverse incentives for unwed births, a myriad of social pathologies, and an explosion of federal and state spending. Since federal welfare programs began on a large scale in the 1960s, unwed births have increased from less than 10 percent to nearly 40 percent. Approximately 70 percent of African-American children are now born out of wedlock.

Freedom Solution: Phase out federal welfare programs, and give block grants to states to partner with churches and charitable groups to assist the poor. Use federal block grants to assist states in setting up safety net programs to provide support for poor and disabled citizens.

Entitlements

The federal government takes a substantial portion of our paychecks throughout our lives with the promise of providing a nominal income and adequate health care upon retirement. Unfortunately, none of this money has been saved to provide the promised services.

With more retirees and fewer workers now than ever, there is not enough money to keep our promises to seniors. Social Security and Medicare are the biggest budget busters at the federal level, and they will bankrupt our nation if they are not restructured.

Freedom Solutions: *Social Security*—Keep benefits the same for current retirees and those near retirement. For younger workers, offer a choice of defined contribution (401k-type) plans that reduce the future liability for the federal government but give workers real retirement savings.

Medicare—Offer Americans a choice: sign up for the current Medicare plan, or accept a defined Medicare benefit that can be used to pay for a personal health insurance plan of their choice. This would allow workers the option of keeping their private health plan when they retire, and it would save the federal government money.

On to 2012

While I plan to direct my efforts toward electing more conservative members to the Senate, the states will also play a critical role in saving freedom by demanding a return to federalism. The states must continue to fight for the repeal of ObamaCare and other federal programs that threaten their sovereignty and solvency.

We must also elect a president who will tell Americans the truth: federal government must do less—much less. No more promises about how the federal government is going to create jobs, improve our schools, provide health care for everyone, build our roads and bridges, and define our values. Republicans must nominate a presidential candidate with the character and courage to take on every special interest group and to focus the nation on one interest: *America*.

Tea Party groups and grassroots activists must also continue to support real conservatives in Republican primaries for Congress and Senate. We must give our next president a Congress that is ready to make the hard decisions to save our country.

And most important, we must amplify the clarion call of our forefathers to stand and fight for freedom. We are not in a partisan political battle; we are at war against those who do not respect or understand the principles of freedom that have made America the greatest nation in the history of the world.

Freedom is what happens when millions of people make their own decisions about what they value and what they do. I will be praying that millions of Americans make the decision to fight for freedom in 2012.

And beyond.

Notes

1. Taken from the inaugural speech of President Obama in November 2008.

2. Rick Santelli speaking on the floor of the Chicago Mercantile exchange on February 9, 2009.

3. Ibid.

4. John O'Hara, *The New American Tea Party* (Hoboken, NJ: John Wiley & Sons, 2011), 12.

5. Ibid.

6. "White House Enemy No. 1: Rush Limbaugh," March 5, 2009, Reuters.com.

7. Editorial from author titled "How Republicans Can Build a Big-Tent Party," *The Wall Street Journal.*

8. Release from Brad Woodhouse on August 4, 2009.

9. Taken from a San Francisco Chronicle blog on August 4, 2009.

10. See http://www.washingtontimes.com/weblogs/potus-notes/2009/aug/04/a-transcript-of-gibbs-manufactured-anger-line.

11. Jim DeMint, "What I Heard in Honduras," The Wall Street Journal.

12. John Miller, "Senator Tea Party," *National Review*, February 24, 2010.

13. Article titled "Jim DeMint's Bid to Embrace Tea Party Irks Senate GOP Colleagues," *Politico*, March 12, 2010.

14. James Rosen, "Jim DeMind Leads Righward Shift of GOP Candidates Nationwide," McClatchy newpapers, May 16, 2010.

15. David Brody, "Mitch McConnell, Wayne Newton, Jim DeMint, and Justin Bieber," Christian Broadcasting Network, May 2010.

16. Kristen Wyatt, "GOP Noticing Ken Buck's Outsider Senate Bid," AP, June 4, 2010.

17. Manuel Roig-Franzia, "In South Carolina, Greene Is Mystery Man Despite Winning Democratic Senate Nod," *The Washington Post*, June 11, 2010.

18. Jim DeMint, *American Spectator* (July–August 2010).

19. Joe Miller, "Help Joe Miller," *National Review*.

20. *Politico* magazine published Charles Krauthammer's remarks from FOX News Special Report with Bret Baier on September 13, 2010.

21. Response to an editorial from author in *The Washington Post*.

22. "The Tea Party Is Now More Powerful than President Obama," *The Telegraph* (UK), September 26, 2010.

23. John Stanton, "Republicans Take 'No Comment' Approach to DeMint," *Roll Call*, October 13, 2010.

24. Karl Rove, "Election Summary," *The Wall Street Journal*.

25. Jim DeMint, "Welcome, Senate Conservatives," *The Wall Street Journal*, November 3, 2010.

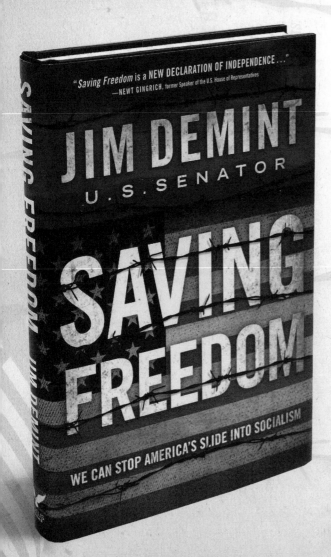